C000298052

SAINTS OF THE ISLES
a year of feasts

RAY SIMPSON

kevin
mayhew

The Celtic Prayer Book is published in four volumes:

Volume One
Prayer Rhythms: fourfold patterns for each day

Volume Two
Saints of the Isles: a year of feasts

Volume Three
Healing the Land: natural seasons, sacraments and special services

Volume Four
Great Celtic Christians: alternative worship

First published in 2003 by

KEVIN MAYHEW LTD
Buxhall, Stowmarket, Suffolk, IP14 3BW
E-mail: info@kevinmayhewltd.com

KINGSGATE PUBLISHING INC
1000 Pannell Street, Suite G, Columbia, MO 65201
E-mail: sales@kingsgatepublishing.com

9 8 7 6 5 4 3 2 1 0

ISBN 184417 078 0
Catalogue No 1500592

Front cover: St Mark and his symbol, from *The Lindisfarne Gospels* by
Janet Backhouse. Reproduced by courtesy of the Bristish Library
Cover design by Angela Selfe
Edited by Katherine Laidler
Typesetting by Louise Selfe

Printed and Bound in China

For the Churches and households of Britain,
Ireland and the English-speaking world
from The Community of Aidan and Hilda

Contents

Introduction

If we feed our minds on great persons we are more likely to become a great people.

If, as a multi-ethnic society, we know about the great souls who have lived on the soil which is our home, we are more likely to bond and grow well.

A popular British television series in which people voted for their top ten Great Britons awarded points for such things as leadership, legacy, ideas, courage, and compassion, but it missed two important categories: faith and selfless service. As a result, some manipulative types crept into the lists. The final programme concluded that none of the winners did well in all the categories, so a computer simulated a composite character made up of the best of them all – the complete human being.

The book in the Christian Bible entitled *The Acts of the Apostles* has gripping stories of great human beings who were guided by God. It ends, however, before Christianity reached the Celtic lands. The stories in this book could be entitled *The Acts of the Apostles, Volume Two*. They bring home-grown saints, as well as some universal ones, into our living rooms and workplaces. These hold clues to what it means to be a complete human being.

The book provides an introduction to a saint, a prayer, a Psalm, an Old Testament and a New Testament reading for each day of the year.

It can be used by individuals as a daily inspirational companion, and by churches and households as a resource for particular saints' days.

Saints and post-modern people

The Celtic Christian tradition seeks to reconnect people on the streets with the saints, and people in the churches with the streets.

At first sight, the world of saints seems far removed from post-modern attractions. Western culture at the start of the third millennium makes an idol of instant celebrities, then takes every opportunity to destroy the reputations of the living and the dead, and is in denial about death.

This could change overnight following a mass terrorist disaster.

Meanwhile, three facts may help us to reconnect:

1. There is something about the great personalities in this book which we can trust. Post-moderns mistrust history because they think it must have been doctored to suit the person who wrote it. Those who told stories or wrote *Lives* of saints did tend, until recent years, to highlight virtues which we do well to emulate, but to gloss over flaws. This was either to inspire others to goodness or else to promote the institution with which that saint was associated. Human, down-to-earth qualities tend to surface more in the stories of Celtic saints than in some others, but even their saints were mainly drawn from the leading strata of society. For these reasons we include some glorious exceptions, draw out particular, homely qualities, and reflect these in the headings, rather than rigidly use stereotyped titles. Thus terms such as monastery, abbot and bishop, which conjure up a very different image today than they did in the early centuries when monastic churches were like informal households and

their leaders like much loved parents, are not uniformly used. Different ways of describing the same thing are sometimes used, such as faith community (instead of church or monastery), leader or guide (instead of abbot or bishop).

The Bible accounts often record weaknesses as well as strengths of God-honourers, in the hope that we will learn to be real with ourselves and with God. These, and prophets, not all of whom were saintly, are also included among the entries.

2. The devotion which contemporary pop idols inspire meets the same psychological need that the respect for saints once met, and can meet again. This psychological need can be valid and God-given.

It is illustrated by the public mourning which followed the funeral of Diana, Princess of Wales, which allowed many people to express feelings which had been bottled up for years. In the three months following Diana's death there was a 50 per cent reduction in admissions to psychiatric hospitals and clinics.

3. The 'let-down' factor is vastly greater with pop idols. The saints do not let their fans down, and they point them to reality, not fantasy. So we hope that the present situation will be turned round, and that *Saints of the Isles*, Volume Two of *The Celtic Prayer Book* will contribute to this.

Saints, the Bible and the Celtic tradition

During the second millennium churches became divided in their attitude to saints. The Celtic tradition, which developed before abuses distorted this issue, is true both to the New Testament and to the experience of the Church in persecution and pilgrimage.

All Christians are called to be saintly, meaning holy. Some people are more saintly than others. The New Testament writer to Hebrew Christians taught that they were surrounded by a cloud of witnesses; that is, the dead were living witnesses, aware of what was going on (Hebrews 11:1–12:2). That is why, when a first-century Christian was buried in a catacomb, their grieving relatives inscribed prayers on their tombs asking an apostle to pray for them. That is also no doubt why St Columba taught Christians to make friends of the dead.

Some 'churchgoers' of Jesus' day thought of past God-honourers as dead and gone. Jesus taught them to change the way they perceived them. 'God is not the God of the dead but of the living,' he said, referring to the likes of Abraham (Mark 12:26, 27).

Those who are close to God become free to leave their earthly attachments behind when they die, and so to journey nearer the heart of God. For this reason Scripture forbids mortals to summon spirits of the dead back to earth, for this would be to re-attach them to our earthly egos (Leviticus 19:31; 20:26).

However, purified souls in heaven, who are set free from having to do what human wills demand, delight to speed anywhere at God's command. Thus sometimes a saint in heaven appears to us as a gift of God in a time of need, or as a surprise when we least expect it.

Since the time that Moses and Elijah appeared to Christ in order to strengthen him (Luke 9:28-36), Christ-like people have from time to time appeared to people living on earth.

The Martyrdom of Ignatius is an eyewitness account of the third bishop of Antioch, who was thrown to the lions some 80 years after Christ's transfiguration: 'Some of us saw the blessed Ignatius suddenly standing by us and embracing us, while others saw him praying for us, and yet others saw him dropping with sweat, as if he had just come from great labour, and standing by the Lord . . . When we had compared our several visions together, we sang praise to God.'*

Sulpicius Severus tells how Martin of Tours appeared to him in glory after his death: 'He appeared to me with that aspect of form and body which I had known so well; though he could not be observed all the time he could be clearly recognised . . . I felt his hand placed on my head with the sweetest touch, while amid the solemn words of blessing, he repeated again and again the name of the cross so familiar to his lips . . .'

In sixth-century Ireland the village folk gathered round their beloved Abbess Moninna as she lay dying. She told them: 'The apostles Peter and Paul have been sent to guide my soul to heaven and they are here with me now. I see them holding a kind of cloth with marvellous gold and artwork. I must go with them to my Lord who sent them. God hears your prayers. He will give a life to one of you. I

---

* *The Martyrdom of Ignatius,* Ante-Nicene Fathers (Grand Rapids, William B. Eerdmans Publishing Company, 1981) Volume 1.

pray God's blessing on your wives, children, and homes; I leave you my badger skin coat and my garden tools. I have no doubt that if you carry these with you when enemies attack God will deliver you. Do not be sad at my leaving you. For I truly believe that Christ, with whom I now go to stay, will give you whatever I ask of him in heaven no less than when I prayed to him on earth.'

Cuthbert of Lindisfarne was seen walking from Holy Island's parish church into the twelfth-century Benedictine Priory with the vessels for Holy Communion 500 years after his death. Indeed, he was seen again over Durham during the 1939-1945 War, protecting the city from air attack.

Canon Kate Tristram, Librarian at Marygate House, Holy Island, is a dispassionate academic, yet one day she 'heard' Aidan and Cuthbert, the island's two greatest saints, say to her, 'We are alive, you know. You can talk to us if you want to.'

In the Celtic tradition, which values imaginative prayer, Christians take to heart Paul's teaching that 'we are fellow citizens with the saints and the household of God' (Ephesians 2:19). To them, there is no barrier between their own households and the great, eternal household. They visualise the saints being with them in their homes and in their boats:

> Who are they on the middle of the floor?
> John and Peter and Paul.
> Who are they by the front of my bed?
> Sun-bright Mary and her Son.

Carmina Gadelica (85)

In the days of the Celtic Mission a person who had attracted others to holiness was declared a holy one or saint by the local bishop at their funeral. This is still the practice in Eastern Churches.

The practice of specially remembering a saint on the anniversary of their death, which was thought of as their birthday into heaven, was established in the early British Church.

> When in the Acts of the Apostles the apostles came together in one place, Solomon's Porch, which became a focus of peace and unity, crowds came who were made whole from diseases even by the shadow cast by the apostles. And truly, up to this day, wherever Christians gather together for the yearly festival of an individual, the Lord never ceases to perform mighty works.
>
> On this splendid festal day of St Samson, at God's inspiration mighty works of God that are just as great have without doubt been witnessed. For this reason we recognise that God has endowed Samson with an everlasting quality and an unhampered freedom. As we celebrate the heavenly kingdom on his day we perceive the next life with a clear, keen insight. For we firmly believe that he is engaged in another, better, unending life among the saints of God, whom we see shining forth among us, strong and mighty in the Lord.
>
> From *The Life of Samson of Dol*

A prophecy about to be fulfilled?

King Edward of England, Confessor of Christ, died on 5 January 1066. According to his *Life*,* some time before he died he had a vision in which two deceased monks he had known in Normandy appeared to him and foretold that, since the people in high office were not what they seemed, but in reality served devils rather than God, one year and one day after Edward's death God would ravage

---

* *Vita Aedwardi Regis*, c. 1065-1067, Nelson Medieval Texts, 1962

the land with sword and fire. Exactly one year and one day after his death William the Conqueror, who led the Norman invasion which oppressed the church and people, was crowned king. In the vision Edward then asked the messengers when there would be forgiveness so that God's design could be shown to the people. They replied: When a green tree, if cut down in the middle of its trunk and the part cut off carried the space of three furlongs from the stock, shall be joined again to the trunk by itself and without the hand of man or any sort of stake, and begin once more to push leaves and bear fruit from the old love of its uniting sap, then first can remission of these great ills be hoped for.'*

We believe that the present renewal of the Celtic Christian tradition, with its organic reconnecting of the strands in Christianity that became separated, is a sign that the fulfilment of this prophecy is near.

---

* Quoted on page 251 of *Saints of England's Golden Age* compiled by Vladimir Moss, Center for Traditionalist Orthodox Studies, California, 2000.

About this book

A spiritual key

Each entry draws out one inspiring quality in the saint of the day, and reflects this in the Bible readings.

The aim of each prayer is to give thanks for that quality and to ask God to inspire us by it.

The calendar

The book starts with a calendar (pages 23-36) of the saints of Britain, Gaul and Ireland in the period of the undivided Christian Church (broadly, the first millennium) and of the universal saints of the undivided Church which are observed in Anglican, Orthodox or Roman Catholic calendars today. A few calendar saints are omitted because, in the light of modern scholarship, we now know that they have been confused with another person of the same name, or that they committed unholy acts.

A saint's day in bold print indicates that full, fourfold patterns of worship for that saint are included in Volume Four of *The Celtic Prayer Book*.

Generally, as already noted, a saint is celebrated on their death day, not their birthday, because that marks their birth into the fullness of resurrection life.

A few saints whose dates we don't know, whose dates clash with some other significant day, or who are commemorated on the day their remains were placed in a popular shrine, are celebrated on a day other than their death. The calendars of the various branches of the Church have different dates for a few saints. This book keeps a rough balance in choosing between these dates.

The daily introductions, prayers and readings

The main part of the book consists of the daily introduction, prayer, Psalm, Old Testament and New Testament reading for each day of the year.

When there is more than one saint in the calendar on any day, one of them is transferred to the nearest 'spare' day. Readers or churches may reverse these according to local preference.

A few lesser-known saints, a few later ones who have 'won a place' in the Celtic tradition, and various angels are also included. God-guided personalities in the Bible make up the remaining 'spare' days.

These transfers and additions are not indicated in the calendar, but are all listed in the index which concludes the book.

Not all the entries are of equal worth. For a few of them we depend upon legend for the human interest. This is indicated in the text.

The prayer endings

In order to keep the prayers sharp and heartfelt, we have not provided standardised endings. This frees readers to use their own preferred endings. A typical Anglican ending is:

... through Jesus Christ your Son, our Lord,
who is alive and reigns with you,
in the unity of the Holy Spirit,
one God, world without end.
Amen.

A typical Orthodox ending is:
   . . . to you we ascribe glory,
   to the Father, and to the Son, and to the Holy Spirit,
   both now and ever, to the ages of ages.
   Amen.

A typical Roman Catholic ending (if any is used) is:
   . . . we make our prayer through our Lord.

Other churches use varied or spontaneous endings, often:
   . . . through Jesus Christ, our Lord.

Use at the Eucharist

If this book is used at the Eucharists of Anglican, Orthodox or Roman Catholic Churches, a passage from a Gospel which reflects the theme needs to be chosen when a Gospel reading is not included here.

Names of countries

The terms Brittany (France), England, Scotland and Wales are sometimes used for the sake of simplicity, although these did not exist in the early centuries of the first millennium. The name of Brittany was Armorica. Britons were at first those throughout Britain who were not the English – the invading Anglo-Saxon colonists. The Irish, some of whom were at first known as Scotti, colonised part of north-east Britain and gave their name to Scotland.

Old Testament and apocryphal Books

The Protestant Old Testament consists of the selection of Jewish Scriptures in Hebrew, begun by the Pharisees, which was completed in the sixth century after Christ. Roman Catholics and Orthodox include the selection of Jewish Scriptures in Greek which were selected some two centuries before Christ. These are quoted by Jesus and New Testament writers. This lectionary includes a few extracts from these (Wisdom, Ecclesiasticus, Judith and Tobit) and one brief extract from the Ethiopian Book of Enoch, one of the Jewish pseudepigraphical writings which is not now in the apocrypha of any of the main Church streams although it is quoted by New Testament writers and early Church Fathers.

Readers who do not wish to use apocryphal readings may wish to choose an alternative from the Scriptures that all branches of the Church accept.

A Calendar of Saints' Days

Saints' days observed by Anglican, Orthodox or Roman Catholic Churches in Celtic lands

An entry in bold print indicates that full, fourfold patterns or worship for that saint are included in Volume Four of *The Celtic Prayer Book*

January

1	Basil, monastic founder, Bishop of Caesarea, d. 379
2	Seraphim, monk and staretz of Sarov, d. 1833
3	**Malachi, prophet, fourth century BC**
4	Abraham, father of Jews, Christians and Muslims, 2000 BC
5	**Paul of Thebes, the first Christian hermit, d. 353**
6	**The Wise Three**
7	**Cedd of Lastingham, Bishop of the East Saxons, d. 664**
8	Brannoc, abbot, founder of Braunton, sixth century
9	Ceowulf, king and monk of Northumbria, d. 764(?)
10	Hilary, Bishop of Poitiers
11	Benedict Biscop, Abbot of Wearmouth, d. 689
12	Aelred, Abbot of Rievaulx, d. 1167
13	**Mungo (also known as Kentigern), monk, evangelist, bishop, founder of Glasgow, d. 612**
14	Abbot Moses and the martyrs of the Sinai desert
15	Ita, spiritual mother of Killeedy, near Limerick, Ireland, d. 570
16	**Fursey, abbot, enlightener of the East Angles, d. 650**
17	Antony, monk and abbot of Egypt, d. 356
18	Moling, monk and founder of a ferry, d. 697
19	Branwalader (Brelade), missionary monk of Cornwall and the Channel Isles, sixth century
20	Sebastian, Roman martyr, d. 300
21	Fechin, founder of Irish monasteries, d. 665

22	Christ the Pantokreter (Prayer for Unity)
23	Remigius, Bishop of Rheims, d. 353
24	Francis de Sales, d. 1662
25	The conversion of the apostle Paul, first century
26	Timothy and Titus, Paul's mission partners, first century
27	Conan, first Bishop of Sodor and Man, d. 648
28	Isaac, Bishop of Nineveh, seventh century
29	Gildas the Wise, Abbot of Llaniltud and Brittany, d. 570
30	Gregory of Nazianzus, d. 389
31	Maedoc (Aidan) of Ferns, soul friend, d. 626

February

1	**Brigid (or Bride), Abbess of Kildare**
2	The dedication of the infant Christ, first century
3	Saints and martyrs of Europe
4	Ive (or Ia), sixth or seventh century(?)
5	Simeon, prophet, first century
6	Mel, evangelist of Ardagh, d. 488
7	Anna, prophet, first century
8	Elfleda, Abbess of Whitby, sister of King Egfrith, d. 714
9	Teilo, Bishop of Llanduff and Llandeilo Fawr, sixth century
10	Trumwine, missionary, Bishop of Abercorn and monk at Whitby, d. 704
11	**Caedmon of Whitby, first English songwriter, 680**
12	Ethilwald, monk, Bishop of Lindisfarne, d. 740
13	Apostles Aquila and Priscilla, first century
14	Cyril and Methodius, Apostles of the Slavs, died resp. 869 and 885
15	Oswy, King of Northumbria, d. 670
16	Five Egyptian and other martyrs, d. 309
17	Finan, monk of Iona, Bishop of Lindisfarne, d. 661
18	Colman, monk of Iona, Bishop of Lindisfarne, founder of Irish monasteries, d. 676

March

20	**Cuthbert, monk, evangelist and bishop of Lindisfarne, d. 687**
21	Enda, pioneer of Irish monasteries, d. 530
22	Jacob, father of Israel's twelve tribes, eighteenth century BC(?)
23	Joseph, saviour from famine, seventeenth century BC(?)
24	Judah, first head of one of Israel's tribes, eighteenth century BC(?)
25	Pregnancy of Mary, first century
26	Miriam, sister and preserver of the baby Moses, sixteenth century BC(?)
27	Tyfil, a child saint, sixth century
28	Moses, leader of Israel's march to freedom, sixteenth century BC(?)
29	Gwynllyw and Gwladys, lovers in love of the King of Life, sixth century
30	John of the Ladder (Climacus), monk and Abbot of Mount Sinai, d. 649
31	Joshua, God-guided military leader, fourteenth century BC(?)

April

1	Tewdric, prince and hermit, fifth-sixth century
2	Caleb, God's spy, fourteenth century BC(?)
3	Deborah, prophet, thirteenth century BC
4	Isidore, Archbishop of Seville, d. 636
5	Derfel (or Cadarn), monk, sixth century
6	Brychan, father of a great Christian family, sixth century
7	Brynach, soul friend of Brychan, sixth century
8	Saints and martyrs of the Americas
9	Madrun, mother, fosterer of churches, sixth century
10	Goran, hermit and patron of Gorran, Cornwall, sixth century
11	Guthlac, hermit of Crowland, d. 714
12	Gideon, deliverer of Israel, thirteenth century BC
13	Hannah, mother of the prophet Samuel, twelfth century BC

14	Padarn, founder of early churches in western Britain, fifth-sixth century
15	Ruadhan, one of the Twelve Apostles of Ireland, d. 584
16	Magnus, pirate, earl of Orkney, martyr, d. 1116
17	Donan and the Pictish martyrs, d. 618
18	Molaise, founder of monasteries, d. 639
19	Alphege, Archbishop of Canterbury, martyr, d. 1012
20	Monesan, passionate seeker of God, fifth century
21	Anselm, Archbishop of Canterbury, d. 1109
22	George, martyr, d. 304
23	Saints and martyrs of England
24	Beuno, founder of monasteries in North Wales, sixth century
25	Mark, evangelist, first century
26	Maelrubha, apostle of the Picts, d. 722
27	Machalus, ex-pirate, Bishop of the Isle of Man, d. 498
28	Modan, the Dryburgh Abba of the Sweet Discipline, sixth century
29	Endellion, God's survivor, sixth century
30	Earconwald, Bishop of London, d. 693

May

1	Joseph the worker, legal father of Jesus, first century
2	Athanasius, Bishop of Alexandria, d. 373
3	Philip and James, apostles, first century
4	Asaph, Bishop of St Asaph, d. early seventh century
5	Molua, monk, builder and hermit of Killaloe, died c. 609
6	Eadbert, Bishop of Lindisfarne, d. 698
7	John of Beverley, Bishop of York, d. 721
8	Eithne, prophetic mother, fifth and sixth century
9	Mother Julian, anchoress and mystic of Norwich, d. 1417
10	Comgall, Abbot of Bangor, Ireland, d. 601
11	Indract, seventh century
12	Ishmael, founding father of a great people, seventeenth century BC

13	Samuel, seer and nation shaper, twelfth century BC
14	Matthias, apostle, first century
15	Pachomius, founder of Christian communal monasticism, d. 346
16	**Brendan the Navigator, Abbot of Clonfert, died _c._ 575**
17	Madron, monk and healer of Cornwall, sixth century(?)
18	Carantoc, missionary, sixth or seventh century
19	Dunstan, Archbishop of Canterbury, 988
20	Alcuin of York, advisor to Charlemagne, Abbot of Tours, d. 804
21	Helena, protector of holy places, finder of the Cross, d. 330
22	Helen of Caernarvon, founder of churches, fourth century
23	Aldhem, Abbot of Malmesbury, Bishop of Sherborne, d. 709
24	Vincent of Lerins, pilgrim for the love of the Trinity, d. 450
25	Bede, monk of Jarrow, first English historian, d. 735
26	Augustine, apostle to Kent, first Archbishop of Canterbury, d. 604 or 605
27	Melangell, hermit and founder of Pennant-Melangell refuge, d. 590
28	Cummian the Tall, abandoned child, great scholar of Clonfert, d. 661
29	Buryan, Irish lady, saint of Cornwall, fifth century(?)
30	Jonathan, King David's friend, tenth century BC
31	Mary and Elizabeth, soul friends, first century

June

1	Justin, philosopher and martyr, d. 166
2	Ronan, monk of Cornwall and Brittany, sixth century(?)
3	Kevin, hermit and founder of Glendalough, d. 618
4	Petroc, Abbot of Padstow, hermit, sixth century

August

1   Neot, monk and hermit, d. 877

2   Germanus, Bishop of Auxerre, d. 446

3   Ignatius of Loyola, founder of the Society of Jesus,
     d. 1556

4   John (Jean-Marie) Vianney, Cure d'Ars, d. 1859

5   **Oswald, king and 'martyr', d. 642**

6   Elijah, Moses, and three apostles with Christ
     on the mount, first century

7   Haggai, prophet, sixth century BC

8   Lide (or Elidius), hermit of the Isles of Scilly, tenth
     or eleventh century(?)

9   Daniel, government officer, sixth and fifth century BC

10   Lawrence, martyr, d. 258

11   Blane, monk and bishop, sixth century

12   Muredach, bishop and founder of Innismurray,
     sixth century

13   Hananiah, Mishael and Azariah, sixth and fifth
     century BC

14   Fachanan, Abbot of Ross Carbery, sixth century

15   The Resurrection of the Virgin Mary

16   Armel, monk and intercessor of Brittany, sixth century

17   Nehemiah, steward, rebuilder of the walls,
     fifth century BC

18   Ezra, Secretary of State, restorer of Jewish Law,
     fifth century BC

19   Micaiah the truth-teller, tenth century BC

20   Oswin, king, patron of mission, d. 651

21   Thaddeus, apostle, first century

22   Esther, Queen of Persia who saved the Jews
     from extinction, fifth century BC

23   Irenaeus, teacher and Bishop of Lyons, d. 200

24   Bartholomew, apostle, first century

25   Ebbe, d. 683, and the enshrining of Hilda

26   Fiacre the gardener, d. 670, and Ninian

27   Monica, Mother of Augustine of Hippo, d. 387

28   Augustine of Hippo, bishop and teacher, d. 430

29   The beheading of John the Baptist, first century

| 30 | Sebbi, king and monk, d. 694 |
| **31** | **Aidan, apostle to the English, d. 651** |

September

1	Drithelm, the man who came back from the dead, d. 700
2	Giles, hermit of Provence, seventh century
3	Gregory the Great, d. 604
4	Phoebe, church deacon, first century
5	Cuthbert's enshrining, 698
6	Bega, abbess, seventh century
7	Eanswyth, founder of England's first convent, d. 640
8	The birth of the Virgin Mary, first century
9	Ciaran of Clonmacnoise, d. 545
10	Finnian of Moville, d. 579
11	Deiniol, abbot, d. 584
12	Ailbe, founder abbot, early sixth century
13	John Chrysostom (the 'golden-mouthed'), d. 407
14	The true Cross
15	Cyprian, Bishop of Carthage, martyr, d. 258
16	**Ninian, founder abbot of Whithorn, missionary to Picts, died _c._ 432**
17	Hildegaard, mystic of Bingen, d. 1179
18	Edith of Wilton, d. 984
19	Theodore, Archbishop of Canterbury, d. 690
20	Honorius, Archbishop of Canterbury, d. 653
21	Matthew, apostle and Gospel writer, first century
22	Ceolfrith, Abbot of Jarrow, d. 716
23	Adomnan, Abbot of Iona, reformer of women's rights, d. 704
24	Sergius, abbot and builder of Russia, d. 1392
25	Finbarr, bishop and patron of Cork and Barra, d. 610
26	Cadoc, monastic founder and spiritual guide, died _c._ 577
27	Attracta, indomitable Irish pioneer, fifth century
28	Wenceslas, martyr, Prince of Bohemia, d. 929
29	Michael the Angel Force leader
30	Jerome, Bible translator and scholar, d. 420

October

1   All angels
2   Guardian angels
3   Seraphim
4   Francis of Assisi, founder of Franciscans, d. 1226
5   Edwin, king and martyr, d. 633
6   Thomas, apostle, first century
7   Iwi, hermit and miracle worker, seventh century
8   Enshrinement of Aidan
9   Denys, martyr, died *c.* 250
10 Paulinus, bishop, d. 644
11 Kenneth (Canice or Cainneach), died *c.* 600
12 Wilfred, bishop, d. 709
13 James the Deacon, seventh century
14 Ethelburga, Abbess of Barking, d. 675
15 Teresa of Avila, founder of Reformed Carmelites, d. 1582
16 Gall, fisherman hermit in Switzerland, d. 630
17 Frideswide, Abbess of Oxford, d. 727
18 Luke, apostle and evangelist, first century
19 The Angel Michael's appearance at Mont St Michel
20 Acca, monk and Bishop of Hexham, d. 732
21 Tuda, Abbot and Bishop of Lindisfarne, d. 664
22 Donatus of Ireland, Bishop of Fiesole, died *c.* 876
23 James, brother of the Lord, first century
24 Maglorius of Sark, founder of monasteries, d. 575
25 Crispin and Crispinian, shoemakers and martyrs, d. 287
26 Alfred the Great, king and founder of monasteries, d. 899
27 Eata, Abbot of Lindisfarne and Bishop of Hexham, d. 686
28 Simon and Jude, apostles, first century
29 Hilarion, monastic pioneer of Palestine, d. 372
30 Raphael and the Seven Angels
31 Local saints (Halloween – Eve of All Saints)

November

1   All Saints
2   All souls and ancestors
3   Cadfan of Bardsey, fifth century
4   Winefride, healer, seventh century
5   All saints of Ireland
6   **Illtyd, founder and Abbot of Llanilltyd Fawr, sixth century**
7   Willibrord, apostle of Frisia, Archbishop of Utrecht, d. 739
8   Tysilio, Abbot of Meifod, seventh century
9   All saints of Wales
10   Justus, Archbishop of Canterbury, d. 627
11   Martin, monk and merciful Bishop of Tours, d. 397
12   Machar, spiritual father of Aberdeen, sixth century
13   Cadwalader, king and protector of British Christians, d. 664
14   Dyfrig (Dubricius), bishop in Hereford and Gwent, hermit of Bardsey island, d. 560(?)
15   Malo, rugged apostle of Brittany, seventh century
16   Margaret, queen and patron of Scotland, d. 1093
17   **Hilda, Abbess of Whitby, Mother of the Church, d. 680**
18   Mawes, bishop and healer in Cornwall and Brittany, fifth century
19   Egbert, Archbishop of York, d. 766
20   Edmund, king and martyr, d. 869
21   Eucherius, solitary and Bishop of Lyons, d. 449
22   Gregory, Bishop of Tours, d. 594
23   **Columbanus of Ireland, Abbot of Luxeuil and Bobbio, d. 615**
24   Enfleda, Abbess of Whitby, d. 704
25   Alnoth of Stowe, hermit and martyr, died *c.* 700
26   Aedh MacBric, founder of monastic churches, sixth century
27   Leonard, Abbot and hermit, sixth century(?)
28   Philip the Deacon, first century

| 29 | Brendan of Birr, abbot, 'chief of the prophets of Ireland', d. 573 |
| 30 | Andrew, apostle, martyr, patron of Scotland, first century |

December

1	Saints and martyrs of Scotland
2	Tudwal, bishop in Wales and Brittany, sixth century
3	Justinian, hermit of Ramsay, sixth century
4	John of Damascus, poet, friend of Muslims, d. 749
5	Birinus, apostle of Wessex, first Bishop of Dorchester, d. 650
6	Nicholas, Bishop of Myra, the original Santa Claus, d. 343
7	Ambrose, Bishop of Milan, d. 397
8	Conception of the Virgin Mary, first century
9	Lydia, Paul's first European convert, first century
10	Saints and martyrs of Asia
11	Edburga, Abbess of Minster, d. 751
12	Finnian, Bishop of Clonard, died *c.* 549
13	Lucy, virgin and martyr, d. 304
14	John of the Cross, virtual founder of the dispersed Carmelite friars, 1591
15	Hybald, Abbot in Lincolnshire, seventh century
16	Ruth, God-honouring ancestor of Jesus, between the fourteenth and the twelfth century BC
17	Jesse, father of King David, forebear of Jesus
18	Samthann, Abbess of Clonbroney, d. 739
19	Winnibald, missionary and Abbot of Heidenham, d. 761
20	Ignatius the God-bearer of Antioch, d. 107
21	Isaiah, prophet, eighth century BC
22	Micah, prophet, eighth century BC
23	David, king, Jesus' forebear, tenth century BC
24	Josiah, king, Jesus' forebear, seventh century BC
24	Mary, Joseph and the shepherds, witnesses of Jesus' birth
25	**Jesus**
26	**Stephen, the first martyr, first century**

A candle lighting for any saint's day

Leader   Light and peace has come into the world
through our Lord Jesus Christ
and through his saints.

All   The light of Christ has come into the world.

Leader   You led your ancient people to freedom
with a cloud by day and a fire by night.

All   The light of Christ has come into the world.

Leader   You led your people out of darkness
through the holy prayers and powerful signs
of (*name of saint*).

All   The light of Christ has come into the world.

Leader   May we who walk in the light of your presence
acclaim your Christ, rising victorious with his
saints.

Reader   Give yourself to the Lord and he will make
your righteousness shine like the midday sun.
Psalm 37:5, 6

Notice the good person, observe the righteous
person.
Psalm 37:37

A candle is lit

Reader   Precious in the eyes of the Lord is the death
of God's saints.
Psalm 115:15

Reader There shall be no more night, because the Lord God will be their light, and they will rule as monarchs for ever and ever.
Revelation 22:5

We do not run life's race alone. Let us call to mind that great cloud of Christ's witnesses who urge us on and inspire us by their example.

They are the righteous who shine like the midday sun. By their deeds, their words, their gifts, they became holy, and God blessed the world with signs and wonders through both their lives and their deaths. The place of their tombs became the place of resurrection. Now, as they stand in the presence of Christ who gave them glory, they pray for us who celebrate their lives.

Sources of divine healing, channels of spiritual gifts, rivers of mercy raising up the poor, symphonies of joy who gladdened our earth, valiant fighters who overcome things that destroy our world.

Martyrs who thought lightly of death, whose blood made holy the land, and whose death illumined the air.

Enlighteners of believers and seekers, patient bearers of troubles –

Rejoice with us, unseen saints and angels with whom we are united in spirit.

There may be a reading of Matthew 5:1-12 or Hebrews 12:22-24.

Reader   When stripped of all, they became rich in spirit.
Being meek, they inherited the land.
Hungering for justice, they were satisfied.
Peacemakers, they were adopted as heaven's
children.
Persecuted, they now exult in glory.

All   Alleluia.

Saints of the Isles

An introduction, prayer and Bible readings
for each day of the year

Basil

Monastic founder, Bishop of Caesarea, d. 379

Basil founded monastic faith communities which combined freedom to follow individual callings with a common framework that had the feel of a household. He became bishop of Caesarea in the fourth century, and a great teacher. He helped people understand the wonderful fact that God and a human being were truly united in Christ, and that the easy line of followers of Arius, that Christ could not be God, missed out on a vital truth. Celtic churches highly esteemed him as a monk and teacher.

PRAYER
Eternal God,
whose servant Basil proclaimed the mystery
of your Word made flesh,
as by the incarnation you gathered into one
things earthly and heavenly,
gather us into the divine glory
that it may shine in us now and through the ages.

READINGS
Psalm 22
Wisdom 7:15-22a
Ephesians 4:1-7, 11-13

Seraphim

Monk and staretz of Sarov, d. 1833

Born in Kursk, Seraphim entered the monastery at Sarov and received permission to live as a hermit in the forest where he shared food with a wild bear. Although he was strong, he allowed thieves to injure him with his own axe rather than use violence himself. For three years he entered total silence back in the monastery. After this, many people were transformed just by one word from Seraphim. He taught: 'Learn to be peaceful and thousands around you will find salvation.' His fame as a staretz, or spiritual guide, spread throughout Russia. A young disciple, Nicholas Motovilov, who experienced the 'warming of the Spirit' while with Seraphim in the snow, wrote down many of his teachings, which emphasised how the Holy Spirit can transform the soul, and the importance of poverty, prayer and service. He has been called 'The Flame in the Snow'.

PRAYER
Eternal Fire,
who lit up the cold stable at Bethlehem
through the birth of your Son,
and enflamed the snows of Russia
through your servant Seraphim,
pour upon the weakness of our nature
the transforming fire of your Presence.

READINGS
Psalm 67; Wisdom 3:1-9; Luke 11:33-36

Malachi

Prophet, fourth century BC

Malachi, meaning 'messenger', is the only name by which we know this prophet who emerged in Jerusalem after its temple had been restored, the early zeal of the returning exiles had faded, and shoddy practices had become endemic. Malachi reminds the people that God loves them, and that their sins consist in offering perfunctory religious observances without conversion of heart. He calls on them to restore dedicated almsgiving, to honour marriage and to prepare for a coming time of deliverance.

PRAYER
Sun of suns,
may your saving power and healing rays come to us.
Make us as free and happy as calves let out of an enclosure.
Bring divided families together again.
Help us to prepare the way for you.

Echoes words of Malachi

READINGS
Psalm 116
Malachi 2:17-3:12
Luke 6:27-36

Abraham

Father of Jews, Christians and Muslims, 2000 BC

Born at Ur, in modern Iraq, before the rise of monotheist religions, Abraham was led by some divine inspiration to venture into the unknown territory of Canaan. Though his wife Sarah was past child-bearing age, he was promised, by a further divine revelation, a child whose descendants would be more numerous than the stars, and told that through him all peoples of the world would be blessed. Christians, as well as Jews and Muslims, recognise Abraham as a spiritual ancestor on account of his faith.

PRAYER
God of the call,
who led Abraham into the unknown
in order to bless all nations
and teach them the dignity of difference,
go before us in our pilgrimage of life;
guide our steps,
and bless the world family of which we are part.

READINGS
Psalm 47
Genesis 12:1-9
Romans 4:1-12

Paul of Thebes

The first Christian hermit, d. 353

Paul is the first Christian hermit known by name. He fled from persecution into the Egyptian desert and lived his long life there alone, until Antony sought him out and communed with him at the end of his life. Jerome wrote a *Life* of this saint. The Northumbrian Cross of Ruthwell and many Irish High Crosses depict these two Egyptian hermits, Paul and Antony.

PRAYER
God who enfolds us in our beginning and our departing,
and in whom alone we find our true identity,
as we marvel that Paul found well-being
in a desert bereft of human accretions,
so we pray that we may grow in our true identity
and be weaned from false addictions.

READINGS
Psalm 26:1-11
Nehemiah 9:13-21
Acts 7:23-38

The Wise Three

Matthew's Gospel (2:1-12) records a visit to the infant Jesus of the first non-Jews to believe in Christ. Guided in part by an unusual star, they came from the east and brought gifts of gold, frankincense and myrrh. Perhaps because they called on King Herod and brought three gifts, later Christian writers suggested that they were three kings. Their names were first mentioned in the sixth century, and by the Northumbrian historian Bede in the seventh: Caspar, Melchior and Balthasar. The Milanese claimed that their relics were brought from Constantinople in the fifth century. These three figures remain an abiding symbol of the power of Jesus to evoke adoration among people from a non-biblical culture who are open to the divine in the natural world.

PRAYER
Infant King,
in the spirit of the three sages
we offer you the gold of our possessions,
the incense of our devotions,
and the myrrh of our daily dyings.
May those we meet in our travels
know that we have been in your presence.

READINGS
Psalm 72:1-11
Isaiah 49:1-6
Matthew 2:1-12

Cedd of Lastingham

Bishop of the East Saxons, d. 664

Cedd was one of four brothers trained at Aidan's Lindisfarne monastery. Sent south to evangelise the East Saxons, he established small Christian communities at Bradwell, Prittlewell, Mersea, Tilbury and Upminster, and was made their bishop. When he was recalled to build a monastery to which the king of Northumbria might come to pray, he chose Lastingham, a site amid steep and rugged hills.

Cedd, who blended Irish and Roman ways and knew both languages, was trusted by both sides to be the translator at the Synod of Whitby in 664, which adjudicated between their rival claims. Bede likened his role to that of the Holy Spirit at Pentecost, who enabled the peoples from various backgrounds to understand the message of Peter despite their different languages.

PRAYER
Thank you for Cedd
who was neither corroded by cynicism
nor cluttered by ecclesial bureaucracy,
but was straightforward, clear, prayerful, confident:
through friendship, gathering others,
through meditation, teaching others,
through prayer, uplifting others.
He served you willingly; so may we.

READINGS
Psalm 52; Isaiah 35; Acts 2:1-12

*or 26 October

Brannoc

Abbot, founder of Braunton, sixth century

Brannoc was a wandering pilgrim from Brittany who sailed round Land's End to Britain. According to legend he had a vision that he was to establish a Christian community at a place where he would find a sow with a litter of piglets. This place became Braunton Burrows, North Devon, whose fields he was the first to cultivate. In the Middle Ages the people of Braunton Burrows celebrated their founder by carving pigs on the roof bosses and bench ends of their new church built over Brannoc's tomb.

PRAYER
In the spirit of Brannoc,
help us to sail the seas of life with you, dear Lord,
and to let the work of our lives
be in response to your call.

READINGS
Psalm 65
Deuteronomy 7:9-13
Galatians 6:7-10

* transferred from 7 January

Ceowulf

King and monk of Northumbria, d. 764(?)

Ceowulf became king of Northumbria in 729, was deposed in 731 and forced to take a monk's tonsure, but was released and continued to rule until 737. He then abdicated and voluntarily became a monk of Lindisfarne. Though his ability as a ruler was questioned, his humility and generosity as a monk was not. He liberally endowed Lindisfarne and as a result the monks drank beer instead of water for the first time! Ceowulf was buried near Cuthbert at Lindisfarne, and people claimed that miracles at his shrine proved his holiness.

PRAYER
God of the call,
as we recall how Ceowulf was willing
to renounce power and prestige
in order to follow his vocation as a monk,
help us to find and follow our most authentic calling.

READINGS
Psalm 115:1-13
2 Kings 22:14-20
1 Corinthians 2:6-16

* transferred from 15 January

Hilary

Bishop of Poitiers

Hilary was elected Bishop of Poitiers in 350, when Arius' teaching that Christ was not divine swept through the church. Hilary, a great teacher and writer, taught that people were created to reflect the moral qualities of the Trinity, and that Jesus and the Father were in essence the same. Although he was exiled for a time, the Church in Celtic lands remained true to the Trinity throughout the Arian controversy. Hilary discipled Martin of Tours.

PRAYERS
All-compassionate Triune God,
keep us from the vain strife of words
and make us consistent witnesses to the truth.
Preserve us in the true and uncorrupted Faith,
that we may always hold to what we pledged
when we were baptised into the Father, Son and Holy Spirit:
that we may have you for our Father,
that we may live in your Son
and in the fellowship of the Holy Spirit.

Hilary, adapted

READINGS
Psalm 43
Ezekiel 34:1-10 or Zechariah 13:7-9
John 8:25-32

* transferred from 13 January

Benedict Biscop

Abbot of Wearmouth, d. 689

Following service with the Northumbrian king Oswy, Biscop Baducing decided to become a monk. After two study tours of Rome, one with King Oswy's son Alcfrith, he became a monk at Lerins. He returned from a third visit to Rome with Theodore, the new Archbishop of Canterbury, and briefly became an abbot at Canterbury. With the help of King Ecfrith he founded the Wearmouth monastery in 674, instituting his version of the Rule of Benedict, after whom he named himself. He brought back from further visits to Rome innumerable books and artefacts and a chanter who taught his monks the Roman uncial script, liturgy and chanting. He then founded the twin monastery of Jarrow. Biscop's library made possible the achievements of Bede.

PRAYER
God of majesty,
Benedict Biscop sought to reflect your greatness
in the liturgies and arts of the Church.
Save us from cramped and penny-pinching attitudes;
may we leave a legacy of beauty
that will for long draw people to you.

READINGS
Psalm 100; Haggai 2:1-9; Revelation 15:2-8

* transferred from 12 January

Aelred

Abbot of Rievaulx, d. 1167

Aelred, whose parents were guardians of St Cuthbert's shrine at Durham, revived a spirit of genuine friendship in his own and other monasteries at a time when uniform codes of conduct stultified spontaneity in relationships. His monastery at Rievaulx, Yorkshire, became the largest in England. He drew inspiration from the biblical writings of John, and from Celtic saints. His own writings include a *Life* of St Ninian and a *Treatise on Friendship*.

PRAYER
Holy and loving God,
who revealed fresh facets of your grace
in the radiant friendship of your servant Aelred,
renew in us the gift of friendship,
so that in loving one another,
we may more deeply reflect on earth
the eternal love of the Trinity.

READINGS
Psalm 131
Proverbs 18:1-16, 24
John 15:11-17

Mungo

Monk, evangelist, bishop, founder of Glasgow, d. 612

Mungo (also known as Kentigern), was reputed to be the grandson of King Loth (from whom the Scottish Lothians take their name). He survived the attempted killing of his pregnant mother who had been raped, and was brought up by the Christian community at Culross. He was consecrated Bishop of Strathclyde in the Irish tradition, and pioneered much Christian mission there, until a resurgence of paganism forced him to flee south. According to his biographer, Jocelyn, he founded a large monastery in Wales before returning north. For eight years he based his mission at Hoddam until he was able finally to return to what is now Glasgow, of which he is the founder. He met with Columba before his death and is buried in Glasgow's St Mungo's Cathedral.

PRAYER
Father,
who through your servant Mungo
caused the light to shine in pagan Britain,
thank you that in both success and adversity
he trusted in your saving power.
Anchor our mission upon the rock
of your goodness and mercy.

READINGS
Psalm 16
Zechariah 13:7-9
Mark 13:9-11

Abbot Moses and the martyrs of the Sinai desert

A robber named Moses reformed his life and lived as a hermit in the Egyptian desert. He became a soul friend to young people who joined him there. One day his desert brothers learned that an armed band was on its way to loot their dwellings and leave them for dead. They urged that they should make a quick escape. 'I have waited so long for this day,' Moses replied, 'my death will be a fitting reminder of Jesus' saying, "Those who use the sword shall die by the sword."' Seven brothers were killed. One brother, however, who hid under some palm fronds observed seven crowns coming to rest on the head of each brother.

PRAYER
God of crowning,
Moses dared much for fleeting gain,
and dared even more for eternal treasure.
Spur us on to give our all
in that adventure which alone is crowned with glory.

READINGS
Psalm 119:89-96
Proverbs 30:4-9
1 Corinthians 9:25-10:13

Ita

Spiritual mother of Killeedy, Ireland, d. 570

Ita was a spiritual guide to many in Killeedy, near Limerick, and established a school for boys, including Brendan. Her spiritual guidance came from the indwelling of the Holy Trinity. These words are attributed to her: 'Three things that please God most are: Faith in God with a pure heart, a simple heart with a grateful spirit, generosity inspired by love. The three things that most displease God are: A mouth that hates people, a heart harbouring resentments, trusting in wealth.'

PRAYER
O Wisdom from on high,
as once you dwelt in Ita,
come now and dwell within us.
Give us a true faith, a pure heart,
a grateful spirit, and a generosity inspired by love,
until we become a nursery for saints in our time.

READINGS
Psalm 119:97-104
1 Kings 3:1-12
James 3:13-18

Fursey

Abbot, enlightener of the East Angles, d. 650

Fursey travelled Ireland with the Good News of Christ, attracted large crowds, and founded a monastery at Killfursa (now named Killarsagh). In 633 he and a few others arrived in East Anglia to convert the pagan Angles to Christianity. The king gave Fursey a base, at Burgh Castle, near today's Great Yarmouth. In a vision during illness he saw four fires – Falsehood, Covetousness, Discord, and Cruelty – that threatened to consume the world. Ever afterwards he confronted people with the choice between life and death with an intensity that made him sweat. After a period as a hermit in the Fens, Fursey travelled to France and established a monastery at Lagny-Sur-Marne. After his death in 650 his body was taken to Peronne monastery which became a large shrine where many miracles were witnessed.

PRAYER
God of the journey,
whose holy scholar Fursey,
impelled by the visions you entrusted to him,
gave his life as a pilgrim for love of you,
spare us your anger,
and help us to heed and speed your word.

READINGS
Psalm 48; Job 33:15-30; Revelation 20:11-21:4;
Matthew 3;13:36-43

Antony

Monk and abbot of Egypt, d. 356

At the age of 20, in about 271, Antony heard Jesus' message: 'If you would be perfect, sell all your possessions, give the money to the poor and you will have treasure in heaven; then come and follow me.' He gave away his wealth and lived a life of prayer, work and hospitality in the desert, overcoming all kinds of spiritual attacks. He became a spiritual guide, and many flocked to the desert to follow his example. He has been called 'the father of monasticism'.

PRAYER
O Christ,
who called your disciples to be perfect
as your Father is perfect,
help us to follow Antony in the way of perfection,
that we may count all things but loss
for the reward of knowing you.

READINGS
Psalm 91
1 Kings 17:2-6
Matthew 19:16-26

Moling

Monk and founder of a ferry, d. 697

Moling went from Leinster to become a monk at Glendalough, Ireland. He was rather serious and did not even permit himself the pleasure of listening to music. Then a visiting harpist went to play music to Moling who was alone in the church. Moling merely stuffed two balls of wax in his ears! But as the harpist continued to play, Moling thought the wax in his ears began to melt, and his hardness began to melt also. He came to understand that music can be a source of goodness as well as of evil. Moling founded his own monastery at St Mullins (County Carlow) and also its ferry service. Later he succeeded Maedoc as spiritual father of Ferns. The bejewelled Book of Mulling, contains a plan of Moling's monastery.

PRAYER
O Son of God, change my heart.
Your spirit composes the songs of the birds
and the buzz of the bees.
Your creation is a million wondrous miracles,
beautiful to look upon.
I ask of you just one more miracle:
beautify my soul.

From a traditional Celtic prayer

READINGS
Psalm 81; 1 Chronicles 13:1-8; Colossians 3:12-17

Branwalader (Brelade)

Monk of Cornwall and the Channel Isles, sixth century

Branwalader, missionary monk, whose name in Welsh means 'raven lord', is known in French as Brelade. He was said to be the son of Kenen, a Cornish king. Renowned as 'a star', he forsook his fame and fortune for the life of a wandering missionary monk. He most likely trained at the Welsh monastery at Llantwit Major where Samson was a fellow pupil. These two were to work together in Ireland, Cornwall, the Channel Isles and Brittany. When the North men laid waste the Breton church where the earthly remains of these two saints were kept, King Athelstan brought them for safe keeping, still together, to his monastery at Milton Abbas, on this day in 935. Many pilgrims come to the Fisherman's Chapel at St Brelade's Bay, Jersey, where Branwalader first prayed, and sense a return to ancient ways.

PRAYER
God of the seas and fisherfolk,
with unwavering faith Branwalader allowed you
to sweep him to varied shores,
where many were swept along by you.
Keep us moving,
with our eyes on the horizons you open up to us,
that we may may be swept along
in the greatness of your plans.

READINGS
Psalm 29; Habakkuk 2:5-14; Acts 27:27-38

20 JANUARY

Sebastian

Roman martyr, d. 300

Sebastian had connections with Milan but was put to death in Rome under the persecution of Christians by the Emperor Diocletian. He was buried in a cemetery on the Appian Way near a basilica which bears his name. His fame came when he was made a figure in a fifth-century fable. In this he is portrayed as a well-built young soldier shot through with arrows aimed at non-fatal parts of his stripped body, so that he died slowly, recovering sufficiently to confront the emperor before being clubbed to death. The image of his pierced body became a centrepiece of Renaissance art. As an example of fortitude, Sebastian became the patron of many military, police and archery associations.

PRAYER
Holy God,
strong and patient, resolute against wrong,
inspired by the martyrdom and the story of Sebastian,
make us firmer in our faith,
and put fibre into our being.

READINGS
Psalm 31:17-24
Deuteronomy 20:1-9
1 John 2:12-17

Fechin

Founder of Irish monasteries, d. 665

Fechin had a God-given ability to cause water to flow in dry places. St Fechin's well, in County Sligo, Ireland, marks the place where he prayed for a source of water for a parched region. At Fore, life was so hard for the monks that Fechin hewed out rock with his own hands until water burst through. At Omly, he immersed the entire pagan population in the waters of baptism. At his death in 665 a friend saw a light so bright that it was believed all Ireland's demons fled for a time.

PRAYER
Living God,
may we strike the rocks of human resistance
until we draw from them waters of salvation.
May we drink deeply of you,
Fount of Life eternal.

READINGS
Psalm 1
Exodus 17:1-7
John 7:37-39

* transferred from 20 January

Christ the Pantokreter

(Prayer for Unity)

Pantokreter is a title given to God in his aspect as the Cosmic Christ who holds together everything that exists. In icons the Pantokreter is often represented as a regal figure sitting outside a sphere that represents either this planet or the entire cosmos. St Paul teaches this, and also that through him God decided to bring the whole created universe back to himself (Colossians 1:20). The Greek word for the last phrase is *oikumene*, and from this comes our word ecumenism. The main Church streams throughout the world pray at this time that the whole created universe may move from fragmentation towards unity in Christ, and that the Church – the Body of Christ – may take the lead in patterning this.

PRAYER
Christ the Pantokreter,
Source of co-operation in the flux and flow of the cosmos,
bearer of the pain of its fragmentation,
we pray for the whole created universe.
Gather all things into one,
and start with us,
by bringing us into true communion
with all your brothers and sisters on earth.

READINGS
Psalm 133
Isaiah 42:1-6
Colossians 1:15-20

Remigius

Bishop of Rheims, d. 353

While Remigius was Bishop of Rheims, Clovis I, king of the Franks, was converted to his wife's Christian faith. He attributed to Christ his victory in battle and his son's healing, and asked Remigius to baptise him and thousands of his household and staff. Remigius observed that Clovis came to 'adore what he had burned and burn what he had adored'. Under the protection of Clovis, Remigius founded many churches. After his death his ministry became legendary. England's King Edward the Confessor and his Norman successors claimed that Remigius had the power of touching for the 'king's evil', transmitted by him to Clovis. Churches in England as well as France were dedicated to him.

PRAYER
Healing God,
who through Remigius touched a king
and guided a people,
give us your touch with the people we meet
and make us sure guides for a searching people.

READINGS
Psalm 20
Habakkuk 2:1-4
Matthew 28:16-20

Francis de Sales

d. 1662

Francis de Sales finds a place in this calendar because he restored the elements of praying and listening to God in the ordinary things of life – elements which were often overlaid following the decline of Celtic spirituality. He was brought up in Savoy and trained in law before he was appointed the Roman Catholic bishop in Geneva. In his many letters of spiritual guidance and in books such as his *Introduction to the Devout Life* he put prayer and meditation within reach of all Christians.

PRAYER
Teach us, O Christ,
according to the counsel of Francis,
to come into your presence as to a king,
to free ourselves from false attachments,
to seek your voice in the silence,
and to dwell on the beauty of the virtues.

READINGS
Psalm 16
Proverbs 9:1-12
1 Corinthians 3:9-17

Conversion of the apostle Paul

first century

The Church began to celebrate the conversion of Paul in the sixth century. Saul thought he was doing God a favour by persecuting Christians, until, while he was on the road to Damascus in order to accuse and arrest more Christians, he had a dramatic conversion, and Christ himself spoke to him in blinding light. Saul lost his sight, but a Christian named Ananias was led by God to pray for him; Saul regained his sight and was baptised. Saul became Paul, the world-shaping apostle of Christ and author of most of the New Testament letters.

PRAYER
May the Father of our Lord Jesus
give you the Spirit who will reveal God to you,
that your minds may be opened to God's light,
that you may know the hope to which you are called,
and how rich are the wonderful blessings
God promises to give you.
Paul

READINGS
Psalm 67
Jeremiah 1:4-10
Acts 9:1-22

Timothy and Titus

Paul's mission partners, first century

On the day following the conversion of Paul, the Church remembers two of his most trusted mission partners, Timothy and Titus. Timothy had a Jewish mother and a Greek father (both Christians), and Paul (as well as Timothy's grandmother) had fostered his faith since he was a child. Two letters Paul wrote to him are preserved in the New Testament. Timothy was ordained, and was an 'ambassador' charged by Paul with difficult tasks. Tradition says that he died as a martyr. Titus was wholly Greek. The close bond between Paul and Titus shows in the requests that he prepare places for his visits, and ordain church leaders. Paul wrote a letter to assist Titus in his difficult leadership role at Crete. It was because of Titus that Paul stood out against compulsory circumcision, but to avoid suspicion from Jews Titus was circumcised. Titus was with Paul during part of his second imprisonment.

PRAYER
God of encouragement,
who by the labours of Timothy and Titus
supported the mission of Paul,
won others to Christ,
and established your people in the true Faith,
help us, like them, to fight the good fight of faith
and lay hold on eternal life.

READINGS
Psalm 100; Isaiah 61:1-3a; 2 Timothy 2:1-8 or Titus 1:1-5

Conan

First Bishop of Sodor and Man, d. 648

Conan was a monk in Ireland where he mentored Fiacre, who then established a hermitage in Brittany. Conan seems to have worked in the Hebrides and the Isle of Man. The Vikings named him as the first Bishop of Sodor.

PRAYER
God our Mentor,
who blessed the work of Conan as a spiritual parent,
help us to grow in our ability to help others.

READINGS
Psalm 33:1-12
Judges 17:7-13
Luke 13:22-30

* transferred from January 26

Isaac

Bishop of Nineveh, seventh century

Isaac was born in Kurdistan, India. After a short time in a monastery he withdrew to the desert and became so highly regarded that he was pressed, and reluctantly agreed, to become Bishop of Nineveh in 670. But when two feuding church members rejected his counsel and told him to leave the Gospel out of the matter, he realised the 'soil was hard', and left to live first among the ascetics in the mountains of Kurdistan and then in the monastery of Rabban Shapur. There he wrote his *Ascetical Homilies*, a spiritual classic that portrays the purpose of human life as loving communion with God. He wrote, 'A person of compassionate heart has a heart aflame for humankind, for the birds, the animals, for the devils, for every creature.'

PRAYER
God of the compassionate heart,
who enflamed Isaac with a gentle love for all,
teach us to be weaned
from the addictive compulsions of our age,
until heaven enters our hearts
and becomes our delight beyond compare.

READINGS
Psalm 119:1-14
Hosea 2:14-23
1 John 4:7-19

Gildas the Wise

Abbot of Llaniltud and in Brittany, d. 570

After training at St Illtyd's monastic college, Gildas moved
to a hermitage in Somerset, perhaps at Steep Holm, where
he wrote his main work, *The Ruin of Britain*, from which
much our knowledge of the sixth century comes. It chronicles
the falling away of the British Church from its original calling. Gildas had a mainland hermitage at Street, near the
Glastonbury monastery with which he was connected.
After a visit to Ireland at the age of 67 he settled in southern
Brittany, at a place in Morbihan now named St Gildas. With
his sister and brother he formed a kind of skete, living
independently but meeting daily for prayer and weekly for
the Eucharist. Here he wrote many letters, of which a few
fragments remain. One of his wise sayings was 'Build like
bees'.

PRAYER
May the holy life and the challenging pen of Gildas
stir us to renew our minds, our Church
and our society in Christ.
May the bright beams of Christ's light
that came to islands stiff with pagan coldness
light up our lives and our lands today.

READINGS
Psalm 119:25-40
Wisdom 5:1-16
Colossians 1:21-29

Gregory of Nazianzus

d. 389

Gregory studied at Athens with his life-long friend, Basil, and they both lived as monks in Pontus. Gregory emerged as the contemplative and theologian. Against his own preferences, he became a priest, and wrote a classic book about the priesthood. He responded to an ill-judged request of Basil, who was now Archbishop of Caesarea, to become a bishop in a difficult diocese, but never fitted in there. He returned to the solitary life, only to be called again, this time to help renew the Church in a Constantinople that had been ravaged by conflict and heresy. He turned his house into a church where his sermons on the Trinity and other subjects became hugely influential. He briefly became Bishop of Constantinople, but his main work was in helping to restore orthodoxy. He died in his home town of Nazianzus.

PRAYER
Triune God,
you restored your Church
by the life and teaching of Gregory Nazianzus.
Raise up contemplatives and teachers
who will call us to be true to ourselves
and true to you.

READINGS
Psalm 16
Ecclesiasticus 39:5-11
Matthew 5:13-19

Maedoc of Ferns

Soul friend, d. 626

Maedoc (or Aidan) – both words stemming from the same root, aed, meaning 'fire' – founded a community at Ferns, County Wexford, Ireland, and others at Drumlane and Rossinver. He had a great capacity for soul friendship. It is claimed that he had friendships with Molaisse, Ita, Columba and even Brigid. There is a tradition that he studied under David in Britain and died in David's arms. There are stories of his long feats of fasting and daily psalm chanting. His crozier can be seen in the National Museum in Dublin, and his hand bell and reliquary are in the library of Armagh Cathedral.

PRAYER
Guardian and Friend,
as we thank you for the numerous people Maedoc befriended
and turned into your friends,
release in us the spirit of friendship
and draw many folk in to the circle of your love.

READINGS
Psalm 15
Ecclesiasticus 6:5-19
John 15:8-17

Brigid

Abbess of Kildare, died *c.* 525

Brigid (or Bride), by her compassion and spiritual wisdom, embodies the Celtic tradition of soul friendship. Her concern for those in need and the generosity of her listening heart remind us that God is very near when we are in the company of a soul friend. She founded the great monastery for men and women at Kildare which became Ireland's most influential centre. She has been described as Ireland's greatest woman and its midwife of faith.

PRAYER
Father of abundance,
who wills your children to seek your kingdom
as their chief treasure and joy,
as we thank you for the rich fruit
of Brigid's generous life,
we pray that you will enlarge our hearts
and increase our fruitfulness.

READINGS
Psalm 92
Leviticus 26:3-13
Matthew 1:31-33

Dedication of the infant Christ

first century

This day marks the completion of 40 days since Christ's nativity, when Mary and Joseph took their infant to the Temple in Jerusalem. Jewish law required the mother to be ritually cleansed. Until that time, she could not enter the sanctuary. On seeing the holy family, the prophetic old man Simeon acclaimed the infant as 'the light to illumine the nations'. The image of Christ as Light of the World led to the celebration of light. In the West this day became known as Candlemas because of the lighting of many candles. In the East it became known as The Meeting, because of the profoundly significant meeting between Simeon and Christ.

PRAYER
Holy and Immortal God,
whose Son was this day dedicated in the Temple,
we dedicate ourselves to you.
May the light of Christ shine through us to the world.

READINGS
Psalm 24
Malachi 3:1-5
Luke 2:22-24

Saints and martyrs of Europe

The Acts of the Apostles describes how Christianity first came to parts of Europe within the Roman Empire. Lydia may have been the first to believe in Macedonia. Armenia was the first entire country to embrace Christianity. Through Cyril and Methodius it spread to Slav peoples. Each country has its share of saints and martyrs, some of them celebrated only in their own land. It can be worthwhile to go through a list of Europe's countries and identify the name of the patron saint and a martyr from each.

PRAYER
Faithful God,
have mercy on the continent of Europe
which was early to welcome the Faith of Christ,
but has often fallen away from it.
May its peoples learn to do today
as its saints and martyrs do in heaven.

READINGS
Psalm 67
Ecclesiasticus 44:10-15
Acts 16:8-15

Ive

Sixth or seventh century(?)

The daughter of a Munster ruler, it seems Ive (or Ia) came to
Cornwall with a group of Irish missionaries. People said they
came on an enormous leaf, referring, perhaps, to their long,
leaf-shaped Irish curragh. Dinan, a local ruler, became her
patron and she established a Christian community on the
north Cornish coast at the place now known as St Ives.
According to some, Ive (Ia) took 777 disciples to Brittany
and was martyred there.

PRAYER
Audacious God,
we thank you for the courage of Ive (Ia)
in her adventures for you.
At times when we fear even to set out,
remind us of her exploits,
and move us, like her, to love you with all our being.

READINGS
Psalm 107:1-9
Ezra 8:21-23
Matthew 21:28-32

* transferred from 3 February

Simeon

Prophet, first century

Simeon is described by Luke the Gospel writer as a just and devout man in Jerusalem who awaited the coming of the Jewish Messiah. This old man attended the daily temple services, and through his reflective habits and attunement to God's ways he developed discernment. Thus this spectator of a mother entering the Temple to dedicate her baby was suddenly impelled to take the baby in his arms and to bless God. He uttered the words which, under their Latin title *Nunc Dimittis,* have become part of the regular liturgy of the world's Churches ever since. Simeon is a sign that ordinary, faithful Christians can have the prophetic spirit.

PRAYER
Let your servant depart in peace
according to your word.
For my eyes have seen your salvation
which you have made ready in the sight of the nations.

Simeon

READINGS
Psalm 119:105-112
Genesis 15:12-15
Luke 2:25-35

Mel

Evangelist of Ardagh, d. 488

There is a tradition that Patrick of Ireland had a disciple and fellow Briton named Mel who was closely involved in the evangelisation of the Ardagh area.

PRAYER
Blessed Lord,
who turned Ireland into a land of saints and scholars,
we thank you for the many people
who carried forward Patrick's great work of evangelisation,
and in particular today for the part played by Mel.
Rekindle in us the spirit that shone so brightly in him.

READINGS
Psalm 33
Isaiah 62:10-12
Titus 1:1-9

Anna

Prophet, first century

Anna was an aged widow who regularly attended the morning and evening services in the temple at Jerusalem, and was given to fasting and prayer. She, like certain other devout believers, earnestly waited for the time when the Jews' promised Messiah would be born. When she heard another worshipper prophesying over a baby who was to be dedicated to God by his mother, she also prophesied and praised God for the fulfilment of his promises. Anna is a sign that the prophetic spirit knows no barriers of age, gender or station in life.

PRAYER
We bless you, dear Lord, for the spirit of Anna,
who told all kinds of people about the infant Jesus.
Give us, like her, insight into our times,
boldness in speaking out,
and joy in the offering of praise.

READINGS
Psalm 84
1 Kings 8:22-30
Luke 2:36-38

Elfleda, Abbess of Whitby

Sister of King Egfrith, d. 714

Elfleda's mother, Enfleda and her father, Northumbria's King Oswy, promised to dedicate their infant to the religious life if they were successful in battle against the heathen invader, King Penda of Mercia. After victory she was entrusted to the care of Hilda, Abbess of Hartlepool, and a few years later both went to Whitby. After Hilda's death her mother and then Elfleda herself became abbesses in turn. Elfleda was a friend of bishops Wilfred and Cuthbert. The latter cured her of paralysis, and prophesied to her that her brother, King Egfrith, would die within a year and her half brother, Aldfrith, would succeed him. Her skill as a mediator was revealed at the synod of the river Nidd in 705 when she secured the reconciliation of Wilfred with both the Church in Northumbria and with the Archbishop of Canterbury. Perhaps not surprisingly, Wilfred's biographer praised her as 'the comforter and best counsellor of the whole province'.

PRAYER
Christ the Reconciler,
may we learn from Elfleda's life to pray:
peace with people of old ways;
peace with people of new ways;
peace with people in all ways.

READINGS
Psalm 16
1 Kings 14:1-5
Matthew 21:33-43

Teilo

Bishop of Llanduff and Llandeilo Fawr, sixth century

Teilo is known as one of the three Blessed Visitors of the Isle of Britain, along with David and Padarn, with whom he worked in fellowship, free from envy. After the plague swept Britain, Teilo led many Britons across the Channel where for seven years he established Christian communities. It is said that 'St Chad's Gospels' originated in Teilo's British family of communities, the greatest of which was at Llandeilo. He is credited with this saying: 'The greatest wisdom in a person is to refrain from injuring another person when one has the power to do so.'

PRAYER
Gentle Lord,
who encouraged the Church by Teilo's example,
warmed by the victory of Teilo's faith,
teach us to forego vengeance at all times,
and to reach out our hands in love to all.

READINGS
Psalm 10 (verses 5-11 may be omitted)
Leviticus 19:1-18
1 John 3:11-18

Trumwine

Missionary, Bishop of Abercorn and monk at Whitby, d. 704

When Archbishop Theodore divided the vast kingdom of Northumbria into five dioceses he appointed Trumwine in 681 as the first bishop of the Pictish lands to the north, recently conquered by the Northumbrians. Trumwine established his see at Abercorn and a monastery at Lothian. He accompanied Archbishop Theodore and King Ecfrith to Farne Island to help persuade Cuthbert to become bishop of another Northumbrian see. However, when the Northumbrians were routed at the battle of Nechtansmere in 685, Trumwine fled with his monks to Whitby, under Abbess Elfleda, where he lived and died.

PRAYER
God of mission,
who sent Trumwine to bring your light into a dark place,
and strengthened him to remain faithful even in setback,
send us out to bring light into dark places,
and help us to be faithful servants in good times and bad.

READINGS
Psalm 119:105-112
Isaiah 49:1-4
2 Timothy 2:1-13

Caedmon of Whitby

First English songwriter, d. 680

Caedmon, a shy and illiterate cowherd who worked on the estates of Whitby abbey, was encouraged to sing God's praises in a vision. He was brought into St Hilda's monastery at Whitby where he put many Bible stories into popular songs in English for the first time. His gift must have been of enormous value in spreading the Faith among the English population through poetry and song. He died as he lived, in holiness and perfect love to all, with smiles and humour. The concept of Middle Earth in Tolkien's *Lord of the Rings* is no doubt taken from Caedmon's poem.

PRAYER
We praise the Guardian of heaven's realm,
the Creator's might and his mind's thought,
the glorious works of the Father.
How of every wonder he, the Lord Eternal,
laid the foundation.
He shaped first for the sons of men heaven as their roof.
He created the Middle World.
Mankind's Guardian, Eternal Lord,
afterwards prepared the earth for us,
Lord Almighty.

After Caedmon

READINGS
Psalm 65
Genesis 1:1-13
Luke 1:46-52

Ethilwald

Monk, Bishop of Lindisfarne, d. 740

A disciple of Cuthbert, Ethilwald became Abbot of Melrose. He succeeded Bishop Eadfrith, scribe of the Lindisfarne Gospels, and sponsored the hermit Billfrith to make the precious covers of the Gospels, which are now lost. His holy life was recognised by his relics being placed with those of Cuthbert. He is at least part author of *The Book of Cerne.*

PRAYER
God of truth, God of beauty,
who called Ethilwald to learn from your saints
and to preserve the glories of your Word,
give us humility to learn your wisdom,
that we may adorn your world with its eternal treasures.

READINGS
Psalm 119:89-104
Deuteronomy 27:1-8
Matthew 13:45-52

Aquila and Priscilla

First century Apostles

Aquila and his wife Priscilla were leading figures in the early Church, and Priscilla (also known as Prisca) is mentioned six times in the New Testament. They were compelled to leave Rome by the Emperor Claudius' decree (Acts 18:2) but it seems they returned later. Aquila, like his friend St Paul, was a tent maker by profession, and they travelled with Paul from Corinth to his mission in Syria and Ephesus. They generously used their home and the Church in Corinth met there. Paul stated that they risked their lives for him and had the gratitude of the Gentile Churches.

PRAYER
Homemaker God,
through the generous use of their home
Priscilla and Aquila saw much fruit in the early Church.
Give us a similar hospitality
that will bear fruit in the lives of others.

READINGS
Psalm 128
Proverbs 9:1-10
Acts 18:1-4, 18-26

* or 8 July

Cyril and Methodius

Apostles of the Slavs, died resp. 869 and 885

These brothers were sent by the Byzantium emperor to evangelise Moravia, at the request of its ruler Rostislav. They translated Scriptures and liturgies into the Slavic spoken language and are regarded as the founders of its written language. Their eastern approach was opposed by the representatives of the more regulated Latin Church. However, the Pope received them with honour. Cyril became a monk and Methodius was consecrated archbishop and sent back by the Pope to Moravia, where he survived persecution. They are symbols of partnership between the eastern and western branches of the Christian Church. Pope John Paul II nominated them as joint patrons of Europe.

PRAYER
Eternal God who fathers and mothers us all,
you gave your servants Cyril and Methodius
tongues to enlighten the Slavs with the Gospel.
Inspire us to share what we have been given.
Make your whole Church one as you are one,
and teach us to honour one another,
until east and west acknowledge one Lord, one Faith,
one Baptism, one Body of Christ,
on earth as in heaven.

READINGS
Psalm 24; Isaiah 49:1-6; Romans 10:11-15; Luke 9:1-6

Oswy

King of Northumbria, d. 670

Oswy succeeded his saintly brother Oswald to the throne of Northumbria, but treated his subjects less well. However, when the pagan ruler of Mercia threatened to invade, Oswy turned wholeheartedly to God, and pledged to give his infant daughter as a nun and prime lands as monasteries if God gave him victory. On achieving victory he honoured these pledges. He gave land for the foundation of the twin monastery of Wearmouth and Jarrow which Benedict Biscop established. Here the monk Bede wrote his many famous works.

PRAYER
Faithful God,
who raises up the humble and brings low the mighty,
as we thank you that in victory Oswy kept his pledge to you,
so we ask you to help us keep our promises.

READINGS
Psalm 118:1-19
2 Samuel 22:1-20
Matthew 5:33-48

Five Egyptian and other martyrs

d. 309

Five pilgrims from Egypt arrived at Caesarea on their homeward journey, after having accompanied some Christians who had been deported to the mines of Cilicia during a period of persecution. Questioned by the guards at the gates, they made no secret of their faith. They were arrested, tortured and asked their names. Instead of giving their family names, they took to themselves names of great biblical prophets: Elijah, Jeremiah, Isaiah, Samuel and Daniel. When asked where they came from, one of them answered, 'From Jerusalem', meaning the eternal city of heaven. They were all beheaded, and the governor then also put Pamphilius and other Christians to death.

PRAYER
Inspirer of prophets,
as we thank you for the courage of the martyrs from Egypt
and for the strength they drew from your prophets,
stir up in us that same prophetic spirit
that it may enable us to stand firm in our time of trial.

READINGS
Psalm 28
Daniel 6:11-24
1 Peter 1:19-21

Finan

Monk of Iona, Bishop of Lindisfarne, d. 661

Finan, an Irish monk from Iona, succeeded Aidan as Bishop of Lindisfarne, and had a similar character and policy. He worked closely with King Oswy, built a wooden church to be like a cathedral, and sent missionaries to Mercia and Essex.

PRAYER
God of ripening purpose,
help us, like Finan, to build your Church,
to sustain its continuity,
and to extend its mission.

READINGS
Psalm 101:1-6
Deuteronomy 4:1-7
John 12:34-36a

Colman

Monk of Iona, Bishop of Lindisfarne
founder of Irish monasteries, d. 676

Colman was an Irish monk from Iona who became Lindisfarne's third abbot-bishop. After the Synod of Whitby, at which he was the spokesman for the Irish ways, he took all his Irish and 30 of his Saxon monks, together with some of Aidan's bones, to Innisboffin, in Ireland. His Saxon monks founded a second monastery at Mayo with an elected rather than a hereditary abbot, which Alcuin praised for its learning.

PRAYER
God of the heartbreaks,
who teaches us that we have no eternal home on this earth,
as you journeyed with Colman
on the sad journey from Lindisfarne,
so journey with us in our heartaches,
and bring new life out of setback.

READINGS
Psalm 7
Jeremiah 8:21-22
2 Corinthians 4:7-15

Archippus

Fellow-worker of St Paul, martyr, first century

St Paul called Archippus a fellow soldier (Philemon 2). He lived at Colossae with his parents, Philemon and Apphia, and perhaps was an elder of the church which met in his parents' home. During the long absence of Epaphrus, who stayed with Paul in Rome, the young Archippus had to bear responsibility for the Colossian church. His zeal as a preacher antagonised unbelievers who dragged him before the governor. Archippus refused to sacrifice to the goddess Diana, and as a result he was beaten, thrown into a pit and buried to his waist. According to tradition, children were incited to run needles into him before he was stoned to death.

PRAYER
God our Tower and our Reward,
who raised up Archippus to leadership
while he was still young,
and raised him yet further
to courageously bear a martyr's crown,
may we grow in leadership
according to the measure you give,
and find the stature of courage in your service.

READINGS
Psalm 127
Daniel 6:11-16
Colossians 4:12-18

Enoch

Holy man and prophet, before dated history

The Bible tells us very little about Enoch, except that he was a descendant of Seth and the father of Methuselah. The two things of greatest interest are his holy life and his glorious exit from earth. Twice the Bible account reminds us that 'he walked with God'. He was also a prophet, declaring God's judgement upon the godless of his time. He is the only member of his family line of whom it is not recorded that he died, but rather that God 'took' him.

PRAYER
God who walks with your people,
and who communed so closely with your friend Enoch,
teach us by his example to walk in intimacy with you,
fleeing from everything that clouds our relationship,
until even death will be but a gentle passing over
into your nearer presence.

READINGS
Psalm 56:8-13
Genesis 5:18-23
Jude, verses 14-23

Melchizadek

Priest and king of Salem, *c.* 2000 BC

Although a mysterious figure, Melchizadek is replete with symbolic significance. He was the king of Salem, which may be the same place as Jerusalem. We know nothing about his birth or death. He is called a priest, before a priesthood had been established among the Hebrews. He appears suddenly as a naturally good person who honoured 'the Most High' and who came out to welcome Abraham on his travels, and gave him bread and wine. When David conquered Jerusalem centuries later he was declared 'a priest for ever after the order of Melchizadek', and the Messiah, David's descendant, was likewise so named. Melchizadek has the honour of pointing us to hospitality as a divine quality that will last for ever.

PRAYER
Most High,
we are in awe at the mystery of your presence in Melchizadek
and with us now.
Forgive us for so glibly diminishing this mystery.
Thank you for Melchizadek's entering
into the stream of divine life with the gift of hospitality.
Be our host for all eternity,
and help us be to others as he was to Abraham.

READINGS
Psalm 110
Genesis 14:17-24
Hebrews 5:1-10

Elwyn

Monk of Ireland and Cornwall, sixth century(?)

Elwyn was an Irish monk who came to Cornwall with a group of Christians who included Breaca, said much later to have been a nun at a convent founded by Brigid. Elwyn is remembered at Portleven (derived from Port Elwyn) at the mouth of the Hayle River, so it is assumed that is where he landed and began his work.

PRAYER
Divine Midwife,
in the mists of time you brought little families of holy souls to introduce you to a people ignorant of you.
Thank you for the likes of Elwyn and Breaca.
Call out families of holy souls today.

READINGS
Psalm 46
Isaiah 33:17-24
Revelation 22:1-5

Polycarp

Bishop of Smyrna, martyr, d. 167

Polycarp was a link between the apostles and succeeding generations, for he was taught by St John and he himself taught Irenaeus. He had been Bishop of Smyrna, Adriatic coast (in modern Turkey) for over 40 years when persecution of Christians began. He was arrested and given the option to renounce his faith and so save his life. He replied, 'I have been Christ's servant for 86 years and he has done me no harm. How, then, can I now blaspheme my King and Saviour?' and was immediately burned alive.

PRAYER
Father of your loved child Jesus,
God of the spiritual powers and of creation,
God of all who live rightly before you,
I bless you that you have thought me worthy
to share Christ's cup of suffering as one of your martyrs
and to rise again in the immortality of the Holy Spirit.
I bless and glorify you
through our eternal high priest in heaven,
your loved child Jesus Christ,
through whom be glory to you,
to him and to the Holy Spirit,
now and for the ages to come.

Paraphrase of Polycarp's dying prayer

READINGS
Psalm 34:1-9, 22; Wisdom 5:15-20; Revelation 2:8-11

Bezaleel

Spirit-filled craftsperson, fourteenth century BC(?)

Moses commissioned Bezaleel to be the chief architect of the Hebrews' movable Tabernacle for the worship of God. His task was to design and execute its works of art. He was gifted to work in wood, metal and jewels. He also trained a workforce, and was said to be filled with the Spirit of God and of wisdom. When the Tabernacle was completed it was filled with the glory of the Lord.

PRAYER
Spirit of God,
who equipped Bezaleel
and inspired him to do everything just as you required,
put a glory in our work,
and may every detail be done just as you desire it.

READINGS
Psalm 27:1-6
Exodus 31:1-11
2 Timothy 2:20, 21

Ethelbert

King of Kent, d. 616

Ethelbert was the first Anglo-Saxon king to become a Christian. He married a Frankish Christian named Bertha, allowed her to revive the ancient Britons' Church at Canterbury, dedicated to St Martin of Tours, and agreed to welcome a mission party from Rome headed by Augustine in 591. Many of his subjects became Christians. Eventually Ethelbert himself professed conversion and built a monastery which became Canterbury Cathedral. He was the first Anglo-Saxon king to lay down a code of laws which, among other things, protected the Christian clergy from harm. An ancient document claimed that 'from his stock there has arisen a numerous and holy race, which shines with virtue through the whole world'.

PRAYER
High King, patient and true,
who brought Ethelbert to gradual faith in you,
may the kingdoms of this world
become the kingdom of your Son,
and your faithful people shine with virtue.

READINGS
Psalm 148
1 Samuel 12:6-15
Matthew 25:31-46

Methuselah

The man who lived longest, before dated history

According to the Bible, Methuselah, the son of Enoch and the grandfather of Noah, lived longer than anyone else in history. He was a means of continuity and of handing down knowledge and traditions that would otherwise have been lost. Thus Noah conversed with the man who conversed with Adam!

PRAYER
Eternal God,
to whom be glory to the ages of ages,
as we marvel at the long life of Methuselah,
we pray that you will bring our lives to their full ripening,
and crown our journey with the life that knows no end.

READINGS
Psalm 8
Genesis 5:21-27
1 Peter 5:1-11

Isaac

Founder of Israel, twentieth century BC

Isaac's name, 'Laughed', was given by God to his parents Abraham and Sarah, because both of them, who seemed long past child-bearing age, laughed when a divine messenger told them they would have a child. This was an essential step in the fulfilment of God's promise to Abraham that he would be the father of nations. When Isaac was 25 he was taken from Beersheba to Moriah where his father, misguidedly, prepared to make a supreme sacrifice of his son to God. Isaac's trust in his father and in God are awesome. After his mother died, Abraham's servant was led by God to find a wife for Isaac named Rebekah. They too were childless until after prayer they were given twins. Isaac's flaws were deceit and favouritism.

PRAYER
God of covenant,
unending in your commitment to us,
out of your call came Isaac.
Keep us faithful to the lines of your plan.
May we neither deviate nor deceive
but, encouraged by Isaac's example,
trust you in all things.

READINGS
Psalm 105:1-9
Genesis 21:1-8
Hebrews 11:17-20

Cassian

Abbot and writer, d. 435

Cassian became a monk at Bethlehem but left with his friend Germanus to study monasticism in Egypt where he was influenced by the teaching of Evagrius Ponticus. He travelled to Constantinople to be ordained deacon, and became a disciple of St John Chrysostom. He returned to the West, where he was ordained priest, and founded both a men's and a women's monastery near Marseilles. Here, at a time of controversy, he emerged as a leader. In contrast to fatalistic teachings that were emerging in the Western Church, he stressed that God has implanted in all humans the possibility for good as much as for evil. His two great works interpreted the Coptic tradition for the West: *The Institutes*, about the monasteries, and *The Conferences,* containing sayings of hermits. These had great influence in Celtic lands.

PRAYER
Holy God,
source of friendship, still centre of the universe,
teach us, like Cassian and holy souls of the desert,
to pray from our hearts by day and night,
until our souls are bathed in light from on high.

READINGS
Psalm 8
Lamentations 3:22-30
Acts 2:23-47

The Unknown Saint

In countries throughout the world, war memorials list the names of those who have given their lives in war. In Britain's Westminster Abbey there is a different kind of memorial. It is simply to 'the unknown soldier'. That soldier represents countless numbers of men and women whose bodies or names were lost but who nevertheless gave their lives. On this day, which is overlooked three years out of four, we remember the untold number of saintly people whose faith is known to God alone.

PRAYER
Eternal Guardian,
who calls each of your children by name,
we remember with gratitude your many faithful servants
who, though they are neither known to us
nor great in this world's eyes,
are like precious jewels to you.

READINGS
Psalm 27:1-10
Genesis 17:1-7
1 Corinthians 1:26-31

David

Patron saint of Wales, bishop, sixth century

David was born on the westerly tip of Pembrokeshire and educated at Ty Gwyn under Abbot Paulinus. Tradition says that David and three friends built a chapel and cell where Llanthony Abbey now stands. While they waited on God there they were guided to build a large monastic centre on the site of the modern St David's Cathedral. David's final words to his people were: 'Be happy and keep your faith, and do the little things that you have heard and seen me do.' Another account adds: 'Always be of one mind . . .' It was said that at his death 'kings mourned him as a judge, the older people as a brother, the younger as a father'.

PRAYER
Teach us, our God and King,
to love you in each person,
to love by noticing the little things,
to love by cherishing the little things,
to love by serving in little things,
to pray by offering the little things,
as David called us to do.

READINGS
Psalm 23
Proverbs 4:10-27
1 Thessalonians 2:7b-12

Chad

Bishop of Lichfield, d. 672

Chad trained at Aidan's Lindisfarne monastery with his three Saxon brothers, and did further training in Ireland. He was asked to become abbot of Lastingham after his brother Cedd, who had founded it, died. Then he was made a bishop of the Northumbrians. Like Aidan before him, he refused special honours and travelled by foot rather than by horse. Later he became bishop of the huge Diocese of Mercia (the English Midlands). Chad built cells at his Lichfield head-quarters and established a monastery at Barton, Lincolnshire. Chad would go into the church to pray whenever he heard wind or thunder. 'Don't you realise,' Chad explained, quoting Psalm 18, 'that God sends wind, lightning and thunder to excite earth's peoples to fear him, to humble their pride and make them aware that they will be judged?' Plague took him and many of his flock, but he saw his brother Cedd coming with angels from heaven to greet him.

PRAYER
Faithful God,
from the first fruits of the English people who turned to Christ
you called Chad to holy learning and high service
as a missionary monk and bishop.
May we learn from his loving discipline
to pattern the ways of Christ in our time.

READINGS
Psalm 18:1-19; Isaiah 4:2-6; Luke 14:7-11

Non

Mother of David of Wales, fifth century

In a field by the shore now named St Non's is a well and the remains of a chapel where, according to tradition, Non gave birth to David, who became Wales' patron saint. It is believed she was raped by a Prince named Sant and that she became, or was already, a nun. She settled in Cornwall and died in Brittany where her fine tomb survives at Dirinon, Finistere.

PRAYER
Holy God who mothers us all,
we give thanks to you for the mother of David
who kept your sayings in her heart
and taught them to her child.
Restore to us belief in the divine vocation of motherhood.

READINGS
Psalm 139:1-18
Deuteronomy 5:16-22
Revelation 22:1-5

Ciaran

Holy wanderer of Saighir, fifth century(?)

Ciaran was known as 'the first-born of the saints of Ireland', and became an early type of the holy wanderer. He was born on Clear Island off the coast of Cork, the southernmost point of Ireland. Clad in skins and living in caves with wild animals, biographers cast him in the role of Ireland's John the Baptist, preparing the way for St Patrick's mission. A wild boar and a wolf became his first 'monks' at Saighir, but this grew into a large people's monastery. It is possible he became its abbot and that St Patrick consecrated him to be a missionary bishop. According to *The Litany of Pilgrim Saints,* 15 people went with Ciaran to the Rhinns of Islay, in Scotland. Their voyage became the first to capture the popular imagination.

PRAYER
Yearning God,
who called Ciaran to be a holy hermit and fiery apostle,
give us strength to step out in faith,
relying on you alone,
that we, too, might be the first fruits
of a new generation of Christ's people.

READINGS
Psalm 119:145-152 ; Isaiah 11:6-9 ; Hebrews 11:32-38

* transferred from 5 March

Piran

Monk, patron of Cornish tin miners, d. 480

It is said that Piran left his home in Ireland in order to share his faith in north Cornwall. A number of his stopping places are still named after him. He established a hermitage at Perranporth and at Perranzabuloe. Although little is known about Piran, his life has inspired many working people throughout the centuries in the West Country of Britain and in Brittany. The Cornish tin miners made him their patron, and the Cornish flag is known as St Piran's Cross, which symbolises the power of light overcoming the darkness of evil.

PRAYER
Father,
with love in his heart and with great courage
Piran left his home and brought the light of Christ
to those in the darkness of another land,
thus ennobling its life and work.
Help us to reverence your creatures.
Bless the work of our hands.

READINGS
Psalm 27:1-7
Jonah 3:1-5
John 9:1-17

Baldred

Northumbrian hermit, eighth century

Bass Rock stands off Britain's east coast, near North Berwick, south of Edinburgh. In the eighth century the hermit Baldred came from Tyningham and made this his home. His prayers were reputed to move heaven and earth.

PRAYER
Rock of ages,
who called Baldred to a wild place where he held fast to you
and let his prayers become a shield over mainland folk,
give us courage to journey with you
into the wild parts of our lives,
and to say prayers that protect the land.

READINGS
Psalm 104:1-12
Job 37:14-24
Mark 1:4-12

Perpetua, Felicity and their companions

Martyrs, d. 203

Perpetua was a young African mother and Felicity was her pregnant slave. With other new Christians they were preparing for baptism, despite the Emperor's prohibition on conversion to Christianity. They were imprisoned, and their transforming experiences of God were recorded and circulated. Perpetua said her prison became a palace. They went to be devoured by lions joyfully as though they were on their way to heaven, singing hymns. The wild animals mauled but did not kill them. Before they were executed they exchanged the Kiss of Peace and witnessed to their faith in Christ, dying most nobly. The commemoration of their death has encouraged the faith of many.

PRAYER
Transforming God,
who made Perpetua, Felicity and their companions
noble in suffering and glorious in death,
keep our gaze steadfastly on heaven,
that we may live valiantly, rise victoriously
and join them in everlasting glory.

READINGS
Psalm 54
Song of Songs 8:6-7
Revelation 12:10-12a

Senan

Single-minded abbot, d. 544

After prolonged waiting on God, Senan was led to establish a remarkable series of monasteries on Irish islands at the mouths of rivers, from the Slaney in Wexford to the coast of Clare. He finally settled on Scattery Island (Inis Cathaig) in the Shannon estuary, where it is said Aidan was a monk before moving to Iona. According to *The Book of Lismore,* St Patrick prophesied that Inis Cathaig had been left wild and uninhabited so that it could become the place of resurrection of a man yet to be born who would be 'splendid, noble, dignified with God and people'. Senan was taken to be that man.

PRAYER
Risen Christ,
who led Senan to his place of resurrection
and worked miracles through his mighty prayers,
raise us up, we pray,
to that place where your Spirit works in us with power.

READINGS
Psalm 44:1-8
Micah 3:5-8
Romans 15:7-13

Gregory

Bishop of Nyssa, writer, d. 395

Brother of Macrina and Basil, Bishop of Caesarea, Gregory married after an outstanding education at Athens, and became a priest. In due course he became a monk, and was chosen as Bishop of Nyssa, a remote outpost of Basil's province near Armenia. His greatest gifts were in pen and pulpit: he wrote a *Life of Moses*, a commentary on the Song of Songs and defended the biblical teaching about the Trinity. He has remained a spiritual writer of great authority.

PRAYER
Living Word of God,
who through Gregory's writings has opened many eyes
to the wonder of who you are,
direct the writers of today to journey into the heart of reality,
and to fall in love with you.

READINGS
Psalm 45
Song of Songs 5
2 Corinthians 13:12, 13

Felix of Burgundy

First Bishop of the East Angles, d. 647

In 630 the Christian King Sigebert returned from exile to rule the East Angles and prompted Honorarius, Archbishop of Canterbury, to invite Felix to come from his native Burgundy to consolidate the Church among the Angles. Felix made Dunwich his diocesan centre, and contemporary bishops of Norwich trace their succession back to him. His fruitful episcopate of 17 years, during which he worked in collaboration with the king, the archbishop and, it seems, with the Irish missionary Fursey who reached out from his base at Burgh Castle, bears witness to his good team building. He founded a school, and the monastery of Soham where he is buried. Felixstowe is named after him.

PRAYER
God of unity, learning and outreach,
as we thank you for Felix's pioneering work in East Anglia,
we pray that we may learn from him
to build sound teamwork, theology and faith.

READINGS
Psalm 34
Deuteronomy 31:7-13
Romans 16:1-16

Constantine

Cornish king, monk, martyr, d. 576(?)

There is some confusion about various leaders by the name of Constantine. We know there was a king of the Cornish people named Constantine who was berated for his violent acts by Gildas, the historian. It may have been this Constantine who, according to John Tynemouth, was converted to Christ in the following way: The hermit Petroc sheltered the stag which Constantine's party were hunting. Constantine was about to attack Petroc in rage when he became paralysed. Petroc then 'released' him. Constantine humbled himself and accepted Christ. In this story he is portrayed as a Prince of Domnonia. Constantine founded three churches: Constantine near Padstow, Milton Abbot in Devon, and Constantine near Kerrier, where he placed himself under the instruction of Petroc. From there he went to the monastery founded by David, and gave faithful service there for seven years before being made a monk.

PRAYER
Great Leader,
who in Constantine overcame dark forces
and drew out royalty of soul,
transform our rage into the gentle love of Christ.

READINGS
Psalm 32; Proverbs 31:1-9; Luke 5:17-26

* transferred from 9 March

Paul Aurelian

Bishop of Pol de Leon, died *c.* 584

Paul was born in Glamorgan of a Romanised Briton, about 480. Against his father's wishes he placed himself at an early age under the guidance of Illtyd, who sent him for a time to the community on Caldey Island. Paul got to know David, Samson and Gildas. It is possible he is the same man as Paulinus, who at the age of 16 set up cells with 12 companions near Llandovery before founding a monastery at Lladdeusant in the shadow of the Black Mountain. Reports of his power and piety led Mark, King of Cornwall, to invite him to preach to his people. He was then guided by God to go to Brittany. It has been conjectured that he first stopped on the islands of Ushant, established some cells on the Ile de Batz off the north coast of Brittany, and finally established his main monastery on the site now known as St Pol de Leon, where he was consecrated a bishop and died at the age of 104. Stories of him overcoming dragons were told and he is thus represented in art.

PRAYER
Mighty God of the Great Adventure,
who called Paul Aurelian to dare anything
and go anywhere for you,
stir up in us that same spirit of adventure,
and crown our lives with your goodness.

READINGS
Psalm 92; Malachi 4:1-4; Mark 1:35-39

Billfrith

Hermit and goldsmith, eighth century

Billfrith was a a hermit and goldsmith who adorned the cover of the *Lindisfarne Gospels* with gold, silver and gems. Though the Gospels survive, the cover is now lost. It is believed his relics were taken to Durham in the eleventh century where he is celebrated with Baldred the hermit on 6 March.

PRAYER
God our Eternal Treasure,
who gives glorious minerals to your creation
and glorious skills to your people,
we bless you for the craft of Billfrith,
honed in prayerful practice.
Raise up skilled craftspeople
who will use creation's gifts and their own
for your glory.

READINGS
Psalm 102:15-28
Exodus 31:1-11
Ephesians 6:5-8

* transferred from 6 March

Eosterwine

Abbot of Wearmouth, d. 686

A royal soldier under Northumbria's King Egfrith, Eosterwine became a monk at Wearmouth, the monastery founded by his cousin, Benedict Biscop. He wholeheartedly entered into the menial tasks such as baking, milking, gardening and harvesting. He was ordained, and Benedict made him abbot during his long absences abroad. The monks found him kind and accessible. He died young, aged 36, while the community was at prayer.

PRAYER
Workaday Christ,
who in Eosterwine found a servant of like mind with you,
help us never to despise menial tasks,
but to find you in the common duties of life
and to see you in the faces of those
with whom we live and work.

READINGS
Psalm 104:10-24
Exodus 2:11-22
Matthew 24:45-51

* transferred from 7 March

Aristobulus

Apostle, first century

The name Aristobulus means 'the best counsellor'. He was the leader of a household church in Rome whom the apostle Paul greeted. Tradition says he was one of the 70 disciples sent out by Jesus who healed the sick and told people about God's kingdom. According to a Spanish tradition, he made his way to Britain in the second year of the Roman Emperor Nero and finally became Bishop of Britonia (modern Montonedo) in Spain. A Greek tradition claims he organised the Church in Britain, but this may be a confusion.

PRAYER
How glorious are those who bring good news, O God,
and who heal the sick in your name.
Thank you for the ministry of Aristobulus,
for his willingness to travel far from home
and to reach out to distant shores.
Save us from hiding ourselves away in our comfort zones;
keep us reaching out.

READINGS
Psalm 147
Isaiah 52:7-10
Romans 16:8-11

Dichu

Farmer and first convert of Patrick, fifth century

Patrick and his team began their mission to Ireland by disembarking at Strangford Lough. A few miles inland, at Saul, they were taken to the home of a local pagan farmer named Dichu who was naturally good. Dichu, thinking they intended harm, was about to kill them, but the moment he saw Patrick's face he saw goodness in it, and invited them to stay. They became friends, Patrick instructed and baptised him, and Dichu remained a life-long supporter. This friendship changed Patrick's mission strategy. He singled out the area where Dichu lived 'for love', and the Faith began to grow there. Towards the end of Patrick's ministry God directed him to return to this area and to proclaim that Dichu's descendants would find divine mercy.

PRAYER
Eternal Goodness,
draw out the good in folk.
Eternal Friend,
draw out the friendship in us.
Eternal Host,
make your home in the place where we dwell.

READINGS
Psalm 18:25-31
Isaiah 26:1-9
Acts 10:34-44

Patrick

Apostle of the Irish, died *c.* 461

Patrick was born on the north-west coast of Britain. When he was a teenager, far from God, an Irish slave raider captured him and for six years he endured forced labour. He turned to God with all his being, and after some years was guided by God to escape. He trained as a priest, perhaps at Lerins in Gaul. At some point he had a vision that the Irish were pleading with him to return and bring them the Good News of Christ. He returned with a small team, and led an immensely successful mission mainly to the north. He set up a diocesan system of pastoral care. His two writings are the earliest autobiographies of Britain. His vulnerability and lack of polished Latin combined with his passion and friendliness enabled him to win for Christ the hearts and imagination of the northern Irish people.

PRAYER
Baptising God,
who in your providence chose your servant, Patrick,
to be the apostle of the Irish,
to boldly confront the kingdom of darkness,
to baptise those who were lost and in error,
and to bring them into the light and truth of your Word,
give us that boldness, keep us in that light,
and bring us to everlasting life.

READINGS
Psalm 5; Hosea 2:19-23; 2 Corinthians 2:14-3:3;
Mark 10:28-31

The daughters of the King of Connaught

d. 432(?)

Soon after Patrick began his mission to the Irish he won the support of Loiguire, King of Connaught, High King of Ireland. The king's virgin daughters came to bathe at a well early one morning and saw, to their amazement, Patrick and a team of priests clothed in white vestments. 'Are you real or from the other world?' they asked. Patrick encouraged them to enquire about the the real God rather than about themselves. His reply to their question 'Who is God?' has become famous as Patrick's Creed. 'Since you are daughters of an earthly king,' Patrick concluded, 'I wish to wed you to the king of heaven.' They asked for instruction, cast off their sins, and were baptised. 'When shall we see Christ's face?' they then asked. 'Unless you taste death and receive the sacrament you shall not see the face of Christ,' Patrick told them. They received the sacrament, and thereupon died. So powerful was the effect that their two druid guides were converted, one at first, the other later. The women were buried beside the well, which is now known as Ogulla Well, near Tulsk, County Roscommon.

PRAYER
King of kings,
who captivated royal virgins
with the beauty of the eternal kingdom,
captivate us with your wonder and glory
that we, with them, may come to see you face to face.

READINGS
Psalm 24; Song of Songs 2:16-3:4; Revelation 19:11-16

Herbert

Hermit of Derwentwater, d. 687

Herbert was a Saxon priest who became a hermit on a little island on Derwentwater in what is now the English Lake District. A close friend of Cuthbert, he used to visit him at Lindisfarne every year. In 686 Cuthbert was in Carlisle and they met there instead. Cuthbert urged him to share everything he needed to and to say goodbye since he, Cuthbert, would die before they met again. Herbert wept and begged Cuthbert to pray that they would share the same 'day of resurrection'. This Cuthbert did. Herbert suffered a long illness and died on the same day as Cuthbert. Seven hundred years later local Christians began to celebrate his day of resurrection on the island now named after him.

PRAYER
Divine Friend,
who contemplated with joy your own creation,
and who called Herbert to the contemplative life,
teach us to contemplate you in creation,
to know the joys of soul friendship
and to reach our day of resurrection.

READINGS
Psalm 4
Proverbs 4:1-14
1 Corinthians 1:4-9

* transferred from 20 March

Cuthbert

Monk, evangelist and Bishop of Lindisfarne, d. 687

Cuthbert was a natural leader. Following a vision of the death of Aidan he became a monk at Melrose and Ripon. He developed many gifts, including those of study, hospitality, preaching, healing, prophecy and pastoral care. When Boisil died, Cuthbert, who had himself recovered from the plague, replaced him as abbot. Following the synod of Whitby in 664 he was appointed to lead the depleted monastery at Lindisfarne. When he was not quite 40, he went to the rocky Inner Farne Island where he lived as a hermit to engage in uninterrupted spiritual battle. Nine years later he reluctantly agreed to become Bishop of Lindisfarne. He returned to Farne Island to die. Eleven years after his death it was found his body had not decomposed. Miracles occurred at his tomb and his shrine drew multitudes.

PRAYER
Tender Father,
who called Cuthbert from tending sheep
to be a shepherd of the people,
help us, inspired by his example,
to heal the sick, to guard unity,
to storm heaven's gates,
and to bring those who are lost home to your fold.

READINGS
Psalms 23 or 121 ; Ezekiel 34:11-16 ; 2 Corinthians 6:1-10;
Matthew 18:12-14

Enda

Pioneer of Irish monasteries, d. 530

Enda became a soldier and then a monk, and trained at the great Whithorn monastery. He returned to Drogheda, established monasteries in the Boyne valley, and finally settled in Inishmore, the largest of the Aran Islands, whose monastic ruins may still be seen. Enda was the earliest organiser of Irish monasticism. He worked closely with his sister Fanchea. Notable Irish Christians sought him out as their mentor, including Ciaran of Clonmacnoise and Brendan.

PRAYER
Mentor and Seeker of souls,
who used Enda to ground Irish Christians
in the learning and fellowship of Christ,
equip your people today in sound learning,
wise counsel and bold experiments in faith.

READINGS
Psalm 78:1-7
Proverbs 15:14-24
Matthew 13:47-52

Jacob

Father of Israel's twelve tribes, eighteenth century BC(?)

Jacob was born of his parents, Isaac and Rebekah, a short time after his twin brother Esau. His name, which means 'Supplanter', epitomises his lifelong struggle with his family and his God to receive the mandate of the older brother. By deceiving his blind father that he was Esau, he became the bearer of God's promise and the inheritor of the land of Canaan. His life is recorded in Genesis 26-50. He was at first selfish and full of intrigue, but he also had a passion to secure God's blessing, and in the end that meant that he allowed God to have his way. Two peak episodes changed his life. At Bethel he saw heaven open and was promised the land of Canaan. At Peniel he wrestled all night with God, and his name was changed to Israel, meaning 'God strives'. He married Rachel and they had twelve sons. These were the progenitors and name bearers of the twelve tribes of the nation of Israel.

PRAYER
God of covenant,
teach us to struggle with you
until we, with Jacob, can say,
'You are here, Lord, in this place,
you protect us wherever we go.'

READINGS
Psalm 46; Genesis 28:10-22; Acts 7:44-46

Joseph

Saviour from famine, seventeenth century BC(?)

Joseph, the eleventh son of Jacob and the first of Rachel, went from rags to riches as a result of his obedience to God. His brothers, jealous of his stature and of his dreams of destiny, left him for dead, but he was rescued and employed by a wealthy man. The man's wife, however, first abused and then accused Joseph and he was put in prison. His gift of interpreting dreams came to the ears of the Emperor who was troubled by dreams. Joseph convinced him he would face seven years of plenty followed by seven years of famine. The Emperor put Joseph in charge of national food supplies. During the famine, when Joseph's family travelled to Egypt to beg for food, Joseph put them through dramatic tests before revealing who he was. Family wounds were healed, and the extended family settled in Egypt.

PRAYER
God of destiny,
who brought Joseph through betrayal
to be a great steward and reconciler,
weave your dreams into our lives,
and make us content with your will,
in bad times and good.

READINGS
Psalm 105:12-22
Genesis 45:1-15
Acts 7:9-16

Judah

First head of one of Israel's tribes,
eighteenth century BC(?)

Judah was the son of Leah and Jacob, who prophesied that his son would lead like a lion the tribes that would spring from his first twelve sons. It was Judah who offered his life as a surety for the youngest brother, Benjamin. His confession before the King of Egypt's Chief Minister (who, unknown to him, was his brother Joseph) has been described as one of the noblest pieces of natural eloquence. The lion was emblazed on the flag of Judah and the Lion of Judah became a title of the Messiah, who was a descendant of Judah's tribe.

PRAYER
Lion of Judah,
who led Judah to lay down his life for his brothers,
and who laid down your life for us,
help us to lay down our lives for one another
and to serve you with the heart of a lion.

READINGS
Psalm 18:35-48
Genesis 44:18-34
Revelation 5:1-10

Pregnancy of Mary

first century

Since there was no record of the precise day of the year on which Christ was born, Jesus was given an official birthday on 25 December to coincide with the winter solstice celebrations. Once this date was fixed in the fifth century it was a natural progression to celebrate the conception of Jesus on a date exactly nine months earlier, 25 March. On this day Christians contemplate the woman who made her womb and her whole being available to the Son of God, and the wonder of God's Spirit working in the deepest parts of a woman's body in order to bring life.

PRAYER
Permeating Spirit,
in the darkness of the womb you brought life,
and lit up Mary with joy.
Graceful her form,
winsome her voice,
gentle her speech,
stately her mien,
warm the look of her eye,
while her lovely white breast heaves on her bosom
like the black-headed seagull on the gently heaving wave.
Echoes the Carmina Gadelica

READINGS
Psalm 139:1-18
Isaiah 7:10-16
Luke 1:26-38

Miriam

Sister and preserver of the baby Moses,
sixteenth century BC(?)

Miriam (which is the Hebrew name for Mary) was the sister of Aaron and Moses. Her baby brother Moses was born in Egypt at a time when its Emperor sought to kill the male infants of its mushrooming Israelite population. Moses was placed in a basket on the river near where the queen was holding a picnic, and Miriam kept watch. When the queen wanted to adopt the baby, Miriam, with flair and daring, offered to get a nurse, who was in fact her mother. Miriam supported Moses as he led his people across the Red Sea. She has been called a prophetess because she led the women in music, dancing and singing. She opposed Moses' marriage to a Cushite woman, perhaps out of jealousy, and contracted leprosy, which was thought to be a consequence. But she received healing through Moses' prayer. Rabbinical tradition suggests she married Caleb and was the mother of Hur. She died and was buried at Kadesh.

PRAYER
With Miriam we sing to you, our God,
for you part the waters that threaten to overwhelm us
and you are glorious in your victories.
Teach us to celebrate your goodness
and enter fully into the dance of life.

READINGS
Psalm 106:1-12; Exodus 15:19-22; Luke 17:11-19

Tyfil

A child saint, sixth century

Tyfil was a nephew of Teilo. When he was still a child he was accidentally killed in the woods by the banks of the River Tywi, beneath the hill to the north-west of Llandeilo, and was regarded as a saint.

PRAYER
Infant King,
who called Tyfil to heaven
while he was yet a child
and who calls us each to exercise a child-like faith,
deepen our trust
and make us ready to meet you at any time.

READINGS
Psalm 148
Judges 13:2-5
Matthew 18:1-5

Moses

Leader of Israel's march to freedom, sixteenth cent. BC(?)

Moses was born when Egypt's ruler had resolved to kill every newborn male in the growing Israelite immigrant population, which he had reduced to slave labour. Adopted by the queen, nursed by his mother, Moses was educated in the royal court. After he killed an Egyptian who had mistreated an Israelite slave, Moses fled to the desert, where he learned deeper lessons from God. At a burning bush God revealed himself as Yahweh, I AM, and called Moses to lead his people to freedom. The story of this mass exodus to a land promised them by God is pivotal to the monotheist religions. Moses instituted festivals such as the Passover, which ever after has recalled his people's deliverance. God was able to use him because power did not go to his head; his will was harnessed humbly to God's purposes. The Torah – the first five books of the Jewish and Christian Bible, which include the Ten Commandments – are largely the work of Moses and later editors.

PRAYER
Yahweh,
through Moses you shaped a people
who became your instrument in the world.
Use us to do big things
and yet to walk humbly with you into old age.

READINGS
Psalm 105:26-45; Exodus 3; Hebrews 11:24-25

Gwynllyw and Gwladys

Lovers, in love of the King of life, sixth century

A dashing romance and a dramatic conversion led to holy callings. Gwynllyw, a ruler in what is now south-east Wales, fell in love with Gwladys, one of the 24 children of the famed King Brychan. She was beautiful and wore silk dresses. Brychan refused to give his consent to marriage so Gwynllyw rode to the court with 300 men and snatched her away. They had a son, Cadoc, who became a radiant Christian and brought them to faith. They dedicated themselves to God and established a prayer centre on the high ground now known as Stow Hill, in Newport, Wales. They bathed daily in the River Usk.

PRAYER
Peace between families,
peace between lovers,
in love of the King of life.

READINGS
Psalm 45:10-17
Song of Songs 2:8-17
1 Corinthians 13:8-13

John of the Ladder (Climacus)

Monk and Abbot of Mount Sinai, d. 649

John was born and married in Palestine and became a monk on the death of his wife. After some years in community he became a hermit, living at Thole like the Egyptian monks, coming with other solitaries to church at weekends. There he wrote *Climacus* (The Ladder) which gave him his name. This book explores the spirituality, vices and virtues of monastic life. At the age of 70 he was pressed to become Abbot of Sinai but after four years he retired to his hermitage, where he died. His concept of the spiritual life as a ladder has inspired many contemplatives and artists.

PRAYER
O Christ, Ladder of Heaven,
you descended to the depths for our sakes
in order that you might accompany us to the heights;
grant that we may not waste our time in byways,
but ascend the ladder with you.

READINGS
Psalm 24
Genesis 28:10-22
John 1:43-51

Joshua

God-guided military leader, fourteenth century BC(?)

Joshua was brought up among the Israelite immigrants enslaved under Egypt. During their long march to freedom, when disobedience to God brought many setbacks, Joshua emerged as Moses' young lieutenant, outstanding in spiritual stature and military skill. He was expert in strategy and espionage, eschewed pilfering and plunder, and sought God's honour above all. He was consecrated by Moses to lead the people into the promised land. The famous walls of Jericho fell down when he actioned an inspiration received as he listened to God. He appointed cities of refuge and set up the Tabernacle for the worship of God. He was said to be filled with God's Spirit. At his death, aged 110, he was deeply mourned. Joshua is a form of the name Jesus.

PRAYER
Lord God Almighty,
who called Joshua to be determined and confident
in the great task to which you called him,
and to love you above all,
may we be careful to love you
above all that competes for our attention,
to be swayed neither by greed nor glamour,
but to give our utmost for your highest.

READINGS
Psalm 95; Joshua 1:1-11; Hebrews 4:1-11

Tewdric

Prince and hermit, fifth-sixth century

According to the *Book of Llan Dav*, Tewdric was a ruler of Glamorgan who in old age handed over power to his son Meurig, and became a Christian hermit at Tintern. He is said to have founded the churches of Bedwas, Llandow and Merthyr Tydfil. In a chance invasion of Saxons he once again put himself at the head of his people and in 595 was mortally injured at the Battle of Tintern. The wounded king was put on a cart drawn by two stags who eventually stopped at the well which may still be seen near St Tewdric's church in Mathern. Here his wounds were washed and he died. Early in the seventeenth century the Bishop of Llandaff opened the stone coffin and observed that Tewdric's bones were not in the smallest degree changed, the skull retaining the aperture of a large wound.

PRAYER
Fount of Life,
even the power and glory of earthly rule
cannot assuage the longing for you.
Teach us, through the life of Tewdric,
to seek you above all things,
and yet to be ready for distasteful earthly duty.

READINGS
Psalm 25
Joel 2:1-13
John 17:20-26

Caleb

God's spy, fourteenth century BC(?)

Caleb was a leader from the tribe of Judah sent out by Moses to spy out the ground before his people's entry into the promised land. When others became discouraged, he was invincible. Through autumn winds, premonitions of snow, threats of stoning, the discovery of hostile giants and the capitulation of colleagues he never faltered. This quality was not just naked courage; it was said he trusted God wholly and perpetually. He was indefatigable. When, at the age of 80, leaders came before Joshua to receive their inheritance, Caleb asked, 'Give me the hill country.' He was not content with the average or commonplace; he scaled the heights.

PRAYER
Great God,
who holds the mountains and valleys in your hands,
as we thank you for the steadfast faith of Caleb,
teach us never to waver in our trust,
but to climb every mountain and overcome every obstacle.

READINGS
Psalm 78:38-55
Joshua 14:6-15
Matthew 17:14-21

Deborah

Prophet, thirteenth century BC

At a time when there was no national government, Deborah was consulted by Israelites from various tribes who wished to settle disputes which they could not sort out locally. She was regarded as a strong, charismatic spiritual mother. She commanded Barak to take the field as Israelite commander-in-chief against the enemy Sisera and accompanied him. Sisera was defeated, and Deborah's song celebrating this victory is one of the oldest pieces in the Old Testament.

PRAYER
Mighty God,
in rough, tough times you can use rough, tough people
to carry out your will.
As we reflect on Deborah,
may we not despair of any situation in the world
but, rather, pray that even in the worst of them
you will raise up Deborahs for our time.

READINGS
Psalm 83
Judges 4
Judges 5

Isidore

Archbishop of Seville, d. 636

Isidore was educated at his brother's monastery and was regarded as the greatest and most learned teacher of his time. He drew up a code of rules for religious orders which were widely followed in Spain. During his 37 years as bishop of Seville he completed the work, begun by his brother Leander, of winning over the Visigoths to the orthodox belief in the Trinity. He decreed that each diocese should establish a seminary or cathedral school. His many writings included history, lives of the saints and biblical personalities, and the completion of the Mozarabic liturgy. These had influence in Celtic lands and Bede the historian, at the time of his death, was translating parts of his book on *The Wonders of Nature.* Before Isidore died he asked one colleague to cover him in sackcloth and the other to put ashes on his head. He raised his hands to heaven, asked forgiveness of his sins, forgave his debtors, gave away his possessions to the poor, and exhorted his people to love.

PRAYER
Divine Teacher, Father, Son and Holy Spirit,
whose presence in Scripture and saint, in creation and liturgy
Isidore discerned and helped others to understand,
save us from a superficial approach
to the mysteries of your presence;
help us to learn and to teach others also.

READINGS
Psalm 25:1-14; Proverbs 1:1-9; 2 Timothy 2:1-16

Derfel

Monk, sixth century

Derfel (or Cadarn) was a soldier who showed heroism at the battle of Camlan in 537. He founded the Christian community which grew into Llanderfel, in Gwynedd, Wales. Later writers say that he became a monk and abbot at Bardsey Island. Llanderfel became a major pilgrim centre. A prophecy about its large wooden statue of Derfel mounted on a horse stated that it would set a forest on fire. It was believed this prophecy was fulfilled when the statue was taken to London to the place where a Franciscan friar named Forest was burned to death.

PRAYER
All-seeing God,
the prayers and prophecies of your saints
often exceed what we can think.
As your power worked strongly
in the life and locality of your servant Derfel,
so may it work here, and in us, beyond our imagining.

READINGS
Psalm 118:1-19
Daniel 2:14-23
Ephesians 1:15-23

Brychan

Father of a great Christian family, sixth century

Brychan was the Christian king of Powys, who gave his name to Brecon, in Wales. According to Welsh hagiology, his was one of the three saintly tribes of Britain. One of the Welsh Triads credits him with having 'given his children and grandchildren a liberal education, so that they might be able to show the Faith of Christ to the nation of the Welsh, wherever they were without Faith.' Many of his large family (24 is mentioned) went on to do great exploits for God, and to take the Gospel to the south-west and to Brittany. Saints who were descendants through marriage include Nectan, Endellion and Morwenna. He clearly had at least one extremely fertile marriage, but one story suggests he tried to keep the child-bearing in check by going to study alone in an Irish monastery for a time. It was said the family had a reunion on the last day of each year.

PRAYER
Fruitful God,
who calls us to reflect your love in the life of our families,
we thank you that the family of Brychan reflected your love
so fully, so widely, and for so long.
May our families reflect your three-fold love
and may believers multiply through our service.

READINGS
Psalm 144:9-15
Genesis 1:26-31
Ephesians 5:25-6:4

Brynach

Soul friend of Brychan, sixth century

Brynach left his native Ireland to become a colleague of David and a soul friend of Brychan. He married Brychan's daughter Corth and had four children. After a pilgrimage to Rome and Brittany he returned to Britain only to find that the Britons were rising up against the Irish who raided their coasts. This strained his marriage and he was expelled from various places. Eventually he was welcomed in Nevern by a ruler related to his wife. He often spent long hours of prayer on the local mountain, and there met with angels; hence it is now called the Mount of Angels (Mount Ingli). Gradually the locals came to value him as a man of God and he established several faith communities. Braunton, in Devon, claims it was founded by Brynach, and it is possible that the anti-Irish campaign caused him to go there, too, at some point.

PRAYER
You who are our strength in adversity,
and who in the life of Brynach
turned extremity into opportunity,
when we meet opposition
help us to keep moving with you
until we find our place of resurrection.

READINGS
Psalm 18:20-36
Malachi 4
Romans 8:31-39

Saints and martyrs of the Americas

Many of the spiritually good aboriginal peoples of North America welcomed and accepted the Faith of those European incomers who respected them as brothers and sisters. The first incomers were from Celtic lands such as Spain, France and Britain. Many were brutal and greedy, but a few came with the pure, defenceless love of Christ. Some of these were killed. The Spanish Franciscan priest, Father Ramirez, walked barefoot and armed only with a cross to convert the Acomas. Another Franciscan, Father Junipero Serra, went to Mexico in 1767 and then to California. He walked over 4000 miles ringing a bell and saying, 'Come, receive the Faith of Christ.' From Britain the Puritans sailed in the ship *Mayflower* and made a peace treaty with the native Americans. From the Russian continent in 1879 came Innocent, whom Orthodox Christians know as Enlightener of the Aleuts and Apostle to the Americas.

PRAYER
God of all peoples, always reaching out,
today we thank you for all those people, known or unknown,
who out of the purest love,
in the friendship of the humble heart
and at risk to their lives,
brought the Faith of Christ to the American continent.

READINGS
Psalm 67; Isaiah 55:1-11; Romans 10:11-15

Madrun

Mother, fosterer of churches, sixth century

Madrun was the wife of Ynyr Gwent, the ruler of the region around Caerwent, Wales. Ynyr welcomed the Irish saint Tathan, who became the soul friend of the family and established a community and school. Tathan must have deeply influenced Madrun. She is thought to be the founder of the church at Trawsfynydd, Merionethshire. According to a popular tradition, she was present with her grandfather and eldest child when the wooden castle, in which the Britons' war leader Vortigern had taken refuge, was burned down by fellow Britons, furious that he had brought in the Saxons as his allies. Madrun fled with the child in her arms to Carn Fadryn, a solitary hill. She founded a church below it. The troubles of her land perhaps caused her to migrate to Cornwall (where she is known as St Materiana). There several churches are dedicated to her.

PRAYER
Triune God who mothers us all,
and who called Madrun to be a spiritual mother
among her own and another people,
draw out in us the love that nourishes, protects and fosters
both those we know
and those who are yet to become our friends.

READINGS
Psalm 116
Proverbs 6:16-23
Mark 3:31-35

Goran

Hermit and patron of Gorran, Cornwall, sixth century

Goran seems to be the hermit also known as Vuron who lived on Bodmin Moor. In the *Life* of Petroc he is described by an angel as a hermit 'winning his daily bread by the labour of his hands and never letting his spirit cease from prayer'. Petroc arrived on the Moor with 12 companions and sought out Goran, who entertained him with 'heaven-sent food'. Goran then decided to move a day's journey south to a more solitary place. He gives his name to Gorran where a cave and well, believed to be his, survive.

PRAYER
Bread of Heaven,
who sustained Goran in his solitude
and in his giving of hospitality,
sustain us in all we do,
and grant that we never cease from inner prayer.

READINGS
Psalm 78:9-29
Exodus 16:1-12
John 6:25-35

* transferred from April 7

Guthlac

Hermit of Crowland, d. 714

After nine years as a Mercian soldier Guthlac, who was of royal blood, became a monk at Repton, where he kept strict discipline and refrained from all alcohol. In about 701 he became a solitary at Crowland on a site accessible only by boat. He tried to emulate the regime of the Desert Fathers, but was at times attacked by Britons who had taken refuge from the Saxons in the Fens. He struggled with temptation, but had the consolation of visions of angels and of his patron, the apostle Bartholomew. He had disciples who lived in nearby cells. After 15 years as a hermit he knew that death was near, and his anchorite sister, Pega, joined his disciples for the funeral. A year later his coffin was opened and his body was found to be incorrupt. His shrine became a centre of pilgrimage and among those who were healed there were Ceolnoth, Archbishop of Canterbury, in 851. His relics were placed in the abbey church of Crowland in 1196. The twelfth-century Guthlac Roll, now in the British Museum, depicts the life of Guthlac in seventeen and a half drawings.

PRAYER
Holy and Immortal One,
who called Guthlac to be a soldier in the spiritual war,
may we learn from his example to so discipline our bodies
that we may become athletes of the spirit
and run our full course in triumph.

READINGS
Psalm 138; Numbers 6:1-8; 1 Corinthians 9:23-27

12 APRIL

Gideon

Deliverer of Israel, thirteenth century BC

Gideon was the fifth judge of Israel and held this post for 40 years during a time when the Midianites, a Bedouin people, threatened to displace Israel. As a strong young farm worker Gideon heard God call him to deliver his people. He checked out whether this really was God speaking by putting out two fleeces and asking God to change their normal dryness or wetness as a confirmation that this was God's will. At God's command he famously reduced his army from 32,000 to 300, and made a sudden night attack which led to a rout. This proved decisive and Israel had peace throughout the rest of Gideon's reign. Certain qualities of Gideon – his humility, confidence in God, and clarity – made him one of the brightest saints of the Old Testament and he is included as one of the heroes of the faith in the New Testament.

PRAYER
Sovereign Lord,
do you really want to use us
to rescue those who are perishing?
We seem so powerless, and we have so little.
Yet if you could so mightily use Gideon,
born of humble stock, pared down to a tiny force,
perhaps you can use us, too.
So help us to do much with little, in your name.

READINGS
Psalm 37:1-18; Judges 6:7-24; Hebrews 11:30-34

Hannah

Mother of the prophet Samuel, twelfth century BC

Hannah was tormented by the other wife of her husband Elkanah for being infertile. So she visited the shrine at Shiloh and poured out her soul to God, vowing that if she was given a child she would dedicate it to full-time service of God. In due course she gave birth to a boy, whom she named Samuel. She praised God in a song which Israelites down the ages memorised. One of those who did so was Mary, mother of Jesus, whose own song on the birth of Jesus echoed that of Hannah.

PRAYER
No one is holy like you, Lord.
You know and judge all that people do.
With you, the strong grow weak and the weak grow strong.
You restore people.
You lift up the poor from the dust
and you even bring the dead back to life.

Echoes Hannah's prayer

READINGS
Psalm 113
1 Samuel 1:9-20
Luke 1:46-56

Padarn

Founder of early churches in western Britain, fifth-sixth century

The Welsh Triads describe Padarn as one of the 'Three Blessed Visitors of the Isles of Britain', along with David and Teilo. He was a cousin of Cadfan and Samson, whom he mentored. Padarn was born in Armorica (Brittany) since his extended family had been part of the Britons' mass exodus there. He returned to Britain, placed himself under Illtyd's instruction, and established a faith community at Petherwyn, in Cornwall. Later he established a community of 120 members at Llanbadarn; this became a diocese, and he was bishop for 21 years. It is believed he was buried at Bardsey. According to some sources, he had skirmishes with Arthur who was slain in 537, and with Maelgwyn who died in 547. We get the impression that Padarn was a spontaneous, genuine person. He was an excellent singer. One of his much quoted sayings was 'What a person does God will judge.'

PRAYER
Overseer of our lands,
you who are always true,
we thank you for the solid faith
and natural enthusiasm of Padarn,
and we ask that we may be genuine in our work,
our friendships and in our use of talents.

READINGS
Psalm 15; Nehemiah 4:6-10; John 14:1-7

Ruadhan

One of the Twelve Apostles of Ireland, d. 584

Ruadhan came from Munster and trained at the great Clonard monastery. He founded the faith community at Lothra, County Tipperary, which numbered 150 monks. An ancient oratory at the parish church of Lothra may well be his. A legend tells how he cursed leaders of the pagan high place of Tara which then became deserted.

PRAYER
Most High God,
who causes the proud to tumble and raises up the lowly,
as we thank you for the life of Ruadhan,
please give us the inner authority of Christ
to surf the waves of ill intent,
to not be bent in the courts of the wicked,
and to make our eternal home on your high ground.

READINGS
Psalm 138
Exodus 17:8-16
1 Peter 1:3-12

Magnus

Pirate, earl of Orkney, martyr, d. 1116

The son of Erling, one of two Vikings who ruled the Orkney Islands off the north coast of Scotland, Magnus was a pirate until he was converted to Christianity. Then he was captured by Magnus Barefoot, king of Norway, and compelled to take part in raids along Britain's west coast. At the holy island of Anglesey he refused to fight, and stayed in his ship reading the Psalms. He escaped to the court of Scotland's King Malcolm 111, and lived as a penitent in a bishop's house. When Magnus Barefoot died he returned to the Orkneys to share the government with his cousin Haakon, but Haakon and his party killed Magnus at Egilsay. Magnus accepted this violent death as a sacrifice and prayed for his attackers. He was thus taken to be a martyr. Miracles occurred at his tomb, and this resulted in him becoming the principal saint of Orkney, Shetland and North Scotland. The cathedral in Orkney is dedicated to him and he is said to have appeared to Robert Bruce on the eve of the battle of Bannockburn (1315) and promised him victory.

PRAYER
Saviour of the seas,
we marvel at your amazing grace in changing Magnus
from pirate to martyr.
Rescue and renew us in the many difficulties of our lives
until we come, with Magnus, to rule with you
as part of your royal kingdom.

READINGS
Psalm 143; Jeremiah 20:1-13; 2 Peter 2:4-9

Donan and the Pictish martyrs

d. 618

An Irish Pict, Donan began his mission journeys around Scotland about 580. Places bear his name throughout Kintyre and the Outer Hebrides. He then founded a faith community on the Hebridean island of Eigg, where he got to know Columba. There, on 17 April 617, Viking raiders burst in on Donan and some 50 of his monks as they celebrated the Easter Sunday Eucharist. Donan asked them to wait until the liturgy was completed, and then begged that he and his companions should meet their death in the refectory, rather than desecrate the church. The raiders set fire to the refectory and killed with the sword any who escaped. Columba had foreknowledge of this event, although it took place some 20 years after his own death. When Donan had asked Columba to be his soul friend, Columba declined, saying it was not fitting that he should be the soul friend of one destined for red martyrdom.

PRAYER
All-knowing, all-merciful God,
whose servant Donan had to forfeit both an easy life
and an easy end,
yet remained faithful to you,
help us to seek no reward
other than that of knowing that we do your will,
that we may join Donan and his martyrs
in the life that nothing can destroy.

READINGS
Psalm 37:1-13; Jeremiah 20:1-16; Matthew 26:47-56

Molaise

Founder of monasteries, d. 639

Molaise was born in Ireland where he was known as Laisren. His grandfather was Aiden mac Gabrain, whom Columba had consecrated King of Dal Riada, the Irish colony in what is now Scotland. Many stories of his miracles have been told. Once, when a snake bit his nurse, the child Molaise signed her arm with the cross and she recovered. While being mentored as a junior by Fintan Munnu, their water supply ran out, so he went to the field and dug through to a spring. His prayers were powerful, even causing a group of attackers to retreat before they had entered any building. The existence of the 'judgment stone' outside his cave on the isle of Arran suggests that he resolved disputes, and he took a healing stone into homes. Arran became known as Scotland's Holy Isle. He returned to Ireland and established faith communities at Old Leighlin and Inishmurray, Sligo. The following was written about Molaise: 'Blessed Molaise, flame of fire, singing with his comely choir.'

PRAYER
Fire of Heaven,
who blazed in Molaise
and through his prayers wrought so much good,
kindle in us that same holy flame,
that we may live to see changes wrought by our prayers,
and one day join the choirs above.

READINGS
Psalm 86; 2 Kings 6:8-17; Mark 9:14-29

Alphege

Archbishop of Canterbury, martyr, d. 1012

Alphege became a monk at Deerhurst, near Gloucester, and later withdrew to live as a hermit in Somerset. Dunstan, Archbishop of Canterbury, recognised his qualities, and made him bishop respectively of Bath and Winchester. In 1005 Alphege was made Archbishop of Canterbury. He retained the simplicity of a monk's life for himself, but gave generously to the poor. In 1011 the invading Danes took him prisoner and placed a huge ransom on his head. Alphege, because he cared for the poor, refused to allow anyone to pay it. His captors brutally killed him at Greenwich in 1012.

PRAYER
God of courage, God of grace,
who, having raised Alphege to high service in your Church,
brought him to a great test,
help us, like Alphege, to retain simplicity
in the midst of the world's affairs,
and to endure all for you out of love for your poor.

READINGS
Psalm 41
Isaiah 43:1-5
Matthew 6:5-13

Monesan

Passionate seeker of God, fifth century

Nothing is known of this courageous God seeker except an entry in Muirchu's seventh-century *Life* of Patrick. She became filled with the Holy Spirit and when someone asked for her hand in marriage she refused. Not even when she was drenched in cold water would she relent; instead she asked her mother and nurse, between drenchings if they knew who was the maker of the wheel by which the world is illuminated. When they told her that it was the sun's maker she became determined to find him and not be united with any mortal. Monesan's parents took her to Ireland to meet Patrick, telling him on arrival, 'We are forced to come to you by our daughter's great desire to see God.' Patrick baptised her in water and the Holy Spirit. She immediately fell to the ground and gave up her spirit. She was buried on the spot where she died, but Patrick prophesied that 20 years later her remains would be transferred in great honour to a place of prayer. This came to pass.

PRAYER
True and Eternal Sun, who led Monesan, through nature,
to seek for you, the Maker of all,
open our eyes to you through the glories of your creation,
and bring the seekers of the world
to be filled with your Holy Spirit.

READINGS
Psalm 139:1-12; Isaiah 44:1-8; Acts 8:14-17

Anselm

Archbishop of Canterbury, d. 1109

Born in Italy, Anselm moved to Normandy, visiting many monasteries and centres of learning, and in 1060 joined Lanfranc's monastery at Bec. He was made prior and wrote several books of meditation and prayers. In 1078 he was elected abbot, for which his sensitive, intuitive mind fitted him. During this time he renewed contact with his former mentor, Lanfranc, who had become Archbishop of Canterbury. On the latter's death, Anselm was asked to succeed him. This was at a time when two popes fought for the See of Peter. Because he refused to support the anti-pope, or England's king, against the true pope, he was twice exiled. Despite his stubbornness, intellectual rigour and personal austerity, he was loved by his monks.

PRAYER
God of Truth,
who in Anselm brought a strong hand
to the helm of Canterbury,
help us to be undeviating in the things that eternally matter,
and to leave the rest to you.

READINGS
Psalm 119:17-24
Ezra 7:6-10
Luke 16:9-13

George

Martyr, d. 304

George was probably a soldier living in Palestine who was martyred at Lydda in about the year 304, at the start of the persecution of Christians by the Roman Emperor Diocletian. He became known throughout the East as 'the Great Martyr'. In subsequent centuries churches in England were dedicated to him, and the story of St George slaying a dragon captured the English imagination. He was made England's patron saint in the fourteenth century.

PRAYER
God of heroic love,
who gave George valour to witness to his risen Lord
even to death,
arm us, who are heirs of all the victories of faith,
to slay the dragons of falsehood, greed, and prejudice.
Raise up among us prophets of speech and pen
to reveal to us the human condition,
to recall us to ways of truth,
and to point us to our destiny.

READINGS
Psalm 126
1 Maccabees 2:59-64
Revelation 12:7-12
2 Timothy 2:3-13
John 15:18-21

* or 23 April

Saints and martyrs of England

According to Gildas, the bright beams of Christ's light reached the Isles of Britain within ten years of Christ's death, and some of these settled in the area around Glastonbury. Alban was England's first martyr. Queen Bertha of Kent was one of the first Saxons to believe in Christ. Alfred the Great was the first Christian ruler to make peace with an invader and help to bring about a united England.

PRAYER
Father,
we bless you for your goodness to the peoples of England,
for those who have maintained
the fabric of our common life in the past
and bequeathed to us a good inheritance.
We thank you for merry England –
for that rejoicing in your presence
amid our ordinary life and landscape.
We thank you for the glories of the English language,
for William Shakespeare, whose birthday it is,
and for our writers and artists in every age.
We confess with shame the sins that have stained our land,
pray that it may it be a land
where none exploits or neglects another,
where a person's word is their bond,
and where we seek the common good.

READINGS
Psalm 90; Deuteronomy 11:8-21; Romans 8:28-39

Beuno

Founder of monasteries in North Wales, sixth century

Beuno is thought to have been brought up in Herefordshire where there is a village named Llanfeuno. His main work was further away from the Saxon settlers, in north-west Wales. He founded a series of faith communities, including those at Anglesey and the Lleyn Peninsular. His main monastery was at Clynnog Fawr. The remains of his oratory still exist. He was the spiritual guide to his niece, Winefride, and is said to be related to both Cadoc and Kentigern. The accounts give an impression of a man of power, influence and temper, who was given land by a series of local rulers for Christian communities but who had to move on when there were disagreements. One of his sayings was: 'Say your Our Father and Creed but to try and run away from death will do you no good.'

PRAYER
Builder of the planets and of paradise,
may the communities and disciples of Beuno still speak to us
as we seek, under you,
to build your kingdom in our generation.
Enable us, with Beuno, to bring the talents and graces you
give into the service of your Church.

READINGS
Psalm 39; 1 Chronicles 29:10-15; 1 Corinthians 3:1-15

* transferred from 21 April

Mark

Evangelist, first century

John Mark was a Jew and a cousin to Barnabas, Paul's colleague. He may have been the young man who followed Christ when his apostles fled (Mark 14:51). The early apostles gathered in his house, perhaps for the Last Supper of Jesus, and certainly for the first recorded prayer meeting after Pentecost (Acts 12:12). He wrote the shortest of the four Gospels, perhaps acting as a scribe for Peter. It seems he was discipled by Peter, who refers to him as his son (1 Peter 5:13). Later, Mark became an assistant to the apostle Paul and to Barnabas when they set out on their great mission tour. However, Paul thought he vacillated, and refused to take him on their next leg of the journey. Barnabas disagreed. However, Mark must have won his spurs since Paul again enlisted him. Tradition says Mark became a bishop and a martyr, and that his body was taken to Venice and buried there, on the site of the magnificent St Mark's Church. The lion, the emblem of Mark's Gospel, is emblazoned on the standard of the Venetian Republic.

PRAYER
God our Teacher,
who instructed your Church
with the doctrine of your evangelist Mark,
help us not to be like children
carried away by the winds of fancy and fashion,
but to be established in the truth of your eternal Gospel.

READINGS
Psalm 119:9-16; 1 Samuel 20:17-23; Mark 14:43-52

Maelrubha

Apostle of the Picts, d. 722

A descendant of Niall of the Nine Hostages, this Irish prince became a monk at Bangor at an early age and was made abbot. In 671 he embarked on a mission to the people of northern Britain (today's Scotland). He sailed from Skye to Applecross, where he established a faith community that always kept close links with Bangor. From there he evangelised Skye and penetrated as far north as Lough Broom. He also built a church on an island in Lough Maree where his spring was famous for its healing properties. He went as far north as Skail, in Sutherland, where he died, aged 80. His companions carried his body back to Applecross. Two round stones in Applecross churchyard mark the supposed site of his grave. The well on the island of Lough Maree was a centre for healing for many years.

PRAYER
Sending God,
in the spirit of Maelrubha
help us to cross frontiers for you
and to knit together a fellowship
across the waters that divide us.

READINGS
Psalm 135; Joshua 1:10-18; Luke 7:24-28

* transferred from April 21

Machalus

Ex-pirate, Bishop of the Isle of Man, d. 498

In *The Life of Patrick*, written by Jocelyn in 1195, the
legend is recounted that Machalus was a pirate in Ireland
who, after his conversion, was told by Patrick to put to sea
in a coracle without oars as a penance for his misdeeds. He
landed on the Isle of Man and it seems he lived out a Christian
life to the full, for in due course the Christian community
of that island asked him to be their bishop. The Martyrology
of Oengus describes him as 'a rod of gold, a vast ingot, the
great bishop Maccaille'. There is a holy well near a natural
landing place on the eastern shore of Man, beside which is
the church dedicated to St Maughold, the Manx version of
his name.

PRAYER
God of a thousand places,
we thank you for Machalus,
a jewel in the crown of your Church.
Help us to be true and glorious like gold,
because we learn the way of penance
and are willing to be purified in your fires.

READINGS
Psalm 21
Proverbs 8:1-11
1 Peter 1:3-9

Modan

Dryburgh Abba of the Sweet Discipline, sixth century

Dryburgh, on the Scottish borders, had one of the most famous monasteries in Britain. Here Modan became a monk in 522. He gave himself to six or seven hours of prayer every day. He delighted to carry out his work eagerly and cheerfully. People said they'd never seen anyone so divested of self will. Modan was pressed, against his own inclination, to become abbot. Firmness in carrying out every detail of the discipline was tempered by sweetness and calm. There was such a divine anointing on his speaking that even his reprimands gave pleasure. Modan began to reach out to the region and preached the Faith at places such as Stirling. He also retired to a hermitage in the mountains near Dumbarton for 30-day vigils, and he spent the last years of his life there.

PRAYER
Sweet Saviour,
who made Modan a delight
even to those who needed discipline,
help us to do our work with joy,
to say our piece with sweetness,
and to give pleasure by our wholeheartedness.

READINGS
Psalm 119:89-104
Proverbs 16:16-24
Ephesians 6:5-9

Endellion

God's survivor, sixth century

Endellion was a daughter of the famous Brychan, and settled in Cornwall at a place called Trenkeny. She lived a very basic life, surviving on the milk of one cow. The legend grew up that the neighbouring landowner put the cow away when it strayed on to his land, and that Endellion's godfather, who was a great man – some said Arthur himself – took revenge on this bad neighbour. Endellion, however, prayed for her bad neighbour and revived him. Behind the story a gentle, prayerful Endellion emerges. St Endellion's Church, to the west of Port Isaac, is thought to be where she lived. A chapel on Lundy Island was dedicated to her, and she may well have had a hermitage there.

PRAYER
Gentle Christ,
who sustained your caring servant Endellion
on the milk of a cow and the milk of your Word,
sustain us in our times of need,
and sweeten us so that we show the milk of kindness
to difficult and sour-faced people.

READINGS
Psalm 81
Isaiah 7:17-22
Mark 8:1-10

Earconwald

Bishop of London, d. 693

Earconwald used the resources of his royal family to found monastic churches at Chertsey and Barking. He led the former, and his sister Ethelburga was abbess of the latter. He gained a reputation for holiness. Theodore, Archbishop of Canterbury, made him Bishop of London, which included the East Saxons of today's Essex and Middlesex. He helped Theodore and the difficult Bishop Wilfred to be reconciled shortly before Theodore's death in 690. Bede reported that miracles came from the couch in which he was carried in his declining years. His remains were taken to St Paul's Cathedral, London.

PRAYER
Great Reconciler,
you have taught us that peacemakers are blessed.
As Earconwald helped two colleagues
to make peace with each other,
so help us to reconcile those who are divided.

READINGS
Psalm 122
Genesis 33:1-11
2 Corinthians 5:16-21

Joseph the Worker

Legal father of Jesus, first century

Joseph was the husband of Jesus' mother, Mary, and legally Jesus' father. A carpenter by trade, he trained Jesus in the skills of the workplace. Joseph was guided by God in a dream to take Mary and the baby to Egypt for safe keeping. They returned to Nazareth where they brought Jesus up. The route of the Holy Family in Egypt is now visited by many pilgrims. He was a caring, faithful and affirming father and husband. Since he disappears from accounts after Jesus reached the age of 12 it is assumed he died before Jesus. He is regarded as a patron of fathers and of families. The Roman Catholic Church celebrates Joseph the Worker on May Day, when millions of workers throughout the world unite and celebrate.

PRAYER
Craftsperson of the world,
who entrusted your Holy Child
to the care and guardianship of Joseph,
make whole our homes by your Holy Spirit,
that parents and children may live together
in the unity of your love.

READINGS
Psalm 89:19-29
2 Samuel 7:4-16
Matthew 1:18-25

Athanasius

Bishop of Alexandria, d. 373

Throughout his life Athanasius fought to uphold and clarify the belief that God is Triune, and to oppose the Arian movement which denied that Christ was eternally divine. He praised the Church in Celtic lands for remaining true to the Trinity. When he was but a bishop's secretary, Athanasius made a suggestion at the Church's Council of Nicea, which was adopted. His stand brought him persecution. He was appointed, deposed and then restored as Bishop of Alexandria and was a prolific author. His *Life of Antony*, the founder of desert monasticism, circulated in the Celtic monastic churches, and desert spirituality caught the imagination of the Celtic people. Athanasius focused on the struggle against the powers of evil, and thought that ascetic spiritual disciplines and celibacy were two important ways of restoring the image of God in humans.

PRAYER
Father, Saviour, Spirit, eternal and triune God,
valiant was your servant Athanasius
in the struggle for truth and purity.
In the light of his sacrifice,
we rededicate ourselves to you,
praying that, joined to Christ, truly human, truly divine,
your threefold love may be reflected in our lives.

READINGS
Psalm 115:1-11; Isaiah 43:8-13; John 14:9-17

Philip and James

Apostles, first century

Philip and James appear in the lists of Jesus' twelve apostles in the first three Gospels, but in John's Gospel Philip has a more prominent role. He is the third apostle Jesus calls, and he then introduces his friend Nathaniel to Jesus. Philip is the spokesperson for the other apostles, who question their ability to feed 5000 people, and at Jesus' final Passover meal he starts a dialogue which leads to Jesus' farewell discourse. James is the son of Alphaeus, and is sometimes known as James the Less to distinguish him from James, the brother of John. Philip and James are celebrated on the same day because their remains are entombed in the same church in Rome.

PRAYER
Almighty God,
whom truly to know is everlasting life,
help us to know your Son as the way, the truth and the life,
that, following in the steps of your apostles Philip and James,
we may walk in the way that leads to life everlasting.

READINGS
Psalm 119:1-8
Isaiah 30:15-21
John 14:1-14

* or 1 May or 14 November

Asaph

Bishop of St Asaph, d. early seventh century

The boy Asaph, whose grandfather came from the north of Britain, was mentored by Kentigern when he fled from the north and founded a famous monastery that numbered over 900 members in the Llanelwy area where Asaph lived. The boy was handsome and took his name from the Old Testament choir leader under King David. Once, following his custom of praising God naked in the river, Kentigern became so frigid with cold that he asked Asaph to bring coals from the fire to warm him. There was no container to do so, so the trusting Asaph carried them in his tunic. To everyone's amazement it was unharmed. Kentigern mentored and ordained Asaph and, when he was able to return to the north, left him in charge of his monastery. With the consent of everyone Asaph was also made bishop. Today St Asaph's Cathedral stands on that site.

PRAYER
Light of the faithful,
who set Asaph to be an eager helper,
shepherd and guide of your people,
help us to walk in his steps and to help others to do likewise.

READINGS
Psalm 29; 1 Chronicles 16:1-13; Hebrews 13:1-8

* transferred from 1 May

Molua

Monk, builder and hermit of Killaloe, died *c.* 609

Molua founded his monastery at Killaloe where he was noted for his hands-on coaching of young recruits. Molua was not afraid to reprove a person, but he always tried to do it with gentleness. Once the king of Leinster arrived with 400 of his men and demanded that they be instantly fed. Molua patiently explained why that would be difficult. The king insisted, and food was brought as quickly as was possible. The first morsel the king tasted stuck in his gullet for 24 hours, preventing him from either eating or sleeping. The king learned his lesson and from that time on he became thoughtful and generous towards the community. Molua's main disciple was Flanna, who succeeded him. His hermit's oratory on Friars Island was re-erected before the area was submerged by the Shannon hydroelectric works.

PRAYER
Understanding Maker,
help me to take the time to sit in the shoes
of the other person:
to listen to what they feel,
to refrain from the too-hasty judgement
and yet not collude with the slipshod
but to help see a thing through.

READINGS
Psalm 25:1-15;
Proverbs 4:10-19;
Luke 6:37-42

Eadbert

Bishop of Lindisfarne, d. 698

Bishop of Lindisfarne from 688, with a devotion to Cuthbert, Eadbert spent every Lent either as a solitary on Thrush Island (Lindisfarne) or on Inner Farne. Bede writes that he was 'well known for his knowledge of the Scriptures, his obedience to God's commandments, and especially for his generosity in alms giving. For each year, in accordance with the Law, he used to give a tenth not only of all his beasts but also of his grain, fruit and clothing to the poor.' His body was carried with Cuthbert's around Northumbria to save the holy relics from the Viking raids on Lindisfarne.

PRAYER
Almighty Giver,
who chose Eadbert to be a faithful pastor
and Bishop of Lindisfarne,
grant that our bishops and pastors today
may speak your word
and be generous-hearted towards the people.

READINGS
Psalm 119:57-72
Genesis 14:17-24
Matthew 7:24-29

John of Beverley

Bishop of York, d. 721

John was one of five monks trained by Hilda of Whitby who became a bishop in the English church. In 687 he was consecrated Bishop of Hexham, where he showed special concern for the poor and disabled. One mute young man began to speak after John taught and prayed for him. He regularly resorted to a hermitage. He became Bishop of York in 705, and Wilfred, who had long had designs on the See of Hexham, replaced him there. Yet John, unlike others, never allowed enmity to develop between him and Wilfred. As Bishop of York he founded a monastery in a forest, which is now Beverley. He retired there four years before his death. Signs and wonders accompanied his ministry, which both Bede and Alcuin record. King Athelstan invoked his prayers and Julian of Norwich drew inspiration from his life.

PRAYER
Lover of the poor,
whose likeness shows most specially
in those with disability of body,
we bless you for the love, faith and prayer of John.
May we, like Mother Julian,
draw inspiration from this lovable saint,
that we may become more Spirit-filled
and more humane towards others.

READINGS
Psalm 22:22-31; Deuteronomy 15:7-11; Luke 14:12-14

Eithne

Prophetic mother, fifth and sixth century

Eithne was said to be descended from Cathoair Mor, the most famous of the kings of Leinster, Ireland. She married King Fedelmid, who was descended from Northern Ireland's legendary Niall of the Nine Hostages. They made their home in Garton, in today's County Donegal. There she conceived. In dreams before their baby's birth an angel brought her a beautiful robe in which all the colours of the flowers were portrayed. After a time the angel asked for the robe back and as he receded the cloak spread across the sky until it covered a great region. 'Do not grieve,' the angel told her 'for you will bring forth a child of such beauty of character that he will be honoured as a prophet and will win countless souls to the heavenly country.' Eithne interpreted her own dreams. 'I will bear a son whose teachings shall extend throughout Ireland and Britain,' she prophesied. The great Columba, founder of many Irish monasteries and of Iona, in Britain, was her son.

PRAYER
Triune God who mothers us all,
and who raises up prophets through marriages
that are made in heaven, as we thank you for Eithne
we pray for marriages that are made in heaven
and for babies who will lead others to heaven.

READINGS
Psalm 8; Daniel 2:14-23; Ephesians 3:7-21

Mother Julian

Anchoress and mystic of Norwich, d. 1417

An unknown woman became an anchoress in a cell attached to the Church of St Julian, Norwich, and that is how she has come to be known as Mother Julian. She had a servant and a cat, and at certain times people sought her guidance at the cell window. At the age of 30, when she seemed to be suffering from a terminal illness, she experienced a series of 16 visions, which revealed aspects of the love of God. In one vision Christ is referred to as our Mother; in another, a little thing the size of a hazelnut in her hand was revealed to exist and to last for ever because God loves it, and all things have being through the love of God. Following her recovery she spent the next 20 years of her life reflecting on the meaning of the visions. She recorded these in the first book written by a woman in English, *The Revelations of Divine Love*. She helped to recover contact with the feminine aspect of God which had nearly been lost in the centuries following the decline of Celtic spirituality.

PRAYER
Most Holy God,
the ground of our beseeching,
when we fret and fear
teach us that all manner of things shall be well,
all manner of things shall be well.

READINGS
Psalm 27:1-8; 1 Kings 19:9-13a; 1 Corinthians 13:8-13

Comgall

Abbot of Bangor, Ireland, d. 601

Comgall founded Ireland's largest monastic church and college at Bangor, in the north of Ireland. St Bernard later called this 'the vale of angels' and over 3000 monks learned, worked, and chanted praise there. Its library has furnished us with much of what we know of Irish Christianity at that time. Comgall prepared for his life's work by spending several years as a hermit on the shores of Lough Erne in the west of Ireland. The regime he introduced, and which 30,000 people followed, was very demanding. His rule encouraged people to love Christ, hate wealth, be kind to others, and to advance a step a day. He stressed the value of the soul friend. He trained, and eventually agreed to send out Columbanus on his great missionary task.

PRAYER
All-kindly Father,
call us to sacrificial service;
all-kindly Christ,
train us in your disciplines;
all-kindly Spirit,
steep us in your praise.
As Comgall's monks transformed their valley,
so may we transmit your presence
and turn round the values of our world.

READINGS
Psalm 135; 1 Chronicles 9:22-33; Galatians 5:16-26

Indract

seventh century

Indract probably brought a stone altar on a boat from Ireland to Cornwall. At a site near Plymouth he planted his staff into the ground and it eventually grew into an oak tree. There he planted also a faith community, which was well supplied with fish from a pond. He and his companions moved to the Somerset marshes, where they were attacked and all but one were killed. The one who survived claimed that every year, on the anniversary of their death, a pillar of light rose from earth to heaven, and many people came out to gaze and remember Indract. In the eighth century the Saxon king of Wessex had a vision of Indract that caused him to have his body placed in a pyramid of stone in the old wattle church at Glastonbury.

PRAYER
God of Life,
who turned Christ's tree of death into a tree of life,
and who changed the tragedy of Indract's death
into a victory sign for the people,
change our despair into hope,
and help us to turn every difficulty into an opportunity.

READINGS
Psalm 92
1 Chronicles 16:23-33
1 Peter 3:13-22

* transferred from 8 May

Ishmael

Founding father of a great people
seventeenth century BC

Ishmael was the son of Abraham by Hagar, an Egyptian. He received a divine promise that he would have twelve sons and become a great nation. Abraham tenderly loved Ishmael, but because his wife Sarah, who bore him Isaac, was jealous of Hagar, he reluctantly agreed they should separate. The separation between these two sons has produced bitter divisions up to the present time between Arabs, who claim descent from Ishmael, and Jews, who claim descent from his brother Isaac. Yet all are children of Abraham, and from God's point of view it is possible to see, in the love which both Abraham and God had for Ishmael, a divine provision for the 'dignity of difference'. The name Ishmael means 'God hears', and he is a monument to God's goodness in answering prayer.

PRAYER
God of a hundred names,
who, for love of Ishmael and his people through the ages,
commit yourself to developing their greatness,
forgive us for our jealous divisions
and help us to honour one another
and seek the common good.

READINGS
Psalm 82
Genesis 17:15-27
Matthew 21:33-43

Samuel

Seer and nation shaper, twelfth century BC

Samuel was the earliest of the Hebrew prophets after Moses. A 'famine of hearing the words of God' ended when he, as a boy apprentice at the shrine of Shiloh, three times heard a voice in the night. The third time his mentor, the old priest Eli, explained it must be God's voice, and told Samuel to say, 'Speak, Lord, for your servant is listening.' Samuel went on to be the person of greatest authority in the land. When it became clear that the people wanted a king, and that God allowed this, Samuel was led to anoint Saul as the first king, and later, when Saul had dissipated his spiritual capital, he anointed David as his successor. Power did not corrupt Samuel, in part because he kept a Nazirite rule of life. He acted as an intercessor, a priest and a judge. The widespread affection the nation had for him is evidenced by the grief shown at his death.

PRAYER
Only true King,
may we heed the call of Samuel
to remember the great things you have done,
to serve you, listen to you
and obey your commands with all our hearts,
so that you will not abandon us
but make us your own people.

READINGS
Psalm 99; 1 Samuel 12:13-25; Acts 3:11-26

Matthias

Apostle, first century

The number of primary apostles Jesus appointed was twelve, just as God had called into being twelve tribes of Israel. So when Judas, one of the twelve, committed suicide after betraying Jesus, the eleven remaining apostles knew it was necessary to choose another to fill the vacancy. The institution of the apostles needed the number twelve to be complete. The new apostle had to be someone who had known Jesus and who had also seen him in resurrection form. Matthias was the person chosen.

PRAYER
Holy Spirit,
who led the apostles to fill the place of Judas
with your faithful servant Matthias,
may your Church be preserved from false apostles
and may its ministries be complete
and served by true and worthy servants.

READINGS
Psalm 138
Ezra 6:13-18
Acts 1:15-26

* or 9 August

Pachomius

Founder of Christian communal monasticism, d. 346

A pagan Egyptian conscripted into the army, Pachomius was moved by people who gave soldiers food parcels, and enquired about them. 'They are people who love one another and they are called Christians,' he was told. He vowed to become a Christian, and on leaving the army became a desert hermit. Others were attracted to live nearby, and after a few years he used his outstanding administrative skills to organise large communal monasteries. They were divided into houses according to the craft practised by the monks, such as agriculture, tailoring and baking. They sold their produce in Alexandria. They had a centralised rule, and Pachomius was like a commander-in-chief. His rule influenced those of Basil and Benedict.

PRAYER
God of order born of love,
who through Pachomius drew people to live
in colonies of heaven as bees live in hives,
come into our disordered world
and build colonies of heaven suited to our time.

READINGS
Psalm 122
Exodus 18:17-26
Philippians 3:17-4:1

* or 9 or 14 May

Brendan the Navigator

Abbot of Clonfert, died *c.* 575

Brendan was born near Tralee, fostered by Ita and educated by Erc. His main activities were in south-west Ireland, where he became a monk and later abbot. He founded monastic communities at Clonfert, which had 3000 monks, Annadown, Inishadroun and Ardfert. He wrote a Rule which was used for several hundred years. He was a great traveller, and stories of his faith-filled seafaring ventures must have circulated, for it was Brendan who was chosen as the hero in the visionary travel saga written at least three centuries later, *The Navigation of St Brendan*, which uses stories of miracle and pilgrimage to illustrate the seasons of the Church year. Its popularity has etched Brendan in the imaginations of Christians who desire to be venturers for God. While on a visit to his sister Brig, he said, 'God is calling me to the eternal kingdom; and my body must be taken to Clonfert . . .' A prophet spoke of 'the age of Brendan who was without crime, who was sage, prophet and priest'.

PRAYER
Pilgrim God,
we thank you for Brendan's drawing together
of families and friends into communities of divine service,
and for his adventures for you on land and sea.
Awaken in us the spirit of heroic love
and lead us into the endless adventure.

READINGS
Psalm 107:1-9, 23-32; Jonah 2 ; John 21:1-14

Madron

Monk and healer of Cornwall, sixth century(?)

We know more about Madron's legacy than about his life. The Cornish town of Madron is named after him, and the well and chapel there have been a place of healing prayer over the centuries. In 1641 a cripple who had walked on his hands for 16 years spent the night at the altar of the ruined church, and next morning bathed in the stream that flowed through the chapel from the well. After sleeping on St Madron's 'bed' for 90 minutes he felt bodily sensations and walked better. After two more visits he was completely cured.

PRAYER
Healing God,
who longs to make us whole in body and mind,
we thank you for the wholeness
Madron left imprinted on his place of prayer,
and for the miracles you have wrought there since.
Cure us of all that cramps our being,
and raise us up to walk with you in resurrection faith.

READINGS
Psalm 30
Genesis 20:14-18
Acts 3:1-10

Carantoc

Missionary, sixth or seventh century

It is thought Carantoc came from Ireland to Britain. He established a monastic community in Somerset, and is patron of Llangranog and Carhampton. Later he led a group who evangelised central Cornwall, and he is patron of Crantock. In due course he emigrated to Brittany, where he was known as Caredec. Centuries later someone wrote a story in which Carantoc cast his portable altar on the River Severn in the belief that God wanted him to settle wherever it landed. He sailed to the western edge of Bridgewater Bay in order to look for it, and was met by the young 'King' Arthur who told him he would show him where the altar had landed if he would tame the dragon that was terrifying that area. Carantoc confronted the beast; it bent its head in obeisance and no one was disturbed by it again.

PRAYER
God who calms the fears of humans and of beasts,
and who draws souls to you,
we thank you for Carantoc's zeal, fearlessness
and freedom to be led by you.
May your peace descend deeper into our hearts,
and your love reach out to others through us.

READINGS
Psalm 91; Isaiah 65:17-25; Luke 10:17-22

* transferred from 16 May

Dunstan

Archbishop of Canterbury, d. 988

Dunstan lived near Glastonbury monastery and spent time at the court of the Wessex king. At the urging of a saintly uncle he entered the monastery, devoting his work time to music, illuminating and metalwork. In 943 the new king made him abbot which launched a revival of monastic life in England. He rose to eminence and King Edgar made him chief minister and Archbishop of Canterbury. Dunstan helped to bring balance, discipline and education to the whole of the English Church.

PRAYER
Great Overseer,
you raised Dunstan to restore discipline in your Church
and to give counsel to rulers.
May we not lack gifted leaders
and those who build up your Church
in cohesion and right living.

READINGS
Psalm 21
Exodus 31:1-5
Matthew 24:42-46

Alcuin of York

Advisor to Charlemagne, Abbot of Tours, d. 804

Alcuin lived in Northumbria, joined the cathedral school at York and eventually became its leader. In 781 he went to Aachen as advisor to Charlemagne, the Holy Roman Emperor, on religious and educational matters and as head of the Palace School, where he established a major library. In 796 he became abbot of Tours. He wrote poetry, revised the Church's Bible lectionary and wrote numerous letters and prayers that have been prized by many.

PRAYER
Eternal Goodness, deliver us from evil.
Eternal Power, be our strength.
Eternal Wisdom, scatter the darkness of our ignorance.
Eternal Pity, have mercy upon us,
that with all our hearts, mind and strength
we may seek your face;
and bring us into your presence.

Alcuin

READINGS
Psalm 123
Isaiah 61:10-62:3
John 4:19-24

Helena

Protector of holy places, finder of the Cross, d. 330

Helena was mother of the Roman Emperor Constantine, who embraced Christianity after seeing a vision of a cross in the sky. She was a devout Christian, a benefactor of churches. In 326 she made a pilgrimage to the Holy Land, and provided the resources to build a basilica on the Mount of Olives and another at Bethlehem. It was thought she retrieved part of the cross on which Jesus died. This is the subject of Cynewulf's finest poem, *Elene.* In the Eastern Church she is commemorated on this day together with Constantine.

PRAYER
You who made the instrument of shameful death
the means of transformation,
and who led Helena to seek you in holy places
and to find your cross,
go before us in our pilgrimage of life,
purify our desires
and lead us in the way of the true cross.

READINGS
Psalm 122
Isaiah 58:12-14
Acts 17:1-9

Helen of Caernarvon

Founder of churches, fourth century

Facts about this interesting and possibly pivotal figure are uncertain. She was a British princess, and perhaps the daughter of King Coel of Colchester, of the nursery rhyme 'Old King Cole'. Clemens Maximus, Roman Emperor in Britain, Gaul and Spain 383-388, had a dream which led him to marry her. She is reported to have organised the building of the Roman roads that traverse Wales from north to south, and which are still collectively known as Sarn Helen. Some believe that she founded one of the earliest large monastic communities in Britain. Churches in Wales are dedicated to her and she is remembered in Llanelan in Gower and at another Llanelan near Abergavenny. She was reputed to have had five children, one of whom was called Constantine. For this reason, suggestions that she is the same person as Helena (21 May) continue to be made.

PRAYER
Your hand, O God,
has guided your people in each land.
We thank you for the far-sighted building
of roads and faith communities
in the early years of the Faith in Britain,
and for all that we know about Helen and people like her.

READINGS
Psalm 127; Nehemiah 2:11-20; Matthew 7:24-29

Aldhem

Abbot of Malmesbury, Bishop of Sherborne, d. 709

A member of the Wessex royal family, he became a monk at Malmesbury, and then its abbot, combining the skills of administrator and writer. His Old English verses, sung with harp accompaniment to draw people to church, were praised by King Alfred. He established faith communities at Frome and Bradford-on-Avon. When the growing Wessex diocese was divided in 705 he became the first bishop of its western half, Sherborne.

PRAYER
You, O God,
are enthroned on the praises of your people.
As Aldhem's harp songs drew folk to you,
so may our talents,
offered now to you,
draw people still.

READINGS
Psalm 33
2 Kings 3:11-20
Revelation 14:1-5

* transferred from 25 May

Vincent of Lerins

Pilgrim for the love of the Trinity, d. 450

On his retirement as a Gaul army officer, Vincent withdrew to the small island of Lerins. Patrick is thought to have studied here and it was becoming known as the holy island of Europe. Here Vincent took the name Peregrines, to express his belief that all of life should be lived as a pilgrimage. He had felt that life's fleeting moments run out like water that is cut off from its source, and that he must redeem time. He used his space for reflection to renew his mind and to write in order to renew the Church. He longed for the Church, which was being pulled in different directions, to be rooted in Scripture and to reflect the loving communion at the heart of God – the Trinity. He declared that whatever has been believed in all places, at all times by all faithful Christians, is what must be believed – the rest should not be imposed. It has been said that he let 'the inward beauty of his mind sparkle in every page of his book'.

PRAYER
Three of limitless love,
may your beauty be seen in us.
May our lives be rooted
in what you have revealed to us in the Scriptures.
May we redeem the time.
Thus shall we honour Vincent;
thus shall we please you.

READINGS
Psalm 115; Exodus 20:1-17; Mark 1:1-12

Bede

Monk of Jarrow, first English historian, d. 735

From the age of 7, Bede was educated at the Northumbrian monasteries of Wearmouth and then Jarrow, where he was a monk for the rest of his life. He said that his special delight was 'to learn, to teach and to write'. He wrote works on orthography, metre, computistics, a chronology of history and 25 commentaries on Scripture. His most significant contributions were his *Ecclesiastical History of the English People*, without which we would know little of the Irish Mission and early Saxon Church, and his *Lives* of saints, most notably of Cuthbert. As his death approached he was translating a work of Isidore and the Latin John's Gospel. An account of his dying has touched the hearts of many. He dictated the last sentence to the boy who was his scribe and said, 'Now it is finished.' Then, after reciting 'Glory be to the Father, to the Son and to the Holy Spirit', and while still kneeling in prayer, he died. It was Ascension Day.

PRAYER
Light of our forebears, rock of their lives,
help us, with Bede, to study your noble works
that we may discern your hand among us.
Help us, like him, to persevere in well-doing day after day,
that we, with him, may join our ascended Lord.

READINGS
Psalm 78:1-8; Ecclesiasticus 39:1-10; John 21:20-25

Augustine

Apostle to Kent, first Archbishop of Canterbury, d. 604 or 605

The great Gregory, of St Andrew's monastery in Rome, wanted to lead a mission to the many English colonists (Anglo-Saxons) in Britain who were not yet evangelised. Owing to a sudden crisis he dispatched Augustine, the prior of his monastery, to go in his stead. Augustine was reluctant but he and his team of monks finally landed in Kent in 597 and were well received by its King Ethelbert whose wife, Bertha, was already a Christian. God worked miracles through Augustine. Augustine tried, but failed, to persuade the indigenous British bishops to accept a uniform church organisation. However, in succeeding generations the Roman organisation replaced the looser, federated basis of the Celtic churches, and he is established as the first of a long line of archbishops up to the present.

PRAYER
Lover of souls, who desired to turn Angles into angels
through the ministry of Augustine,
and who used him to establish order
in the Church of the English,
teach us to seek your face above all,
and to create teamwork
with those from different backgrounds
who also serve you.

READINGS
Psalm 98; Isaiah 49:22-25; Luke 10:17-20

Melangell

Hermit and founder of Pennant-Melangell refuge, d. 590

Melangell fled from her native Ireland to avoid a forced marriage. God led her to a place in Britain. There she once sheltered under her cloak a hare whose hunters crashed in upon her. The local ruler, who led the hunt, was so impressed that he granted her that land as a sanctuary for ever. She made it into a sanctuary of prayer for the rest of her life. By the start of the third millennium Pennant-Melangell, in Wales, had revived as a place of prayer and healing.

PRAYER
Hold us, dear Lord, like Melangell, captive to your love.
May we, like her, seek no provenance apart from you.
All she needed came from your hand and she flourished.
Alive through you to her holy calling of prayer,
she gained the land in Pennant
that you have hallowed ever since.
Give us the land, O God;
teach us to pray; hallow the place where we now live.
Draw us into that place where we are safe at last
in the centre of your heart.

Pennant-Melangell pilgrim, Jane Clarke

READINGS
Psalm 91:1-4
Numbers 35:9-15
Matthew 23:37-39

Cummian the Tall

Abandoned child, great scholar of Clonfert, d. 661

Brendan's great monastery at Clonfert grew to about 3000 monks. His three immediate successors as abbot are commemorated thus in the Feilire of St Aengus of Tallaght: Fintan the Melodious, Senach the Rough, Colman, son of Comgall, the Guileless. The fourth successor was Cummian. He is regarded as Ireland's most distinguished seventh-century scholar. He had, however, a hard start to life: abandoned outside the convent founded by Ita at Killeedy, he was named Cummian after the basket in which he was found. The phrase 'the tall one' was added to distinguish him from another Cummian. He had a reputation as both a saint and a scholar. He wrote a famous letter trying to get his brothers in the Ionian monasteries to bring their date for Easter into line with the rest of the world. His Epistle and Penitential reveal his wide learning and wisdom in moral matters. A long Protection Prayer (Lorica) is thought to have been written by Cummian at the time of the yellow plague, of which the prayer below is an extract.

PRAYER
May Mary's son cover us!
May we be under his protection tonight!
Wherever we go, may he guard us well . . .
Cummian

READINGS
Psalm 119:97-112; 1 Chronicles 27:25-34;
Matthew 13:47-52

Buryan

Irish lady, saint of Cornwall, fifth century(?)

An Irish princess, said to be a friend of Patrick, it is thought Buryan came to Cornwall with Piran, landing on the coast near the present St Ives. The name Buryan means 'Irish lady' in Cornish. A parish in Penzance is dedicated to her. King Athelstan built a church in her honour after his successful tenth-century expedition to the Scilly Isles. A Hymn for St Buryan extols 'one glorious within who came to teach our land Christ's law . . . Throughout her days God's little flock she tended, a faithful shepherdess.'

PRAYER
Wind of heaven,
as once you blew your saint to a new shore,
blow us where you will.
As Buryan, glorious within, let love defend her sheep,
help us to form safe places of love
where your children may grow.

READINGS
Psalm 107:21-32
Micah 2:12-13
John 3:1-8

Jonathan

King David's friend, tenth century BC

Jonathan was the eldest son of Israel's King Saul who, because he loved both God and David with all his heart, risked his jealous father's fury in order to protect David's life. Jonathan was sufficiently humble and perceptive to know that he would never succeed his father as king, and that under God David would. With total selflessness he supported David, and they made a covenant to lay down their lives for each other. Of his children, we know only the name of Meshibotheth, a cripple whom David cared for after Jonathan's death. Jonathan, who showed courage and prowess in battle, was slain on the battlefield with his father. David's elegy for his friend is one of the most moving in history (2 Samuel 1:22). Jonathan personified many of the graces New Testament writers extol.

PRAYER
Covenant God,
we thank you for Jonathan, glory of Israel,
swifter than an eagle, gracious and loved.
Teach us the arts of true friendship and wholehearted living,
and grow in us the graces of the Holy Spirit.

READINGS
Psalm 133
1 Samuel 20:1-16
2 Peter 1:5-11

Mary and Elizabeth

Soul friends, first century

Some months after she became pregnant Jesus' mother Mary visited her cousin Elizabeth, who was also pregnant. The Holy Spirit was so powerfully upon them that Elizabeth's baby, John, leapt in her womb, and Mary was inspired to sing a song whose words were later recorded and included in the Bible and the Churches' liturgies. In Luke's account, John's leaping in the womb is a way of saying that the last of the Old Testament prophets bears witness to Christ as the promised Messiah. Thus this links the Old and the New Covenants of God.

PRAYER
Blessed Lord,
by your grace Elizabeth rejoiced with Mary,
who shared her life with Jesus
from the warmth of her womb
to the silence of the grave.
Now that Jesus has become one with us,
may we become one with him.
Inspired by the example of Elizabeth and Mary,
may we welcome the Spirit whom he sends.

READINGS
Psalm 113
Zephaniah 3:14-18
Romans 12:9-16
Luke 1:39-49

Justin

Philosopher and martyr, d. 166

Justin, born of a pagan family, became a noted apologist for the Christian Faith and wore the dress of a professional philosopher. He was convinced non-believers would become Christians if the doctrines of Christianity were sufficiently clearly expounded. The record of his martyrdom survived and has inspired many up to this day.

PRAYER
Transforming God,
through 'the foolishness' of the cross
you taught Justin to confound
both the vanities of philosophy
and the terrors of death.
Ground us so firmly in the faith of Christ crucified
that we, too, may in all things be more than conquerors.

READINGS
Psalm 16
1 Maccabees 2:25-28
1 Corinthians 1:18-25

Ronan

Monk of Cornwall and Brittany, sixth century(?)

The monk Ronan travelled from Cornwall to Brittany where he steadfastly refused inducements to renounce the life of a holy hermit. It was decided he would be buried wherever the oxen pulling his cortege chose to stop. The great church and crafts village of Locronan now mark the place of his shrine.

PRAYER
Faithful God,
we thank you that your servant Ronan
remained loyal to the end.
May the fragrance of sanctity
which lingered long in his adopted land
be revived again by the yearly remembrance of his life.

READINGS
Psalm 40
Isaiah 43:1-5
Matthew 5:1-8

* transferred from 1 June

Kevin

Hermit and founder of Glendalough, d. 618

As a child Kevin was educated by monks. After ordination he settled as a hermit by the Upper Lake of Glendalough, County Wicklow, Ireland, which today is marked by 'Kevin's Bed', his tiny cave 50 feet above the lake, and by a bronze-age rock tomb which he re-used as a church. As disciples gathered round him these premises became too small and they settled by the Lower Lake. After his death a flourishing 'monastic city' grew around the Lower Lake monastery, which is perhaps the world's best preserved Celtic monastic city. There are famous stories about Kevin, such as his praying with hands stretched out in the shape of Christ's Cross, and allowing a bird to nest and hatch its egg in the palm of his hand. The story that he tamed the feared monster of the lake, by allowing it to curl around his body while he prayed, has been used by guides in Glendalough's revived pilgrimage centres as a symbol of Christ taming our inner monsters.

PRAYER
Give us courage to journey, like Kevin, into the wild places, for you who created each wild thing, created us.
Teach us, as you taught Kevin,
that if we journey with you to the place of our greatest fear, it can become the place of our greatest strength.

READINGS
Psalm 104:16-21
Hosea 2:16-23
Matthew 3:1-6

Petroc

Abbot of Padstow, hermit, sixth century

Petroc founded a monastery at Padstow (Petroc's Stowe) with the help of the Christian Cornish king Constantine. His holy rule, which included praying while standing in the river, drew others to join him. In due course he built himself a hermitage further inland at Little Petherick. In his old age he settled with twelve companions in beehive huts on Bodmin Moor, where he became friends with the wild animals. He became a much loved saint of south-west Britain, and there are stories of his saving sailors from shipwreck.

PRAYER
O Gentle Christ of Bodmin Moor,
who blessed Petroc's monks and friends of fur,
protecting Saviour, strong to save,
whose arm can bind the restless wave,
hear our cry, O Trinity,
for those at risk on land or sea.

READINGS
Psalm 103
Lamentations 3:22-32
1 Kings 19:1-16
Matthew 6:19-34

Boniface of Crediton

'Apostle of Germany', Archbishop of Mainz, martyr, d. 754

Boniface became a learned monk at Exeter, refused church posts in England, and became a missionary bishop in the Roman tradition to the Germans and French. For three years he helped the aged Willibrord in Frisia. He evangelised and was made Bishop of Hesse. He helped to reform the Church in France. He became Archbishop of Mainz and was martyred by hostile pagans. His strengths were his courage, zeal and administrative skill.

PRAYER
Redeemer God,
we thank you for calling Boniface to lay down his life
for the German people,
and for his zeal and learning.
Raise up those who will destroy the strongholds of idolatry
in the hearts of people and institutions.
May the German people be able
to receive that same gentle love of Christ
which works all things together for good.

READINGS
Psalm 115
Isaiah 49:5-10
Acts 20:24-28

Colman

Bishop of Dromore, sixth century

Born in Ulster, Colman spent much of his working life in County Down and founded the monastery of Dromore, where he was also bishop. There he probably taught Finnian of Moville. His influence in Scotland is honoured there. It is said he was born in Scottish Dal Riada at Kintyre. It seems that either he or his disciples established faith communities there. There is also a belief that he founded faith communities in Wales at Llangolman and Capel Colman in Dyfed.

PRAYER
Set us free, O God, like Colman,
to cross frontiers for you.
Make us open to others in listening,
generous to others in sharing
and sensitive to others in praying.
Echoes a prayer of Brother Bernard, SSF

READINGS
Psalm 96
Isaiah 12:4-6
1 Timothy 6:11-21

* transferred from 7 June

Eadfrith

Illuminator of the Lindisfarne Gospels, bishop, d. 721

Eadfrith was a monk of Lindisfarne who became its abbot and then its bishop. It was he who transcribed and illuminated the Lindisfarne Gospels, which were dedicated to God and St Cuthbert in 698. This masterpiece of the Celtic Golden Age reveals extraordinary scholarly and artistic qualities. Drawing together Irish, continental and Anglo Saxon influences, it has been described as the first manifesto of the English Church, and Eadfrith himself has been described as 'the first personality in English art history'. He died on this day in 721 and his relics were taken with those of Aidan and Cuthbert eventually to be buried in Durham.

PRAYER
Divine Artist,
you endow us with gifts and call us to serve.
Anoint us by your Spirit that we, like your servant Eadfrith,
whose inspired fingers moved the bird's feather
over the stretched, brown skin of calf,
may make good use of our gifts
and be worthy of our calling.

READINGS
Psalm 45
Exodus 31:1-11
Luke 12:35-44

* transferred from 4 June

Ephrem of Syria

Hermit, theological teacher and writer, d. 373

Born in Nisibia, Mesopotamia, he was baptised and joined its cathedral school, of which he later became head. He emerged as a great poet, teacher, orator, commentator and defender of the Faith. After the Persians captured Nisibia in 363 he became a monk, living in a cave near Edessa. There he wrote commentaries on Scripture and put his words to popular songs which were then incorporated into the Church's liturgy and translated into several languages. In 370 he visited Bishop Basil, whose brother Gregory wrote in his praise. In 372 he organised charity to victims of famine. He died soon afterwards in his cave.

PRAYER
O Lord,
create quiet in your churches.
Blend and unite the contentious sects,
still and rule the conflicting parties,
and may there at every period be one true Church,
and may her righteous children gather themselves together
to confess your graciousness.

Ephrem

READINGS
Psalm 96
Isaiah 5:1-7
Colossians 3:12-17

* transferred from 9 June

Columba

Founder of Irish and Ionan monasteries, d. 597

Columba (or Columcille) was born into one of the great families of sixth-century northern Ireland. A brilliant organiser, poet, songwriter and prophet, he developed the tender simplicity of his Master, and became the leader of a network of monasteries and a strategist for the kingdom of God. After training at Moville monastery he transferred to Finnian's famed Clonard monastery, where he was ordained a priest. He spent some 15 years establishing up to 300 churches and monasteries throughout his home region before sailing to Iona and founding its great monastery. From there much of the highlands of Scotland was evangelised. Daughter monastic houses were founded. Columba wrote many poems and songs, and his singing could be heard from afar. After his death Aidan took a mission from Iona south to Lindisfarne, inspired by the life and disciplines of Columba, which was to have immeasurable influence in England.

PRAYER
Mighty God,
whose servant Columba established strongholds of the Faith in the Western Isles,
keep us strong in that faith,
bold in that outreach, and ablaze with that fire
which marked Columba and his communities.

READINGS
Psalm 34:1-14; Lamentations 3:19-33; 1 Corinthians 14:1-18

Nathan

Prophet, tenth century BC

Nathan was a distinguished prophet who lived during the reigns of Israel's kings David and Solomon. He is known to the world for his bringing home to David, with great clarity and courage, the enormity of his sin in having sexual intercourse with the wife of a leading soldier, and, when she found she was pregnant, arranging for her husband to be deployed at the front where he would be killed. Nathan appealed to the better side of David, created a scenario of injustice and asked him what punishment he would advise for the misdoer. Then he told David, 'You are that man.' This led to deep repentance by David of which Psalm 51 is a sign. It was also Nathan who advised David that God wanted his son, not him, to actually build the great temple which David had long planned. Nathan wrote a history which is now lost.

PRAYER
Pilgrim God,
who through Nathan rebuked misdoing
and reminded your people
that you always seek to lead them on,
restore honesty to our public life;
may our churches never be a pretext for resisting your Spirit.

READINGS
Psalm 51
2 Samuel 12:1-14
Hebrews 4:12, 13

Barnabas

Apostle and encourager, first century

Barnabas was a wealthy Levite from Cyprus who sold his estate and gave the proceeds to the early Church in Jerusalem, which held all things in common. When the persecutor-turned-Christian Paul arrived in Jerusalem, and was shunned as a spy, it was Barnabas who befriended him and introduced him to the apostles. The Jerusalem apostles sent Barnabas to Antioch to guide the Christians there in their relations with non-Jewish converts. He promoted the concept of them being one in Christ. Later, when Paul had joined the Antioch leader's team, the Holy Spirit called the two of them to embark on mission tours. Barnabas is known as 'the son of encouragement'.

PRAYER
Father of compassion,
who called Barnabas to encourage others,
and graced him with particular gifts,
inspire us by his example
to be generous in our judgements
and unselfish in our service,
that your Church may be built up
through the love of your Son
and the power of your Spirit.

READINGS
Psalm 112
Job 29:11-16
Acts 11:19-30

The Saints of Africa

The first non-Jewish Christian was probably an African, Simon of Cyrene, who walked with Jesus to his death, bearing the cross which Jesus could no longer carry. Christianity was early established in Ethiopia and in North Africa, where desert monasticism spread like wildfire from the fourth century. Monks from North Africa were the first to visit Ireland, and they remained an abiding inspiration in Celtic lands. Through the centuries Africa has produced many saints and martyrs, and, in our own time, perhaps more than any other continent. Notable among these is Uganda's Archbishop Janani Luwum who stood up for the people against the abuses of the tyrant Idi Amin, who then had him killed.

PRAYER
God bless Africa.
Through the lives of her saints
and the blood of her martyrs,
bring to birth a society free from hate, greed or fear,
where the land itself is blessed.

READINGS
Psalm 72
2 Chronicles 9:1-12
Acts 8:26-39

Elijah

Prophet, tenth century BC

Elijah, a Tishbite from Giliad, suddenly bursts upon the scene as a fearless, God-centred prophet who rebukes the godless and reawakens his nation to its calling. He rebukes kings. He intercedes so effectively that even droughts and famines are affected by his prayers. He establishes a school of prophets on Mount Carmel. He falls prey to depression, but learns to listen to God's still, small whisper on a mountain. He exits this world in a trail of glory. Inspired by his example, many communities, such as the Carmelites, have sought to root their lives in discipline, silence and service. The Jews came to believe that Elijah would return before the Messiah came, and this belief is reflected in their annual Passover meal.

PRAYER
Lord God Almighty,
wean the people from the false gods of fortune,
fame and fantasy;
teach our world that we have to reap what we sow;
raise up children to serve you as the living God;
and grant us, in the spirit of Elijah, to go to you in glory.

READINGS
Psalm 74:1-12
1 Kings 19:1-18
James 5:13-20

Dogmael

Saint who helped children to walk, d. early sixth century

Dogmael began his life in Pembrokeshire, Wales, where many churches are dedicated to him under variations of his name. A late account suggests that saints Tydecho and Tegfan for a time helped him build up a faith community at Llandudoch. At some point, like so many others, he emigrated to Brittany. He is a patron of St Domineucin Ille et Vilaine. Stories about him led people in Brittany to pray to him to help children walk.

PRAYER
God of Dogmael, Guardian of the children,
we pray for children who falter and stumble through life.
Come to them in your mercy,
help them to grow in stature
and to walk well with you.

READINGS
Psalm 78:1-8
Joel 2:15-17
Mark 5:35-43

Elisha

Prophet, tenth century BC

The young Elisha left a peaceful occupation in the Jordan Valley to train with Elijah's school of prophets. His ministry as a prophet lasted 50 years under six kings. He emerges as Elijah's successor, performs signs and wonders, but is more of a seer in the mould of Samuel than was Elijah. Like Elijah, he constantly sought to recall his people to the worship of the one Lord God Yahweh, as Moses had taught. He healed people and brought about miracles by a word or an instruction, as when he told a commander of a neighbouring country to bathe seven times in a river and he would be healed of leprosy. Perhaps the most famous story is of the couple who provided him with a room, whose oil was replenished, who were given a baby, and whose dead boy was restored, all following his prayers.

PRAYER
God of signs and wonders,
you teach us through your servant Elisha
that these come only through the continual
washing of the eyes.
Wash our eyes and take our ears:
teach us to listen,
not to the surface babble of a sick society,
but to the deep, pure truth that comes from you.

READINGS
Psalm 105:1-15; 2 Kings 4:1-7 (or 1-38); Luke 4:23-30

Ismael

Bishop of Menevia, sixth century

A tiny church in a wood by the village of Ismael, near Milford Haven, marks the site where Ismael had his hermit's cell and around which his teaching monastery grew. Ismael was the son of Budic, a prince of Brittany, and emigrated to Britain with his two brothers. They all became disciples of Dubricius, Teilo and David. Teilo consecrated Ismael to succeed David as Bishop of Menevia.

PRAYER
Discipler of souls,
we thank you for the great blessings
brought to us by families such as Ismael's,
who bent themselves to holy learning
and gave themselves to fostering the Faith.
Inspire us by their example
to learn all we can and to build all we can.

READINGS
Psalm 133
Genesis 45:1-15
Matthew 12:46-50

Nectan

Hermit and martyr of Harland, sixth century

The eldest of 24 children of Brychan, saintly king of Powys, Nectan sailed from Wales with many relatives to establish a hermitage at Hartland Point in North Devon. This had a strong and godly influence. He lived as a forest solitary, only meeting his fellow settlers on the last day of the year. He was killed by a cattle thief whom he sought to convert to Christ. The belief grew that the blood from his severed head imparted healing properties to the local spring.

PRAYER
Holy God,
who led your servant Nectan
to plant the Faith of Christ in virgin land
and to reach out to others in the victorious Spirit of Christ,
may the Tree of Death become the healing Tree of Life
in barren and violent places today.

READINGS
Psalm 49:1-15
Isaiah 26:19-27:6
2 Corinthians 5:1-10

Govan

Hermit, sixth century

Govan is said to have lived as a hermit in the cleft of the rock where there is still a little chapel at St Govan's, Wales. Either the same saint, or perhaps a disciple who bore his name, migrated to Brittany and his skull is still preserved in the church of St Goban, to the west of Laon.

PRAYER
Great God,
as once you spoke with Elijah,
so also you met with Govan in the cleft of a rock.
You who speak in stillness and storm,
speak to us, make us holy, and move us on.

READINGS
Psalm 62
1 Samuel 24:1-7
Mark 1:40-45

* transferred from 20 June

Sundar Singh

Sadhu of India, d. 1929

Sundar Singh was a Sikh who converted to Christianity after seeing a vision. He travelled tirelessly through the subcontinent as an Indian-style sadhu, or holy man. Like many Celtic wanderers for the love of God centuries earlier, he came to feel that church was not meant to be static, and that he could fulfil his vocation only by wandering.

PRAYER
Loving God,
you called Sundar Singh to love you with all his being
and to serve you throughout his life;
may this holy pilgrim inspire us in our pilgrimage of life
to trust you above all else
and daily to increase in the wisdom of the heart.

READINGS
Psalm 119:97-112
Deuteronomy 6:4-7
Acts 26:9-18

Julius and Aaron

First British martyrs, third century

These are two of the first three Britons to be recorded as martyrs for the Faith of Christ. Julius and Aaron were martyred in Caerlon in what is now South Wales.

PRAYER
Immortal God, mighty and strong,
by whose power the martyrs Julius and Aaron
triumphed over suffering
and despised death
for joy of the crown that awaited them,
strengthen us to endure hardship and wax valiant
that we, with them,
may receive the reward of everlasting life.

READINGS
Psalm 116:1-5
Wisdom 3:1-9
Luke 12:1-9

Adam and Eve

It is fitting to think of Adam and Eve on this solstice day (the summer solstice in Celtic lands), for in the story with which the Bible begins, Adam, whose name means Mr Earth, and his wife, Eve, are in the first place symbols of human beings flowing in their pristine potential, at one with God and creation. After they do something that they know is wrong, they become symbols of human beings who cover up who they really are and who run away from reality. The Bible presents Jesus Christ as a second Adam who restores our lost innocence, and tradition sees Jesus' mother, Mary, as a second Eve, who co-operates with, rather than rebels against, God.

PRAYER
Great Creator,
whose glory is seen in human life coming fully alive,
help us to live fully human lives for you,
in the power and strength of Jesus Christ,
truly human, truly divine.

READINGS
Psalm 8
Genesis 2:4b-25
1 Corinthians 15:12-22

Alban

One of the first British martyrs, third century

Alban, who came from the city now named after him (St Albans), offered himself for execution in the place of a Roman soldier who had converted to Christ and sought shelter with Alban.

PRAYER
All-compassionate One,
in whose sight the death of your saints is precious,
and who gave Alban grace
to lay down his life for another
out of love for you,
help us to follow him in the constancy of our faith,
that we may receive with him the crown of righteousness.

READINGS
Psalm 56
Wisdom 5:14-16
2 Timothy 2:3-7

Etheldreda

Abbess of Ely, d. 679

Etheldreda was the daughter of the godly King Anna of the East Angles. Although forced to marry, she felt called to be a 'bride of Christ', remained a virgin, and on the early death of her husband retired to the Isle of Ely, her dowry. In 660, for the sake of political alliance she had to marry the 15-year-old Ecfrith, King of Northumbria. He at first agreed she could remain a virgin but after 12 years changed his mind. She refused all bribes and advances, and, aided by Bishop Wilfred, left Ecfrith to become a nun at Coldingham under her aunt Ebbe, before leaving to found a double monastery at Ely in 673 on the site of the present cathedral. In a family of wealth and excess, she lived simply in woollen clothes, on one meal a day, and devoted many hours to prayer. Seventeen years after her death her body was found to be incorrupt.

PRAYER
King of all,
who called Etheldreda to an earthly throne
that she might advance your eternal kingdom,
give us a purity of heart like hers,
that we may be fruitful in good works
and attain a crown of peace.

READINGS
Psalm 73
Proverbs 22:1-13
2 Corinthians 6:14-7:1

24 JUNE

John

Prophet, forerunner and baptiser, first century

The Bible story of John, the son of Elizabeth, cousin of Jesus' mother Mary and of the priest Zechariah, begins with his leaping in his mother's womb when Mary, pregnant with Jesus, visits them. From this moment, and not just through his years as a desert hermit and public crusader, he has been regarded as forerunner of Jesus the Messiah, an Elijah figure. It was understood that God's Spirit moved powerfully in him before his birth to grace him as a last link between the Old Testament prophets, who anticipate and point to Christ, and the new covenant inaugurated by Jesus.

PRAYER
God of prophecy,
give us something of the spirit of John the Baptist:
his moral courage,
his contentment with simplicity,
his refusal to be fettered by this world,
his reaching out to the people,
his perseverance to the end.

READINGS
Psalm 85
Isaiah 40:1-11
Luke 7:18-28

Moluag

Founder of Lismore and other monasteries, 530-592

Moluag trained as a monk at Bangor, Northern Ireland, and at the age of 32 founded a monastery on the island of Lismore, in Scotland, a year before Columba settled on Iona. It was said Columba wanted to found his own monastery there. Instead he visited Moluag and preached there. Moluag made missionary journeys to the Isles of Skye and the Outer Hebrides, and he or his Lismore monastery founded daughter communities at Fort Augustus and Glen Urquhart on the shores of Loch Ness. His fine pastoral staff of blackthorn, enshrined in gilded copper, is preserved at Lismore.

PRAYER
Sending God,
the folk of the shore lands now praise you
because once your servant Moluag
heeded your call to them.
Bless today the places he made holy,
and stir us to journey with you to plant faith in new places.

READINGS
Psalm 97
Isaiah 41:1-10
Acts 28:1-15

Bartholomew of Farne

d. 1193

Born at Whitby of Scandinavian parents, he gave up a somewhat dissolute life and became a priest in Norway. After three years as a parish priest back in England he became a monk at Durham and took the name Bartholomew. Following a vision of Christ on the cross stretching out his arms to him, he went as a hermit to the island of Inner Farne, continuing a line started by St Cuthbert. He remained there for 45 years. Like Cuthbert, he was known for his constant cheerfulness, and sang with fine voice as he tended his crops, cow and manuscripts. He was difficult to live with, but was generous to all, and rich visitors were so awed by his godly presence that they gave up oppressive practices.

PRAYER
God of creation,
each thing that grows you call into being.
God of the Church,
each member you call into a holy vocation.
As we thank you for Bartholomew,
and for all the hermits of Farne,
we pray that we may serve you
in the holiness and truth of our calling.

READINGS
Psalm 97; Isaiah 41:1-10; Acts 28:1-15

* transferred from 25 June

Cyril

Bishop of Alexandria, d. 444

Cyril, who became patriarch of Alexandria in 412, was the moving spirit of the Church's third Ecumenical Council at Ephesus in 431. He played an important part in the development of Christian doctrine of the Trinity, of the Real Presence of Christ in the Eucharist and the place of Mary in the Incarnation of God's Son. The Ephesus Council ruled that Mary should be called Theotokos, or Bearer of God, to emphasise that Jesus in his flesh was truly divine. Although Cyril sometimes got caught up in antagonisms that were not edifying, there is no doubt that God used his precision, accuracy, skill and zeal to move the Church forward. His views were opposed to those of Nestorius, who thought that Christ was two separate Persons, one human and one divine. They reflected the teachings of Athanasius and Basil, to which the Churches in Celtic lands were faithful.

PRAYER
God of love,
give us a mind forgetful of past ill-will,
a pure conscience, sincere thoughts,
and a heart to love our brothers and sisters.
Echoes the Coptic Liturgy of St Cyril

READINGS
Psalm 110
Haggai 2:10-23
John 1:1-14

Ananias

A link in a chain, first century

Ananias was a Christian in Damascus who had an unusually specific vision in which God gave him instructions to go to a particular house and ask for a visitor who had been recently blinded. Ananias was to lay hands on this person and pray for his sight to be restored. The problem was that this man was a notorious persecutor of Christians, and Ananias had every excuse to dismiss this vision. He dialogued with God, with whom he clearly had an intimate relationship. God made clear that he had called this man, whose name was Saul, to be a great Christian missionary. So, overcoming his fears, Ananias did as he was told. As he laid hands on Saul something likes scales fell from his eyes, he was able to see, and he was baptised. We know nothing else about this local church member; he was a link in a chain, but what a link!

PRAYER
Holy Spirit,
remind us through Ananias' faithful act
that big doors swing on small hinges,
and that if we can't be a door,
we can at least be a hinge for you.

READINGS
Psalm 146
2 Kings 4:18-37
Acts 9:1-19

Peter

Leader of Jesus' twelve apostles, first Bishop in Rome, first century

Simon was a fisherman, son of Jonas, brother of Andrew. Jesus enlisted him and renamed him Cephas, the Aramaic word for Peter, meaning Rock. Jesus said that on this rock he would build his Church. Peter was often the first to launch out for Christ, but at first wobbled in the heat of opposition. He wept bitterly for denying that he knew the arrested Jesus. Following his resurrection Jesus asked Peter three times if he loved him, and commissioned him to feed his sheep. Peter headed the group of apostles who led the early Church among the Jews, and consulted with Paul when the latter emerged as a leader among the non-Jews. Early tradition agrees that Peter went to Rome to oversee its church and there was crucified upside down.

PRAYER
Great Shepherd of the human flock,
who told Peter you would build your Church
on his rock-like faith
and ordained him to feed your sheep,
help all bishops and overseers
to be unwavering in their faith
and to be true shepherds of their people.

READINGS
Psalm 125
Zechariah 4
Matthew 16:13-19

Austell

Friend and co-worker of Mewan and Samson, sixth century

Austell speaks to us of tender and delightful friendship that is content to take second place. He was a disciple of Mewan and came with him and Samson from South Wales to Cornwall. It seems he helped Samson establish a faith community at Golant, near Fowey, for he planted his hermitage nearby where now stands a church dedicated to him. St Austell's in Cornwall is named after him. Austell followed Mewan and Samson to Brittany, and was alongside Mewan as he established a faith community there. The famous abbey of St Meen now stands on the site. When Mewan was dying, Austell stood by with streaming eyes. The aged abbot bade him not be discouraged, since he would follow him in seven days. When Austell died seven days later the brothers, in tribute to their longstanding friendship, lay Austell by his abbot. When the stone tomb was later opened they found that Mewan, whom they had laid on his back with arms folded over his chest, had moved to one side so as to allow space for his companion.

PRAYER
Triune God,
who calls us to reflect your three-fold friendship,
as we thank you for Austell's gift of friendship
we pray that you will increase this gift in us.

READINGS
Psalm 15; Proverbs 18:16-24; John 15:9-17

Serf

Monk, apostle to Fife, sixth century

Tradition says that he established the monastery at Culross, on the northern shore of the Firth of Forth, and there fostered the infant Kentigern 'like another Samuel, committed and assigned to him by God' (Jocelyn). He became the apostle to Fife.

PRAYER
We thank you for Serf's holy life,
his fostering of young vocations
and planting of faith communities in hostile territories.
Fan into flames the embers in such places today
and fire us by his example.

READINGS
Psalm 119:73-80
1 Samuel 2:11, 18-20
2 Timothy 4:6-16

Solomon

Wise king, ninth century BC

The boy Solomon was greatly influenced by his godly and beautiful mother, Bathsheba, and by Nathan, the prophetic advisor to his father, King David. Solomon was showered with divine gifts: immense stores of wisdom, ability to govern, powers of observation, and humility as well as wealth. He was chosen as the heir of David who would oversee the building and the grand opening of the temple in Jerusalem. He wrote many proverbs, and people like the legendary Queen of Sheba travelled far to meet him. Yet his many wives, whose questionable religious traditions he provided for, gradually eroded his cutting edge and his claim to sainthood. He is included in this roll call because God was pleased with his humility at the time of his enthronement in asking for wisdom more than power and wealth.

PRAYER
O Lord my God,
I am only a little child
and do not know how to carry out my duties.
So give your servant a discerning heart to fulfil my duties
and to distinguish between right and wrong.

Echoes Solomon's prayer

READINGS
Psalm 111
1 Kings 3:4-15
Luke 11:29-32

Germanus

Bishop of Man, d. 475

In an attempt to disentangle conflicting references to saints with the name of Germanus, the scholar Baring-Gould has suggested the following. Born in Brittany about 410, where he may have met Patrick during his training, Germanus went to Ireland and worked with Patrick. At the age of 30 he came to South Wales and lived in the monastery founded by Illtyd. Following a meeting with Patrick during his visit to Britain in 462, Germanus gave a lead in the turbulent period of intrigues and massacres between groups of British Christians, pagans and Saxons. Once he took a group on to a rock and fasted against King Gwrtheyrn, who had slaughtered 300 British leaders, and Gwrtheyrn soon fled. Having rid the land of tyrants he blessed Cadell and Ambrosius who took their place; he reported back to Patrick who consecrated him Bishop of the Isle of Man in 466. There he converted a robber to Christ.

PRAYER
God our Champion,
who enabled Germanus to give bold leadership
in turbulent times
and to overcome evil with good,
build up our fibre,
that we may be more than conquerors
through Christ who gave himself for us.

READINGS
Psalm 18:25-36; 1 Samuel 7:2-12; Acts 14:21-28

Martin of Tours

His ordaining and enshrining, fourth and fifth centuries

While Martin was leading his first monastic community at Liguge, living on bare essentials and dressed in rough clothes, citizens of Tours decided they wanted him to fill their vacant bishop's post. He was not interested, so they arranged for him to visit a sick person, where he was forcibly conveyed to the church. He was indeed consecrated as bishop, but refused to sit on a throne. Instead he produced a cow stool, and asked his clergy to use cow stools also as they symbolised the simplicity and pastoral care which was their calling. He was buried at Tours where his remains were later enshrined. His tomb became the principal place of pilgrimage of the Franks and 4000 French parishes and many in other lands are dedicated to him. His emblems are a globe of fire and a goose, both symbolising the Holy Spirit.

PRAYER
Wild Goose of the Almighty,
who comes down to earth and stirs up everyday life,
keep us down to earth, like Martin,
in daily imitation of the One
who had nowhere to lay his head
but who lay down his life for his sheep.

READINGS
Psalm 119:165-174
Numbers 27:15-20, 23, 24
John 10:11-18

Moninna of the Scottish Borders

fifth century

Several holy women of this name have become confused by those who record history. It seems probable that one of them was an Irish abbess whom Aldfrith, son of Northumbria's King Oswy, visited in 670 when he fled to Ireland. It is possible he sought her help in his struggle between lust and power on the one hand, and love of God on the other. When Aldfrith became Northumbria's king in 685 he asked Moninna to take charge of the large monastery for men and women developed by Hilda at Whitby, and there to mentor his sister Elfleda. After a brief stay Moninna returned to Ireland, but her brother Ronan, who was a missionery in Northumbria, asked her to send sisters to help him in his work in the present Scottish borders. These, or perhaps Moninna herself, studied at Whithorn, and founded hermit faith communities in Musselburgh, and perhaps in the seven towns in the region fortified by Arthur.

PRAYER
Wise guardian of peoples,
thank you for the communities of prayer Moninna planted in Ireland and Scotland,
and for the light she brought to those in government.
May we not squander this precious birthright,
but rather build upon her example.

READINGS
Psalm 119:87-104; Ecclesiasticus 37:7-15; 1 John 5:14-20

Morwenna

fifth century

It is believed that Morwenna was one of the children of the saintly king Brychan whose family settled in North Cornwall. A foundation stone or portable stone altar which she carried hit a rock and water gushed forth. God used such signs of creation to guide her to establish a church in a place different to the one she first envisaged. She may have established her first hermitage at Marhamchurch, but ended her days in the quiet valley that was named after her, Morwenstowe. She is remembered as a teacher and may have founded a school of disciples at Kilkhampton.

PRAYER
Holy Three, one God who mothers us all,
you called Morwenna,
and through her new life sprang up
among a parched and pagan people.
May your life pour into us
and flow out to a parched and pagan world.

READINGS
Psalm 127
Nehemiah 9:9-15
Matthew 13:31-33

Palladius

First bishop in Ireland, fifth century

Pope Celestine sent Palladius to be the first bishop of those who had become Christians in the south of Ireland. It has been surmised that Palladius was a monk in Constantinople and in the Egyptian desert before going to Rome. Previous to his Irish mission, Palladius may well have accompanied Bishop Germanus to Britain and then reported back to the Church in Rome. He seems to have landed and worked mainly in Wicklow, where three churches claim to be founded by him. He left Ireland for Scotland, perhaps on account of the hostility he encountered. Stories that he preached in Scotland for 23 years are uncertain, but he died there, at Forddun, near Aberdeen.

PRAYER
All-seeking God,
who never rests until every soul knows you,
we thank you for Palladius' willingness to preach and pastor
in foreign lands,
never to return to his earthly home.
Teach us by his example always to reach out to others
until we reach our eternal home.

READINGS
Psalm 65
Isaiah 42:1-5
Romans 10:11-15

Boisil

Abbot of Melrose, d. 661

As prior of Melrose, Boisil attracted the young Cuthbert to his monastery in 651, and became his mentor. Boisil was also known for his preaching journeys to neighbouring villages. In 659 he became abbot. On Cuthbert's return to the monastery in 661 Boisil caught the plague. He and Cuthbert read through the Gospel of John before Boisil died. (In accordance with Boisil's prophecies, Cuthbert himself recovered from the plague, and agreed to be made a bishop in later life.) After his death Boisil appeared in a prophetic vision warning King Ecfrith against attacking the Picts. The site of Boisil's monastery is Old Melrose, some two miles from the existing ruins of the later monastery. A large fragment of his eighth-century shrine is at Jedburgh Abbey. The village of St Boswells is named after him.

PRAYER
Living God, who ever speaks,
we give thanks for your servant Boisil
and for the gift of prophecy.
Increase in us sensitivity to your voice,
that the spirit of authentic prophecy may flourish in your Church today.

READINGS
Psalm 49:1-15; Deuteronomy 18:14-22; John 21:20-25

* transferred from 7 July

Maelruain

Abbot of Tallaght, d. 792

Maelruain founded a monastery at Tallaght (now a suburb of Dublin) in 774 and became the most influential leader in the Culdee Reform movement. This restored prayer and soul friendship as the centre of monastic life, and monks were required to remain celibate and not to wander off. The earliest Irish lists of martyrs (those of Oengus and Tallaght) and the earliest surviving Irish liturgy (the Stowe Missal) were compiled under his direction. One of his sayings is: 'Labour with devotion is the most excellent work of all.'

PRAYER
Holy God,
at a time when your people fell away from you,
you called Maelruain to restore the disciplines
of faith and worship.
Inspired by his example,
help us to follow your path in singleness of purpose.

READINGS
Psalm 119:65-80
Leviticus 19:1-18
Jude 14-25

* transferred from 7 July

Sunniva

Irish princess, founder of Norway hermitage, sixth or seventh century(?)

According to legend, Sunniva was an Irish princess who embarked with several companions in search of a haven to live consecrated lives in exile for Christ. They crossed Scotland and sailed until they alighted on an island named Selje off the west coast of Norway. Living in caves and subsisting on fish, they lived a rhythm of prayer and work. The neighbouring ruler Jarl Haakon heard about it and came after them. They fled to caves, and masses of rock avalanched down and blocked anyone's entrance or exit. Many years later Sunniva's incorrupt body was found. Tales spread fast that here was the shrine of a saint, and it became a popular place of pilgrimage. In 995 King Olaf is said to have built a chapel in her honour. In 1170 her relics were moved to Bergen. Five ruined churches survive on the island.

PRAYER
Blest are the pure in heart, for they shall see their God.
Blest were those women who crossed the sea
and made holy a hard place.
May we be blest, O God.
Make us pure in heart.

READINGS
Psalm 24; Exodus 20:18-21; 1 Corinthians 5:7-11

* transferred from 7 July

Benedict

Abbot, author of Benedictine Rule, patron of Europe, d. 550

Benedict was born at Nursia, studied at Rome and became a hermit at Nursia. Disciples joined him which incurred local opposition, so he moved to Monte Cassina where he completed his Rule for monks which became the dominant Rule in the western Church and later led to the Benedictine Order. The Rule drew on the desert monastic insights but made them moderate, orderly and workable in an attempt to create long-term stability. Elements of his Rule were introduced into some Northumbrian monasteries in the time of Bede.

PRAYER
Lord,
enable us, after the example of Benedict,
to live as one family
in the stability of obedience to you.

READINGS
Psalm 119:57-64
Isaiah 33:2-6
Matthew 19:27

Amos

Shepherd with a prophet's call, eighth century BC

Amos was a shepherd in Judah during the reign of King Uzziah. He was not a professional prophet but God called him to go north to Israel, which enjoyed a time of prosperity, security and outward piety. Amos saw that this was limited to the wealthy and that it fed on injustice and oppression of the poor and less able; religious observance was insincere, and security more apparent than real. With passion and courage he explained that God would discipline the nation. He called for justice to flow like a stream, and said that if it did, God would be merciful to those who survived a coming disaster.

PRAYER
You who made the Pleiades and the Orion,
who turns light into darkness and darkness into light,
who brings to nothing the powers of this world,
have mercy on the poor and weak,
raise them up,
and start to do this through me.

READINGS
Psalm 94:1-15
Amos 5:4-15
Luke 11:37-51

Hosea

Prophet, eighth century BC

Hosea prophesied in the northern kingdom of Israel, after Amos, during the troubled times before the fall of Samaria in 721. He has been named 'the prophet with the sorrowful heart'. Through the wrongs he personally suffered, especially though a wife who became a prostitute, he more deeply understood the nature of Israel's sins against God. If Israel was like a prostitute, God was like a true lover. He predicted disaster (which indeed followed), called for justice, and yet held out the possibility (in the moving words of chapter 11 of the Book of Hosea) that God's constant love for his people could restore their relationship.

PRAYER
Forgive us, Lord,
that our love for you has so often vanished
like the morning dew.
Restore to us the deep cords of affection,
that we may find a love tryst with you
that no one and no thing can break.

READINGS
Psalm 89:1-18
Hosea 11:1-11
1 John 4:7-21

Hezekiah

King of Judah, eighth century BC

Hezekiah is one of the best and most faith-filled kings in history, even though his kingdom was always threatened by a super-power. His virtues are even more remarkable in the light of the dreadful crimes of his father, King Ahaz. The start of his rule at the age of 25 signalled a period of spiritual revival, during which Hezekiah was advised by that great prophet Isaiah. Hezekiah cleared away false gods and restored the laws taught by Moses. When the Assyrian super-power announced it was to invade, 185,000 Assyrian soldiers died outside the walls following Hezekiah's prayers and Isaiah's prophecies. When he became terminally ill, he was given a 15-year extension of life as a result of the prayers he wrung from Isaiah. However, this extension of life, and the national prosperity that his reforms made possible, caused him to 'take his eye off the ball' and he became somewhat self-sufficient.

PRAYER
Lord God, enthroned between the cherubim,
you alone are God over all the kingdoms of the earth.
You have made heaven and earth.
Open your eyes and see.
Listen to the one who insults you and lays waste to nations.
Deliver us, that all kingdoms on earth may know
that you alone are God.

Hezekiah (2 Kings 19:15-19)

READINGS
Psalm 124; 2 Kings 18:1-12; Matthew 17:14-21

Swithun

Bishop of Winchester, d. 862

Egbert, king of Wessex, chose Swithun as his chaplain and as mentor to his son Ethelwulf who succeeded him. Ethelwulf chose Swithun as bishop of Winchester, the Wessex capital. Swithun became famous for his charitable gifts and his building of new churches. During this time Wessex consolidated its position as the most influential English kingdom. After his death, when a monastic community was established at the cathedral, Swithun's remains were placed there in a shrine. All sorts of cures took place and also prolonged and heavy rainfall. This led to the English saying that if it rains on St Swithun's Day it will rain for 40 days.

PRAYER
Bountiful God,
who enhanced your Church through the life
and labours of Swithun,
and warned your people through rains from above,
send our land showers of blessing through your generosity.

READINGS
Psalm 89
1 Kings 3:16-4:7
Mark 1:29-34

Helier and Marcoul

First hermits of Jersey, sixth century

As a boy, Helier devoted himself to Christ in Tongres (Belgium). Expelled by his pagan father, he travelled to the monastery at Nanteuil (France) and placed himself under the direction of its founder, a fellow Saxon named Marcoul, from whom he gained a love of the hermit life. Marcoul sent him to live as a hermit in a cave high in a rocky part of Jersey. Then Marcoul led a mission to convert Jersey's inhabitants, and founded a monastery there. From this grew the capital town now named St Helier. Marcoul successfully led the islanders to defend Jersey against pagan invaders, but some returned and killed Helier when he tried to preach the Gospel to them.

PRAYER
Faithful God,
whose servants Helier and Marcoul
set more store on serving you
than on life itself,
and whose lives brought transformation to many,
may Jersey be an island of prayer and holiness,
and may we offer service in that singleness of heart
which brings growth to others.

READINGS
Psalm 119:145-152
Obadiah verses 15-17
Matthew 10:32-29

Huldah

Wise guide, sixth century BC

Shaphan, the chief priest in the reign of the godly King Josiah, turned to Huldah for guidance at a crucial moment after some men working on the repair of the Jerusalem temple found a record of the laws God had given to his people in the time of Moses, but of which the present generation was ignorant. Huldah advised that they should accept this book as the Law of God. She then prophesied that after Josiah's death the nation and its capital city would suffer the consequences of living contrary to God's Law. She was married to Shallum, who was in charge of the wardrobe at the court or the temple.

PRAYER
God of gods,
we have chased after idols and illusions,
and we have forgotten your ways.
Restore in our land respect for your laws,
and spur us to use the means of spiritual renewal
that you have provided.

READINGS
Psalm 119:33-40
2 Kings 22:3-20
Luke 16:14-18

Zephaniah

Prophet, seventh century BC

Zephaniah was descended from King Hezekiah. His name means 'Yahweh has hidden', which may relate to his need to hide away during the ghastly reign of Manasseh, who had the prophet Isaiah sawn in half. Zephaniah started to publicly speak out during the reign of his distant relative, the godly King Josiah, who came to the throne as the age of 8. It may well be that Zephaniah had an influence over the young king, and that his messages helped Josiah to root out the remnants of Baal worship and other sleazy practices.

PRAYER
Judge of all the earth,
before whom nothing false can stand,
teach us to be silent before you.
Bring to birth a humble people.
May the day come when all people will look to you.

READINGS
Psalm 37:1-20
Zephaniah 3:1-13
2 Peter 3

Macrina

Mother of a family monastery, 379

Macrina was born in Cappadocia in what is now Turkey. The eldest of ten children, she influenced them for Christ and turned family members into a kind of monastery. Her mother taught her the Bible, household management and spinning and weaving. At the age of 12 her fiancé died and, though she was very beautiful, she decided to refuse all other suitors and be Christ's bride for ever. She taught her famous brothers, Basil and Gregory, to renounce worldly glory and live the life of the Beatitudes. Another brother, Naucratius, handsome and sporting, became a hermit and supported the poor through his fishing expeditions. Macrina and her mother adopted the standard of living of their household servants and retired to Annesi, where they lived as nuns with other women under the direction of her brother, Bishop Basil.

PRAYER
Thank you, Father, for Macrina,
holy, beautiful and purposeful,
and for her pioneering of a family monastery.
May the kindness and rhythm
of our households reflect your love.
Free us from greed,
so that we, too, may bring blessing to others.

READINGS
Psalm 119:25-40; Ecclesiasticus 29:8-13; Matthew 19:16-26

Jeremiah

Prophet, seventh and sixth centuries BC

Jeremiah was the son of Hilkiah, a priest from Anathoth. During his long ministry Jeremiah warned his people of the catastrophe that awaited them as a consequence of their addiction to money, sex and power, and their abandonment of God. This made him unpopular, and he was imprisoned for a time. He agonised with God about the pain his prophetic calling involved. He lived to see his prediction come true with the fall in 587 of a Jerusalem which had been regarded as inviolable. Nebuchadnezzar, the Babylonian king, conquered the land and Jeremiah, along with all the leading citizens, was taken into exile. There he urged fellow exiles to work for the good of the Babylonian cities in which they lived, though he also predicted that after 70 years in exile there would be a return to Israel. Throughout history 'Jeremiah' has been a name for a prophet of doom.

PRAYER
Lord God,
like Jeremiah we feel inadequate
for the tasks to which you call us.
When we don't know what to say, touch our lips;
when we fear attack, protect us;
when we lack confidence,
remind us that you give us, in Jesus,
authority to do as he did on earth.

READINGS
Psalm 31:1-20; Jeremiah 1; Acts 9:1-19

Ezekiel

Prophet, sixth century BC

Ezekiel lived in exile in Babylon (present-day Iraq) before and after the fall of Jerusalem in 587. Following God's call to him to be like a night watchman, he gave messages, in varied, striking and sometimes bizarre ways, to two groups of people: the exiles in Babylon, and his beleaguered compatriots who had been allowed to stay behind in Jerusalem. He warned these about the imminent fall of Jerusalem. He helped both groups to realign their thinking by keeping God's perspective. He tried to comfort those in Jerusalem after its fall, and he raised everyone's sights with a vision of a new temple. His well-known prophecy, likening his people to a valley of dry bones who are resuscitated and given flesh, has been made famous in song and story.

PRAYER
Yahweh,
all the trees know that you are the Lord,
yet the people spurn you and seem headed for disaster.
Take our burned-out lives,
breathe upon us
and raise up a renewed people who will restore your glory.

READINGS
Psalm 147
Ezekiel 37:1-14
John 2:13-22

Mary Magdalene

first century

Mary was one of the women who accompanied Jesus during his ministry, stayed beside him during his crucifixion, and showed such devotion at his tomb that she became the first disciple to meet the risen Christ. Tradition has identified her with the woman who was a sinner (perhaps a prostitute) and who wiped Jesus' feet (Luke 7:37). Legend says she went east with John the apostle and Jesus' mother Mary. She is an icon of healed prostitutes and of contemplatives.

PRAYER
O God, our Desire,
you formed us in our mother's womb
and call us by our name.
In the compassion of your suffering presence
may we know, as Mary Magdalene knew,
that you can make our violated bodies vessels of love.
In the strangeness of human attraction
we put our trust in you,
knowing that we may live with you for ever.

READINGS
Psalm 42
Song of Songs 3:1-4
John 20:1-2, 11-20

23 JULY

Bridget of Sweden

d. 1373

At a time when Christendom was fragmenting, Bridget felt God move her from her native Sweden to the world stage in order to weed out false growths at the heart of the Church. She married Ulf Gudmarsson at the age of 13 and the couple agreed that they should make 'God's will night and day' their aim. A servant said that Bridget was 'kind and gentle and had a laughing face'. Bridget was told in a vision: 'Through you God will be made known to the world.' On becoming a widow Brigid challenged Sweden's king to root out gluttony, lust and pride. He changed his ways only in part, but he gave her land to establish a convent at Vadstena. Bridget then challenged the popes to return to Rome from their pleasure resort in France and to become international peacemakers. She went to live in Rome and became a spiritual guide and a prophet. Bridget spent much time creating the liturgies and rules for a new order.

PRAYER
Lord, show us the way and make us willing to walk in it.
May your will night and day be our aim,
as individuals, families and churches.
Use us to clear out the false growths in our society,
and let us see your kingdom come on earth,
as it is in heaven.

Echoes Bridget

READINGS
Psalm 4; 2 Samuel 10:1-15; Ephesians 5:1-20

Declan

Bishop of Ardmore, d. early fifth century

Declan is one of only four bishops who founded churches before Patrick evangelised in Ireland. He founded the Christian community at Ardmore. Ruins of his monastery and a round tower, together with a holy well and an ancient St Declan's stone, still stand on the shore of the headland by Youghal harbour. Legend states that the standing stones at the Dog's Pass in the Comeragh Mountains mark the place where Declan was offered dog meat disguised as mutton by the pagan tribal leader. Declan was not deceived; they said he even restored the dog to life!

PRAYER
Pioneering God,
as we thank you for the bold initiatives of Declan,
we ask that you will spur us to cross frontiers,
overcome deceptions,
and build up the Faith.

READINGS
Psalm 120
Ezekiel 18:5-9
Revelation 1:4-9

James

Apostle, martyr, died *c.* 44

James was a Galilean fisherman, one of the twelve apostles, and the brother of John. The two brothers and Peter were with Jesus at significant moments in his life such as his Transfiguration and before his betrayal in the Garden of Gethsemane. James was martyred by King Herod Agrippa, probably in 44.

PRAYER
We thank you that James was willing
to leave his family home and all he had
in order to follow Jesus.
Help us, like him, to forsake the attractions of the world,
to respond without delay to your call,
to learn from mistakes,
and to be obedient to the end.

READINGS
Psalm 126
Jeremiah 45:1-7
Matthew 20:20-8

Anne and Joachim

Jesus' grandparents, first century BC(?)

As Christians reflected on the wonder of Mary's call to give birth to Jesus, they felt drawn to honour the parents of Mary, Jesus' grandparents. The legendary second-century Gospel of James, which is not in the Bible, gave them the names Anne and Joachim. The name Anne in Hebrew means 'grace', and thus stands for loving and cherishing motherhood at its best. Visions of Anne visiting places, especially in Brittany, have brought spiritual transformation there, and she is known as the patron of Brittany.

PRAYER
God of Covenant,
who in the deep counsels of your wisdom
entrusted to Anne and Joachim
the preparation of the Blessed Virgin
for her most holy calling,
as we ponder the wonder of your hand on this family,
may we be drawn to trust completely
in your redeeming plans,
and in everything place ourselves in your keeping.

READINGS
Psalm 128
Zephaniah 3:14-18a
Luke 1:68-72

Zechariah

Prophet of the Messiah, sixth century BC

Zechariah was probably brought back from exile in Babylon while still a junior, and as a young man he announced visions he had for the restoration of the destroyed temple. It was probably in his old age that he gave messages about the Jews' messiah and the ultimate fate of the world.

PRAYER
Almighty Lord,
we seek to return to you.
Restore those good things in our national life
that have been eaten away.
Move us out of false walls of comfort.
May you yourself be the fire
that protects, warms and guides us evermore.

READINGS
Psalm 50:1-15
Zechariah 2
Acts 2:29-42

Samson

Flying bishop, d. 565

Samson's parents took him to be educated at Illtyd's monastic school at Llantwit Major. He was ordained and became one of the great travelling missionaries. Samson established a monastery on Caldey Island, and undertook a visit to Ireland where he acquired a chariot which could carry his books. Then, in response to a prophetic challenge, he embarked on a mission to Cornwall, where he dialogued and prayed with those who followed the Druid religion, and marked standing stones with symbols of the new Faith. The last part of his life was as Abbot of Dol, in Brittany, which became a large foundation with many trees Samson himself helped to plant.

PRAYERS
Thank you, Lord,
that Samson's birth, schooling and calling
were the fruit of prophecy.
Thank you that his prayer, heroic acts of witness, courtesy
and wonderful love towards all
won pagans to the Faith,
and patterned a new way of being church.
As we contemplate his life, give us a new direction.

READINGS
Psalm 125
Judges 13:1-7, 24-25
Acts 28:1-10

Martha, Mary and Lazarus

Jesus' friends, first century

These two sisters and their brother Lazarus made their home at Bethany, outside Jerusalem, available to Jesus, and there was a deep bond of affection between them. Jesus, moved by the sisters' grief, restored the deceased Lazarus back to life. The story of Mary sitting at Jesus' feet while Martha was busy in the kitchen has been used as an illustration of the contemplative and the active vocations. It was this family to whom Jesus repaired in the last fateful week of his life.

PRAYER
Tender Saviour,
who enjoyed the company and the coziness
of the Bethany household,
may the goodness of friendship grow in our households:
friendship without guile,
friendship without malice,
friendship without striving.

READINGS
Psalm 40:1-6
Isaiah 25:6-9
John 12:1-8

Silas

Ideal church secretary, first century

Silas (also known by his Romanised name, Silvanus) was a much respected assistant in the first Jerusalem church who had prophetic, writing and organisational gifts. These caused him to be sent by that church to Antioch to welcome new Christians from a non-Jewish culture. When Paul and Barnabas separated after their first mission tour, Paul took Silas as his colleague on his second tour. Silas stayed on at Beroea on his own, and rejoined Paul at Corinth, who later commended Silas's work there. He is associated with the letters Paul wrote from Corinth and may have acted as his secretary. Orthodox Christians include Silas as one of the 70 missioners sent out by Jesus.

PRAYER
God of encouragement,
we thank you that Silas used his many gifts
to build people, bridges and communications.
Help us to do likewise.

READINGS
Psalm 103
Proverbs 18:12-24
Acts 15:22-41

Joseph of Arimathea and the Glastonbury saints

first century

Gildas the Wise, first writer of the Britons, who lived near Glastonbury, claimed that the Light of Christ came to these islands, stiff with pagan coldness, within a decade of Christ's death. After Jerusalem's Christians were scattered the noble Joseph of Arimathea came, according to widespread church tradition, to found a church at Glastonbury. Joseph had the courage and integrity to give Jesus a worthy burial place in his garden cemetery. He is thought to be an uncle of Jesus and a tin trader who was familiar with the Cornish tin trade route. Tradition also says that Aristobulus was Britain's first Bishop and that the British King Lucius invited Fagan and Dyfan to restore the church. Archeologists confirm that the church here is very early, as is a hermit settlement. Glastonbury was then an island, the Avalon that was introduced into the fables about King Arthur. In recent times the mystic Marjorie Milne, who believed that Glastonbury was meant to be the spiritual heart of England, and who prayed three hours each day in its churches, called for the rekindling of Glastonbury's Christian vision.

PRAYER
Holy love, rest on us,
tongues of fire, light on us,
wind of God, carry us where you will.
        Marjorie Milne of Glastonbury

READINGS
Psalm 122; Isaiah 62:1-5; Acts 7:59-8:4

Neot

Monk and hermit, d. 877

A monk of Glastonbury, Neot became a hermit in Bodmin Moor at the place now named after him, where he founded a small monastery. King Alfred sought his counsel, and he is said to have advised that the English School in Rome be revived. He appeared to Alfred in a vision before the battle of Ethandun. He was so small he had to stand on a stool to celebrate the liturgy, yet he stood daily in a well reciting the Psalms. It was said that he ate one fish a day from his well, yet always three fish swam in it. His relics were taken to a monastery in eastern England and that place is also now named after him.

PRAYER
Spacious God,
though Neot was small in stature
you made him great by your boundless grace.
In our littleness, enlarge our wisdom;
in our need, give us provision;
in difficult times, may praise fill our days.

READINGS
Psalm 119:49-64
Proverbs 21:20-31
Matthew 17:24-27

* transferred from 31 July

Germanus

Bishop of Auxerre, d. 446

Following marriage Germanus became governor of a Celtic province of Gaul until he was chosen to become Bishop of Auxerre. He spearheaded two extended missions to Britain. During his second visit he led the British forces in battle against anti-Christian Pict and Saxon invaders. He called on the British troops to advance, shouting 'Alleluia', and this led to the famous 'Alleluia Victory', apparently without bloodshed.

PRAYER
God of steadfast purpose,
who called Germanus to rally Christ's forces
in a neighbouring land,
establish our resolve,
that we may reach out to our Christian neighbours
in their time of need.

READINGS
Psalm 68:1-14
Judges 5:1-11
Revelation 19:1-8

* transferred from 31 July

Ignatius of Loyola

Basque founder of the Society of Jesus, d. 1556

Although Ignatius lived much later than the period of the undivided Church, he reintroduced into the rather juridical mindset of the Western Church the imaginative and intuitive faculties that flourished under the Celtic Mission. While convalescing after a battle injury he was given the Bible and *Lives* of the Saints to read, as well as the romance stories he had chosen. While the romance stories titillated him, the other stories transformed him. He became a Christian, founded the movement whose disciplined members are known as Jesuits, and wrote a classic training manual entitled *Spiritual Exercises*. These help people to bring imagination to bear on Scripture, and to find discernment for life's decisions.

PRAYER
Teach us Lord,
to serve you as you deserve,
to give and not to count the cost,
to fight and not to heed the wounds,
to toil and not to seek for rest,
to labour and not to ask for any reward
save that of knowing that we do your will.
                              Ignatius Loyola

READINGS
Psalm 107:1-22; Ecclesiasticus 44:1-15; Philippians 4:4-9

* transferred from 31 July

John Vianney

Curé d'Ars, d. 1859

John (Jean-Marie) Vianney was born into a poor peasant family, missed much schooling and failed ordination exams. The Vicar-General decided that 'the most unlearned but most devout seminarian in Lyons' should be ordained and he was sent to the remote 'dead-end' parish of Ars-en-Dombes where it was thought he could do little harm. The curé offered himself on behalf of this parish as a sacrifice to God, eating little more than potatoes. He began his great plan of the total conversion of Ars. The church was 'populated with heaven' and there were prayer vigils; the dissolute community was turned round. Soon he was asked to lead missions elsewhere and people flocked to confess their sins. In 1926 the Roman Catholic Church made him the principal patron of parish clergy.

PRAYER
O God, through the life of John Vianney
you teach us that our strength is made perfect in weakness.
Inspired by his example,
may we offer our lives as a sacrifice,
assiduously work to let heaven
in to the grey places of human control,
and learn to commune with you
and your saints by day and by night.

READINGS
Psalm 119:49-63; Ecclesiasticus 6:18-37;
2 Corinthians 12:2-11

Oswald

King and 'martyr', d. 642

For 17 years Oswald, a Northumbrian prince, was in exile while his maternal uncle ruled his country. At Iona, Oswald was baptised and trained as a Christian, and vowed that if he ever gained the throne he would invite Iona to send a mission to convert his largely pagan people. After winning a decisive battle, and following an abortive first mission, he received Bishop Aidan and supported his mission in every way. He himself was a humble, prayerful king, who cared for the poor. He died in battle praying for his soldiers. In the centuries following his death many churches throughout Europe, who were looking for a model of a Christian ruler, were dedicated to him.

PRAYER
High King of heaven,
whose servant Oswald
was the first to model Christ-like rule
among the English people,
redeem our land from the curse of disobedience
and bring it into the wholeness of your just and gentle rule.

READINGS
Psalm 72
Deuteronomy 17:14-19
1 Timothy 2:1-7

Elijah, Moses, and three apostles with Christ on the mount

first century

At about the time Jesus knew he had to face betrayal, trial, torturous death and cosmic conflict, a means of strengthening him for this uniquely testing ordeal was provided by God. Jesus took his inner circle of Peter, James and John to a mountain peak. There, while they drowsed, Elijah, representing the great prophets, and Moses, representing the Law of God, appeared each side of him and communed with him. Jesus' face and garments were transfigured.

PRAYER
Light of the world,
Who, before his agony, revealed to chosen witnesses
your only Son wonderfully transfigured,
help us so to contemplate the radiance of his being
that we may be strengthened to bear all and believe all.

READINGS
Psalm 97
Daniel 7:9, 10, 13, 14
Mark 9:2-13

Haggai

Prophet, sixth century BC

Haggai and Zechariah are the first two named prophets after the people of Israel returned from their 70 years' exile in Babylon. It is assumed they returned in 537 and that Haggai may have been a child. If so, it began to dawn upon him after 16 wasted years that the first bright hopes were receding. There were so few resources, motivators or institutions. Then the Spirit of God came upon Haggai with power. He unerringly put his finger on the root of the malaise: the people were putting their personal comforts first; they were building their homes before building the house of God. So he urged them to begin to rebuild the temple. Later he built up the expectation and possibility of a temple of even greater glory than Solomon's. He assured the leader Zerubbabel that he would be kept safe despite the growing threat from Persia. Looking to the far future, Haggai held out the prospect of a period of peace for a renewed and purified people.

PRAYER
Great Ruler,
in a moment you can shake the entrenched tyrannies
of this world from their thrones.
All the silver and gold of the world is yours.
Forgive us for being so mean,
and help us to use generously
what we have to make a better future for all.

READINGS
Psalm 135; Haggai 1; 1 Corinthians 3:16-23

Lide

Hermit of the Isles of Scilly, tenth or eleventh century(?)

Lide (or Elidius) is the hermit saint of the Isles of Scilly. He settled on and gave his name to the island now called St Helens, where remains of his hermitage and his tomb have been found. It may well be that he is the seer whom Olaf Trygvason visited. A small community lived on this island in the Middle Ages, which became linked with a larger community at Tavistock.

PRAYER
Lord of Light:
self-emptied you came.
Unceasing as sea-surge, you pour your untameable colour.
Baptise into glory our death and our shame.
Ascended, you fling out Love's light
across all your creation again and again.

Anon

READINGS
Psalm 26
1 Samuel 9:1-20
Matthew 6:19-23

Daniel

Government officer, sixth and fifth century BC

An Israelite of noble birth, Daniel was carried captive into Babylon where, with various companions, he trained for the king's service. He retained his spiritual disciplines of thrice daily prayers and abstinence from meat. He gained a reputation as a wise and capable person and as an interpreter of dreams. He successfully occupied government posts under three rulers, but incurred opposition from jealous colleagues who engineered a situation whereby Daniel incurred the death penalty. According to the famous story, the lions that should have devoured him shut their mouths, he was released, and he and his God were valued even more by the king. Rabbinic tradition says that he returned with freed exiles at the end of his life and that he was buried in Susa.

PRAYER
You are wise and powerful.
You control the times and seasons.
You give wisdom and understanding,
and you reveal things that are deep and hidden in darkness.
You yourself are surrounded by light
and I praise and honour you, God of my forebears.

Daniel

READINGS
Psalm 34:1-16
Daniel 6:11-24
2 Timothy 1:1-12

Lawrence

Martyr, d. 258

Lawrence was one of the seven deacons of Rome. According to tradition, when he was asked to hand over the church's treasures, or else to die, Lawrence gathered many poor and sick people who had been helped by the church, and presented these to the authorities as the church's treasure. Later legend says he was then taken to a large grill and slowly roasted alive. The watching Christians sensed a sweet savour, and Lawrence prayed for the conversion of Rome before he died.

PRAYER
God our Treasure,
we thank you for the life-changing deeds and death
of your servant Lawrence.
Change us, that we may serve you in your poor ones,
and go through the fires of testing,
looking only to your joys.

READINGS
Psalm 66:10-20
Tobit 4:5-11
Matthew 6:19-24

Blane

Monk and bishop, sixth century

Blane left his native home at Bute in order to further his monastic training in Ireland. He returned and became a church planter. He was ordained a priest and later a bishop, and founded a monastic church at Kingrath (Bute) where he was buried. Dunblane Cathedral was built on the site of the monastery, and a bell reputed to be Blane's is preserved there.

PRAYER
God of our beginnings,
as we celebrate Blane's call to establish your Church
in his birthplace,
make holy our birthplace
and give us grace to prosper Christian community
in the place where we live.

READINGS
Psalm 80
Malachi 2:4-17
Mark 4:21-32

Muredach

Bishop and founder of Innismurray, sixth century

On the island of Inishmurray, in Donegal Bay, Ireland, you can see the remains of the oratories and the beehive huts of the monastery founded by Muredach. Before that he was the first bishop of Killala.

PRAYER
Bounteous Guide,
who led Muredach to establish community in a fertile land,
bring us to a place of fruitfulness
that we may serve and enjoy you in fullness of life.

READINGS
Psalm 1
Ezekiel 17:22-24
1 Corinthians 15:1-11

Hananiah, Mishael and Azariah

sixth and fifth century BC

These were three young Jewish companions of Daniel who were taken into exile to Babylon and employed by the King of Babylon. They had to be handsome, intelligent, well-trained, quick to learn and free from physical defects. They learned to read and write in Babylonian. They persuaded their superior to let them forego the menus, rich in meat, and to eat just vegetables. God gave them skill in literature and philosophy. However, enemies of these God-honouring Jews reported to the king that they would not worship the Babylonians' golden calf instead of their God. According to the story, the king was furious and ordered them to be thrown fully dressed in to a furnace that was made seven times hotter than usual. The flames burned the guards to death, but the three walked unharmed in the centre of the furnace, and the king saw a fourth figure which he took to be an angel. He released and promoted them.

PRAYER
Praise the God of these three who serve and trust him,
who sent an angel to rescue them.
No other God can rescue like this.
How powerful are the miracles he performs.
God is king for ever; he will rule for all time.

King Nebuchadnezzar

READINGS
Psalm 9:1-14; Daniel 3:8-30; 2 Peter 2:4-10

Fachanan

Abbot of Ross Carbery, sixth century

Fachanan perhaps studied under Abbess Ita. He travelled to Ross Carbery where he founded the first Christian community.

PRAYER
All-pure God,
whose servant Fachanan took jewels from your treasury
to share with people ignorant of you,
teach us to let our light shine in unlit places,
through Jesus Christ our Lord.

READINGS
Psalm 65
Ezekiel 45:1-8
Matthew 5:13-16

Resurrection of the Virgin Mary

Tradition says that Jesus' beloved disciple John took Jesus' mother with him to Ephesus where she died and was taken into great glory. Christians visualise her as leading the procession of Jesus' followers who experience the 'resurrection of the body' as proclaimed by the Bible and the Christian Creeds.

PRAYER
O Christ,
who welcomes into the eternal kingdom
that great procession of believers
who are resurrected in new bodies,
we thank you that Mary, who is always close to you,
leads the way and assures us that we, too,
may be near you.

READINGS
Psalm 45:6-15
Ecclesiasticus 24:7-11
1 Corinthians 15:35-49

Armel

Monk and intercessor of Brittany, sixth century

Armel, who is reputed to have been a cousin of Samson and Cadfan, went to Brittany on becoming a monk. There, with the help of King Childebert, he founded faith communities at Plouarmel and Ploermel. There is a legend that he took some feared wild creature to the top of a small mountain (now named Mont Saint-Armel) and ordered it to dive into the river below. He must have been a person of powerful intercession, for the reputation of his prayers spread widely after his death. England's King Henry VII believed he was saved from shipwreck off the coast of Brittany by Armel's prayers. Consequently there is a statue to Armel in that king's chapel at Westminster Abbey.

PRAYER
Lord Jesus Christ,
you ever live to make intercession for us,
and the members of your Body on earth and in heaven,
joined to you as their head,
seek to pray as you do.
We thank you for the power of Armel's prayers,
and ask that you will direct our own intercessions as you will.

READINGS
Psalm 28
Genesis 18:16-33
Romans 8:18-30

Nehemiah

Steward, rebuilder of the walls, fifth century BC

Nehemiah, a Jewish exile, rose to prominence under the Persian Empire and was cup-bearer to King Artaxerxes I. His deep concern for his people when he heard some had been allowed to return to a Jerusalem in ruins, his dependence on God, dedicated prayers, taking of responsibility for his people's sins, initiative in getting permission to return and supervise the rebuilding of Jerusalem's walls and infrastructure, and his skill and moral strength in overcoming all kinds of opposition, mark him out as a great man.

PRAYER
Lord God,
you faithfully keep your covenant.
My ancestors and I have sinned against you
and not done what you commanded.
Remember your promise that if your people return to you,
you will bring them back.
Listen to my prayers
and all the prayers of people who want to honour you.
Give me success.

Nehemiah

READINGS
Psalm 51
Nehemiah 2
Acts 15:1-18

Ezra

Secretary of State, restorer of Jewish Law,
fifth century BC

Ezra was a Jewish exile who seems to have become a kind of Secretary of State for Jewish affairs in the Persian Empire under Artaxerxes I. In 458 Artaxerxes sent him, along with some valuable gifts for the reconstructed Jerusalem temple, on a temporary mission to enforce the uniform observance of the Jewish law among the returning exiles. After fasting and prayer Ezra set up a committee to sort out the problem of mixed marriages. Perhaps a generation later he returned, after Nehemiah had rebuilt the walls. He gathered large numbers of the people together to read, explain, re-interpret and apply God's Law to their new situation. A profound conversion of heart seems to have taken place. He gained a reputation as a great and inspired reformer.

PRAYER
You Lord, alone, are Lord.
You made the heavens and the stars of the sky.
You made land and everything in it.
You gave life to all.
The heavenly powers worship you.
Remember how much we have suffered.
From prayers of the returned exiles

READINGS
Psalm 119:97-104
Ezra 7
Matthew 5:17-26

Micaiah

Truth-teller, tenth century BC

Micaiah, the son of Imlah, was a prophet in Israel in the reign of the tyrant King Ahab. According to Josephus, he is the unknown prophet referred to in 1 Kings 20:35-43. The record of his interview with King Ahab tells us that the 'spin machine' in Ahab's time was rampant, and no one but Micaiah told the truth. Micaiah was pressed to predict peace when there was no peace. When he told the truth, Ahab put him in prison, but Ahab was killed in battle as Micaiah had predicted. We do not know if Micaiah was released by Ahab's successor.

PRAYER
Eternal Truth,
before you all fantasy shrivels to nothing.
Thank you for the integrity of Micaiah the truth-teller,
save us from manipulating truth
and help us to live in the light.

READINGS
Psalm 119:41-56
2 Chronicles 18
John 5:16-27

Oswin

King, patron of mission, d. 651

Oswin succeeded to the throne of the northern part of Northumbria and, like his uncle Oswald, worked closely with Bishop Aidan to evangelise his people. The historian Bede describes him as 'a man of handsome appearance and great stature, pleasant in speech and courteous in manner. He was generous to high and low alike and soon won the affection of all by his kingly qualities of mind and body.' It was he who gave Aidan an expensive horse which Aidan gave away to a beggar. Aidan prophesied that such a humble king would not reign for long, and shortly afterwards Oswin was slain at Tynemouth by his uncle Oswy, who wanted to control the whole of Northumbria. To assuage his guilt Oswy built a monastery there.

PRAYER
Gentle Saviour,
whose kingly qualities shone through your servant Oswin,
may your gentle and generous ways shine also in our lives,
that we may be a royal priesthood,
to the glory of your name.

READINGS
Psalm 45
Proverbs 30:21-31
Acts 20:25-38

Thaddeus

Apostle, first century

Thaddeus is the name by which one of the twelve apostles came to be known. He was probably at first named Judas, but because the more prominent Judas turned out to be a reviled traitor, it was deemed unhelpful to continue to use this name. The word Thaddeus implies a feminine quality, and it may be that this apostle was warm and intuitive. Eusebius believed him to be one of the 70 sent out by Jesus. Jerome said he was sent on a mission to Abgar, king of Edessa.

PRAYER
We bless you, dear Lord,
that through your apostle, in teamwork with others,
your good news was proclaimed,
the sick were healed,
and you saw the entrenched but unseen powers of evil
fall from the high places.

READINGS
Psalm 112
Isaiah 52:7-10
Mark 3:7-19

Esther

Queen of Persia who saved the Jews from extinction, fifth century BC

Esther was a God-fearing Jew in exile under the Persian Empire, who, no doubt because of her exceptional beauty, was made a queen of King Xerxes. She found herself, in the words of Winston Churchill, 'walking hand in hand with Destiny'. Her great courage and devotion to duty saved her people from being exterminated, and led to the Jewish festival of Purim. The story is told in the biblical *Book of Esther*. She had not learned to eschew revenge, but her call to her people to fast and pray with her, and her willingness to risk her life in order to save others is what commends her to us.

PRAYER
Blessed are you, Lord our God,
King of the universe,
who makes us holy through doing your commands,
and commands us to read the Scroll of Esther.
Blessed are you,
who did wonders for our forebears in those days.
You are our hope in every generation.

From the Purim Prayer

READINGS
Psalm 44:1-8
Esther 4
Mark 13:14-27

Irenaeus

Teacher and Bishop of Lyons, d. 200

As Irenaeus grew up, Polycarp, Bishop of Smyrna (in modern-day Turkey), taught him what he had learned from the apostle John and other witnesses of Jesus' resurrection. While Irenaeus was staying at Rome the largest church in Celtic Gaul, at Lyons, asked him to become their leader following the martyrdom of their previous leaders. He thus brought the spirit of John and the East into the West. He wrote against Gnostics who taught that neither everyday things nor Christ's death were real, and that people could bypass these through a purely spiritual knowledge. Yet he did not fall into the opposite trap of being legalistic. He explained the value of spiritual gifts and taught people to think of the Trinity as the Father embracing the world with the two arms of the Saviour and the Spirit.

PRAYER
Father,
help beginners to reach their potential;
give intelligence to the little ones
and aid to those who are running their course.
Give sorrow to the negligent,
fervour to the lukewarm
and to the faithful a good consummation to life.

Irenaeus

READINGS
Psalm 8; Exodus 3:13-17; 1 John 4:1-12

Bartholomew

Apostle, first century

Bartholomew, meaning 'son of Tolmai', is simply listed in the first three Gospels as one of Jesus' twelve apostles, but scholars generally assume that John's Gospel refers to his first name, and that he is the same person as Nathaniel, whom Jesus called 'a true Israelite'. Early tradition says that he took the Gospel to India and later tradition that he was flayed alive before being beheaded at Derbend, Armenia, by the Caspian Sea.

PRAYER
Lord,
you called Bartholomew, faithful witness, true of heart,
to be your apostle,
and you call us, too.
Help us to be faithful and true
to the end of our days.

READINGS
Psalm 119:1-16
Genesis 28:10-22
John 1:43-51

Ebbe, and the enshrining of Hilda

(Ebbe died 683)

Ebbe was the sister of King Oswald, whom she outlived, and was probably, like him, nurtured in the Faith at Iona. She became the first Abbess of the monastery for men and women at Coldingham (in today's Scotland) where people of noble blood took vows. On the advice of Bishop Wilfred, King Egfrith's virgin wife Etheldreda was separated from him and lived as a nun under her Aunt Ebbe before founding her own monastery at Ely. Ebbe became known as a holy and discerning person. While King Egfrith and his second wife stayed at the monastery his wife became ill. Ebbe counselled that this was because they had put Wilfred in prison, and he was released. In her old age it is thought she spent much time in her own oratory, and the monastery became somewhat lax. So, in an attempt to tighten up discipline, she permitted a monk's prophecy to circulate that the monastery would be burned down by fire, which it was in 686. On this day also the remains of Ebbe's friend Hilda were enshrined at Whitby.

PRAYER
King of all,
we thank you for providing through Ebbe
a vehicle for the spiritual formation of the leaders of her land.
May we, like her, build up a royal priesthood,
and serve our land with faithfulness and discretion.

READINGS
Psalm 68:4-18; Isaiah 49:8-13; Philemon verses 4-20

Fiacre the gardener, and Ninian

(Fiacre died 670)

A patron of gardeners, and always depicted with a spade, Fiacre was an Irish travelling hermit who settled at Meaux, in Brittany. There he is said to have built the first hostel for Irish pilgrims on the continent and maintained a large vegetable garden to feed his guests. The place where he lived and died is now called Saint-Fiacre. He gave his name to French hackney carriages because they often started their journeys from the Hotel Saint-Fiacre in Paris. This day is also an alternative day for the remembrance of Ninian, who also developed a large garden to feed the many pilgrims who visited Whithorn.

PRAYER
Earth Maker,
by whose life we are born and sustained,
as we thank you for the careful tending of Fiacre,
help us to tend this planet, your garden,
to the best of our ability.

READINGS
Psalm 104:24-33
Exodus 23:10-19
Luke 20:9-18

Monica

Mother of Augustine of Hippo, d. 387

Monica was born in North Africa of Christian parents. She was married to a dissolute and violent man whose difficult mother also lived with them. Monica, who had herself overcome a tendency to heavy drinking, won them both over to Christ's ways. Their eldest child, Augustine, also became somewhat dissolute. She turned to extended prayer vigils for him, and followed him when he ran away to Rome and Milan. There he met Bishop Ambrose and a deep moral conversion took place. She died at Ostia while travelling with him.

PRAYER
Faithful God, who ever seeks us,
we thank you for Monica's persistent prayer
and fruitful motherhood.
May many embrace the divine vocation of motherhood,
and may each of us be a fosterer of righteousness.

READINGS
Psalm 121
1 Samuel 1:9-19
James 5:13-20

Augustine of Hippo

Bishop and teacher, d. 430

Born in Algeria, Augustine was brought up by his mother Monica as a Christian but he was not baptised. He had brilliant gifts of rhetoric and teaching, studied Manichaeism for nine years, and gave up Christianity in favour of a profligate life. After a long inner conflict following his meeting with Bishop Ambrose in Milan, he embraced Christ and celibacy, was ordained and made Bishop of Hippo. He became one of the church's most influential teachers and prolific writers, though some teachings influenced by his revulsion towards the flesh are rejected as false. His classic autobiographical *Confessions* continues to change lives.

PRAYER
O God of Beauty, so ancient yet so fresh,
who turned Augustine from the ugliness of sin
to the beauty of holiness,
change our restless hearts
until they find their rest in you.

READINGS
Psalm 51:1-13
Hosea 11:1-11
1 Corinthians 6:9-11

The beheading of John the Baptist

first century

The main celebration for John is on 24 June, the date for observing his birth, but John was also the forerunner of Christ in his death. King Herod, whose immoral behaviour John had challenged, had him arrested and then was inveigled by his wife to put John to death. Jesus, on hearing of John's arrest, took up John's call: Repent, for the kingdom of heaven has come near. He said there was no greater prophet than John.

PRAYER
Holy God,
who upheld John
as he boldly resisted corruption in high places
and suffered for the truth,
strengthen us that we may show neither fear nor favour
in the cause of truth.

READINGS
Psalm 11
Malachi 3:1-7a
Matthew 14:1-12

Sebbi

King and monk, d. 694

After the apostasy of his predecessor, Sebbi, king of the East Saxons, restored the Christian mission to his people and installed Bishop Jaruman. He was noted for his prayer, penance and generous alms-giving. He is reputed to have built the first monastery at Westminster, and to have been buried at the original cathedral of St Paul, London. Sebbi resigned his throne and became a monk shortly before his death.

PRAYER
All-advancing God,
help us, after setback, like Sebbi
to think and pray on the grand scale,
and to reach out prayerfully.

READINGS
Psalm 78:38-55
2 Samuel 7:18-29
Acts 7:44-47

* transferred from 29 August

31 AUGUST

Aidan

Apostle to the English, d. 651

Aidan was an Irish monk who joined the community founded by Columba at Iona. In 631 he was chosen to lead the mission to the largest English kingdom of Northumbria, at the request of its new young king, Oswald. He eschewed the trappings of a bishop's status, walked everywhere, and led an ascetic life of constant scripture meditation. He established a mission monastery at Lindisfarne, and the first school for English boys. He used gifts of money to help the poor or buy slaves their freedom. His mission spread very fast and many clergy poured in from Ireland and elsewhere to establish new monastic churches and pastor the villages.

PRAYER
Holy Spirit,
inspire pastors and carers
that they may tend those they care for
after the pattern of Aidan,
with gentleness and strength.
Set the people free by love, to love.

READINGS
Psalm 47
Isaiah 45:22-25
Matthew 11:28, 29

Drithelm

The man who came back from the dead, d. 700

Drithelm, the head of a godly Northumbrian household, was declared dead, but he came back to life with a vivid recollection of a journey to those in misery and those in bliss in the next world. He radically altered his life, gave his money to his family and the poor, and lived in a solitary hermit dwelling in the grounds of Melrose monastery. Each day he would stand in the river Tweed reciting Psalms, even when it was icy. He became a talking point throughout the region. Bede's account of his vision is the first and fullest account of the variety of life beyond the grave from Anglo-Saxon Britain.

PRAYER
Eternal God,
who drew aside heaven's curtain
for your servant Drithelm
and led him into a life of continual prayer and praise,
reveal to us the choices that make for life or death
and open to us the riches of eternal life.

READINGS
Psalm 9
Ezekiel 37:1-14
2 Corinthians 12:1-5 *or*
Matthew 25:31-40

Giles

Hermit of Provence, seventh century

Giles founded a monastery at a place in Provence later called Saint-Gilles on land given by King Wamba. This became an important centre for pilgrims on their way to both Compostella and the Holy Land. It is said that as an old man Giles placed his monastery under the protection of the pope, who gave him two doors of cypress wood. The frail hermit, lacking other means of transport, pushed them into the sea, and, amazingly, they were washed up near enough to his monastery to be used! There is a story that he sheltered a hind hunted by King Wamba, who unwittingly shot him as well as the hind, but both recovered. This gave rise to a widespread belief that through his prayers Giles would protect the injured. Countless hospitals as well as churches are dedicated to him.

PRAYER
All-merciful One,
help us to follow in loving thought and deed
the pattern of your servant Giles.
Make us concerned for those
who are deprived of their basic needs,
tender towards those who are broken,
and humble towards you.

READINGS
Psalm 31:14-24
Tobit 13:10-13
Matthew 12:9-14

Gregory the Great

d. 604

Gregory became the chief administrator of the city of Rome in 593. Kentigern visited him, following his strategy meeting with Columba, and doubtless talked about the need for Britain's invading Anglo-Saxons to be evangelised. Gregory became a monk, then the Pope's representative to the patriarch in Byzantium, and in 590 was elected pope himself. He styled himself 'the servant of the servants of God', inspired fresh music and chant in the Church's worship, became a peacemaker (for example, with the Lombards), and sent Augustine and 40 monks from his monastery on a mission to the English. History rightly knows him as Gregory the Great.

PRAYER
Servant King,
who called Gregory to pattern your likeness on earth,
and gave him, among many cares,
a longing to convert the English people,
may we ever desire, like him,
to be servants of the servants of God,
to make peace and to reach out to others.

READINGS
Psalm 96
Ecclesiasticus 47:8-11
Ephesians 2:11-18

Phoebe

Church deacon, first century

Phoebe came from Cenchreae which was the port of Corinth. It is likely she was a woman of some means who had used her resources to help many people. She was a deacon, and had been of service to Paul. She made a journey to Rome, probably at her own expense, and took with her the letter Paul wrote to the church there (which is part of the Christian Bible). Paul wrote them an introduction to her.

PRAYER
Spirit of God,
who equips people with the gift of helping
in order to build up the faith communities,
as we thank you for Phoebe and her fellow deacons,
we pray that we may use whatever means are at our disposal
to forward your work on earth.

READINGS
Psalm 112
2 Chronicles 2:11-16
Romans 16:1-2

* transferred from 3 September

Cuthbert

His enshrining, 698

Eleven years after Cuthbert's death a great occasion was planned. Cuthbert's body would be removed from its coffin and placed in a fine new shrine at Lindisfarne, and the Lindisfarne Gospels, a masterpiece of medieval illuminated calligraphy, would be dedicated to God and St Cuthbert. To everyone's astonishment Cuthbert's body was found to be incorrupt. This led to a huge popular following throughout Britain and beyond, and miracles occurred at his shrine.

PRAYER
Holy God of Cuthbert,
bright star of the North,
we would become, like him,
peacemakers and hospitality givers,
open to change and partnership,
Spirit led, in solitude and costly service.
We invite you, as he did, to enter deeply into our lives
and into our very bones.

READINGS
Psalm 139:1-16
2 Samuel 21:10-14
Hebrews 4:12, 13

Bega

Abbess, seventh century

Bega (or Begu) became a friend and disciple of Hilda, who appointed her the abbess of her daughter monastery at Hackness. There Bega, before news of Hilda's death had been received, had a vision of Hilda being escorted to heaven. Legend says that Bega, the beautiful daughter of an Irish king, fled to Northumbria rather than enter a forced marriage. There she founded a hermitage at a place on the Cumbrian coast now named after her, St Bees. A monk there wrote about her relics being transferred to Whitby, and of miracles following. If this Bega was the same person, she must have either begun or ended her Northumbrian days at St Bees.

PRAYER
Gentle God,
in Bega we glimpse the beauty of friendship
and sensitivity offered to you.
Help us to create such stillness in our inner being
that we may become aware of your gracious movements
in the souls of others.

READINGS
Psalm 63:1-8
Genesis 28:10-17
1 Peter 2:1-12

Eanswyth

Founder of England's first convent, d. 640

The daughter of a king of Kent, Eanswyth refused to marry in order to be a 'bride of Christ'. She probably became a novice nun in France before founding a nunnery at Folkestone, which is, as far as we know, the first among the English. Vikings destroyed this, but King Athelstan restored the church. It is thought that her remains were found in a Saxon coffin in the north wall of the present church of SS Mary and Eanswyth, Folkestone.

PRAYER
Eternal Spouse,
who ever woos your people,
as we give you thanks for the first brides of Christ
among the English,
we pray that in every land there may be no lack of people
who respond with all their being to your advances.

READINGS
Psalm 5
Proverbs 4:1-9
1 Peter 3:8-12

* transferred from 31 August

Birth of the Virgin Mary

first century

The festival in honour of the birth of the mother of Christ is celebrated on this day in both the Eastern and Western Churches. Coming just nine months after the celebration of Mary's conception, it acknowledges the preparation by God of his people to receive the Saviour, showing that mortal flesh can be the bearer of Christ to the world.

PRAYER
Holy Spirit of the infinite God,
who enveloped Mary and prepared her body and soul
to be a dwelling place for your Son,
keep us pure and available to your purposes,
that you may live in us without hindrance
and without end.

READINGS
Judith 16:13-16
Genesis 3:1-16
Matthew 1:1-16

Ciaran of Clonmacnoise

d. 545

The son of a travelling carpenter, and descended through his mother from a national bard, Ciaran was born at Connaught, Ireland. He was mentored by Finnian at Clonard and Enda on the Aran Islands where he was ordained priest. After seven years he established his own monastery. The hearts of all Ireland went after him, and he had the gift of harnessing this attraction to God. In response to a prophetic vision he established a community at Clonmacnoise which united people from two hostile tribes. Still a young man, he died of plague only seven months after arriving, yet that foundation lasted a thousand years.

PRAYER
O holy scholar of holy strength,
O overflowing, loving, silent one,
O generous and thunderous giver of gifts,
O rock-like warrior of a hundred hosts,
forgive.

Attributed to Ciaran

READINGS
Psalm 80:8-18
Genesis 18:1-11
Revelation 7:9-17

Finnian of Moville

d. 579

Finnian crossed from Ireland to be educated at the monastic college of Whithorn founded by Ninian. A nearby cave on the coast, where he is reputed to have retired to pray, is named after him. He went back to his native land to establish the faith community at Moville, County Down. There Columba was one of his many disciples. He became famous as a teacher and guide, and founded another monastery at Dromin, Louth. Some scholars believe that the Penitential of Vinnian is his.

PRAYER
Merciful God,
may patience arise from rage,
kindness arise from envy,
restraint arise from backbiting,
joy arise from gloom,
and generosity arise from greed.
Echoes Vinnian's Penitential

READINGS
Psalm 51:1-13
Proverbs 1:1-19
Matthew 10:16-25

Deiniol

Abbot, d. 584

Deiniol was a natural leader who planted hermit cells, discipled others and then moved on. He founded the great monastic centre of learning at Bangor, in western Britain. Bede claimed this had over 2000 monks, 1200 of whom were massacred by Northumbria's King Ethelfrith at the Battle of Chester in 615. With Bishop Dubricius he organised the milestone Synod of Llandewi Brefi. St Deiniol's, Hawarden, Britain's largest residential library, is beside the site of a cell and church founded by Deiniol.

PRAYER
Source of Wisdom,
you left not your people bereft,
but in Deiniol gave to them a student and teacher.
Raise up holy students and teachers
in places now denied them.

READINGS
Psalm 119:97-117
Nehemiah 8:1-8
James 1:1-18

Ailbe

Founder abbot, early sixth century

Ailbe founded a monastery in Munster, Ireland, sixteen kilometres to the west of Tipperary. As bishop he obtained from Munster's King Angus the gift of an Aran island for Enda, which became one of Ireland's foremost centres of spiritual formation. Legend says that Ailbe was the son of a slave girl who was left to die as soon as he was born. A she wolf carried him to her lair and placed him with her cubs where a hunter found him. Years later Ailbe saved the life of a she wolf who was being hunted, which he believed to be the same wolf that befriended him, and the wolf came often to be fed.

PRAYER
Tender God,
who delights to mother us all,
as we thank you for protecting the infant Ailbe
and using him to prepare a way for you,
fill us with wonder at your protecting presence,
and use us to open doors to your kingdom.

READINGS
Psalm 91
Isaiah 11:1-9
John 3:22-30

John Chrysostom

(The 'golden-mouthed'), d. 407

Born in Antioch, John was a brilliant preacher which earned
him the nickname Chrysostom, meaning 'golden-mouthed'.
Against his wish he was made Patriarch of Constantinople
in 398. He exposed corruption among the clergy and the
imperial administration, and reformed the Church. This
brought opposition from the Empress Eudoxia and he was
twice sent into exile, finally dying of exhaustion and hunger
in September 407. He died with the words 'Glory be to
God for everything' on his lips.

PRAYER
God, whose speech is glorious
and who warmed the minds of many
through the golden tongue of John,
may your Spirit put words into our mouths
that open the unsearchable riches of Christ to others.

READINGS
Psalm 119:89-104
Jeremiah 1:1-10
Colossians 4:2-6

The true Cross

Helena, mother of the Roman Emperor Constantine, was a devout pilgrim Christian, and while overseeing excavations in Jerusalem uncovered a cross which many believed to be that upon which Christ was crucified. A basilica named the Holy Sepulchre (known also as the Church of the Resurrection) was built on the site and dedicated this day in 335.

PRAYER
Crucified Saviour,
may we see an image of your unconditional love,
poured out for your children of every race, creed and time
in the life and death upon the Cross of your Son.

READINGS
Psalm 22:1-5, 25-31
Numbers 21:4-9
John 3:13-17

Cyprian

Bishop of Carthage, martyr, d. 258

A barrister and teacher of public oratory in Carthage, Cyprian became a Christian in mid-life and was made bishop only two years later. He would not make decisions without first consulting his flock, and sought to offer reconciliation to penitent Christians who had apostasised during a period of persecution. The Council of Carthage of 251 approved this policy. Yet he himself refused to renounce Christ during a further period of persecution and was exiled, tried and executed.

PRAYER
Faithful God,
who brought Cyprian to faith,
called him to shepherd your flock when days were hard,
and rewarded him with a martyr's crown,
strengthen us by your Spirit to be always firm but fair,
merciful in life and serene in death.

READINGS
Psalm 119:57-64
Ezekiel 34:11-17
Luke 14:27-33

* transferred from 13 September

Ninian

Founder abbot of Whithorn, missionary to Picts, died *c.* 432

Amid the danger and drift following the withdrawal of the protecting Roman troops from Britain, Ninian launched a mission to the northern Picts and founded a community of love among his own British people in Galloway. He had been brought up as a Christian and was trained and ordained a bishop on the continent of Europe. While returning he stayed at the Community in Tours founded by St Martin and was profoundly inspired by it. He established the influential monastic community of Whithorn.

PRAYER
Father,
you called Ninian to make you known
among a northern people,
and to establish loving community among his own people;
raise up among us messengers of light in dark places
and communities of love in blighted places.

READINGS
Psalm 36:1-9
Jeremiah 1:4-9
Matthew 9:35-38

Hildegaard

Mystic of Bingen, d. 1179

Hildegaard was mentored by a solitary nun, Jutta, joined her monastery at Diessenberg and succeeded her as abbess. About 20 years later she moved to a monastery at Bingen founded by an Irish monk. She had ecstatic visions and rekindled the mystical tradition. She also wrote extensively on matters of science, health, the saints and Scripture, and was an artist and musician, who composed fresh chants for worship.

PRAYER
God of vision,
whose servant Hildegaard was caught up
in the marvels of your heavenly courts,
and brought colour to your Church through music and art,
open our eyes to glimpse your glory
and our lips to praise you with songs that are ever fresh.

READINGS
Psalm 104:24-35
Proverbs 8:22-31
1 Corinthians 2:9-13

Edith of Wilton

d. 984

As the daughter of King Edgar of Kent, Edith was brought up at the royal abbey at Wilton. She refused opportunities to become queen, or abbess of the large prestigious monasteries. Instead she lived in simplicity with her mother at Wilton, serving the poor, at home with wild animals, meditating on Christ's passion in her prayer cell. Although she died at the age of 23, many answers to her prayers were claimed before and after her death.

PRAYER
Gracious God of faithful Edith,
as we cherish her example,
reveal to us the royalty of service,
open our hearts to the poor,
and give us perpetual devotion
to the suffering heart of Christ.

READINGS
Psalm 84
Amos 4
Luke 23:50-56

* transferred from 16 September

Theodore

Archbishop of Canterbury, d. 690

Following the divisions between the Irish and Roman Missions among the English which were highlighted at the Synod of Whitby, the scourge of plague, and the death of the Archbishop designate of Canterbury, Theodore, a lay Asiatic monk aged 65, was ordained and sent as archbishop. He travelled throughout the English realms, instituted a unified organisation through the Synod of Hertford, and established a clergy school at Canterbury. It was Theodore who created a missionary Diocese to the northern Picts, and urged Bishop Chad, who had trained under Aidan of Lindisfarne, to travel by horse. This holy, scholarly and tireless man was the first archbishop to command the allegiance of all the English.

PRAYER
God of Unity,
who alone can create order that is life-giving,
may we learn from your faithful servant Theodore
to work for the common good,
to encourage holy learning
and to be faithful stewards
of what you have handed on to us.

READINGS
Psalm 78:1-16
Malachi 2:1-8
1 Corinthians 14:40-15:11

Honorius

Archbishop of Canterbury, d. 653

The Pope sent Honorius from Rome in 601 as part of the second wave of Roman missionaries to Kent. During his 25 years as archbishop he consolidated the work of evangelisation, and approved the sending of the Burgundian Felix to evangelise the East Angles.

PRAYER
May you bring forth abundant fruit
for the increase of the Church,
through faith and good works in the fear and love of God.
Echoes words Pope Honorarius wrote to Archbishop Honorius

READINGS
Psalm 115
Joshua 8:30-35
Matthew 11:25-30

* transferred from 30 September

Matthew

Apostle and Gospel writer, first century

In his despised occupation of a Jew collecting taxes from fellow Jews for the occupying power, he was known as Levi, but in the Gospel that he himself wrote he calls himself Matthew. His emblem as a Gospel writer is a person, because he depicts Christ's lineage. In art he is represented seated, writing his Gospel with an angel guiding him. Varying traditions suggest that he was martyred.

PRAYER
God of insight,
who called Matthew from the selfish pursuit of gain
to live and write so that many would gain eternal riches,
free us from the possessive love of money
that we may reveal the treasures of your kingdom to others.

READINGS
Psalm 119:113-128
Job 28:12-28
Mark 2:13-16

Ceolfrith

Abbot of Jarrow, d. 716

Ceolfrith became a monk at Gilling, North Yorkshire, and then joined the monastery founded by Wilfred at Ripon. He visited learned places and became an expert in church affairs, but his cooking skills meant that he remained the caterer at Ripon. Benedict Biscop invited Ceolfrith to join him at his Wearmouth monastery and soon appointed him prior and then acting superior. In 682 he was made first abbot of the new twin monastery of Jarrow. A plague killed most of the monks, and only Ceolfrith and the boy Bede were left to lead the Latin worship. Yet it soon flourished once again. On the death of Biscop in 689 Ceolfrith became abbot of both monasteries. The number of monks increased to 600 and the great library, which made Bede's work possible, was developed. Ceolfrith resigned in 716 and asked the monks to forgive him for his faults.

PRAYER
Our Father in heaven,
forgive us our sins
as we forgive those who sin against us.

READINGS
Psalm 25
2 Chronicles 6:19-27
Luke 11:1-4

* transferred from 25 September

Adomnan

Abbot of Iona, reformer of women's rights, d. 704

Adomnan was a descendant of Columba who became abbot of the Columban monastery at Iona. His *Life* of Columba is a significant contribution to our knowledge of Celtic Christianity. He negotiated the release of 60 Irish hostages taken by the Northumbrian King Aldfrith. Adomnan initiated a new law, known as Adomnan's Law, which forbade the use of women and children in war, and which protected the rights of women. He tried, unsuccessfully, to bring Iona into line with the western Church's calendar for the date of Easter.

PRAYER
Faithful God,
who through Adomnan
called to mind your hand in your people's journey,
and reached out to establish justice in the world,
stir us again with memory of your mighty deeds
and to acts of justice and mercy.

READINGS
Psalm 133
Micah 3:8-13; 4:5
Luke 4:14-21

Sergius

Abbot and builder of Russia, d. 1392

Born at Rostov of a noble family some hundred years after the Tartars conquered what is now Russia, Sergius fled with his family to Radonezh, near Moscow. Although paganism ruled under the new regime, Sergius' family managed to maintain the daily services and learning of Psalms inside their family home, and the young boy had a conversion. After his parents' death, Sergius and his brother Stephen became monks and restored the monastery of the Holy Trinity. But there was jealousy, so one day Sergius left and trekked alone into the depths of the vast forest, there to build a himself a hermitage. Eventually many others came to live the simple life nearby. He had great prophetic leadership. He advised certain princes to form an alliance, and this enabled them to defeat the anti-Christian powers, which was the beginning of Holy Russia.

PRAYER
Great Protector,
who in days of trouble raised up Sergius
to defend and unite his people,
strengthen our brothers and sisters in the Russian Church,
that holding fast to the faith once delivered to all the saints,
they and their land may be transformed into your likeness.

READINGS
Psalm 36; Wisdom 10:9-14; Luke 14:28-33

* transferred from 25 September

Finbarr

Bishop and patron of Cork and Barra, d. 610

Finbarr's father was a metalworker in Cork, Ireland, who married a slave girl. Finbarr was mentored at Macroom and became a hermit at lake Gougane Barra. Many people flocked to him as a teacher and a wise anamchara (soul friend). Once, when he was settled at Gougane Barra, which it seemed was his 'place of resurrection', some former students arrived to share a dream that this would be their place of resurrection. Finbarr immediately handed over the entire estate to them, and again went wandering on as a lone hermit. Tradition says that he settled and founded a new hermitage at the place that is now St Finbarr's Cathedral, Cork.

PRAYER
Eternal God,
our beginning and our end,
accompany us through the rest of our journey.
Open our eyes to praise you for your creation,
and to see the work you set before us.
Based on St Finbarr's Cathedral Midday Prayer,
Cork

READINGS
Psalm 121
Isaiah 42:16
Matthew 19:27-30

Cadoc

Monastic founder and spiritual guide, died *c.* 577

Cadoc was such a Christ-like hermit that when a hunting party invaded his hermitage and grossly violated his hospitality he remained gentle, smiling, and compassionate. This made such a lasting impression that this story was recycled to explain the conversion of a man such as Illtyd a generation earlier. Cadoc founded a monastery at Llancarfan. Later, Finnian of Clonard joined him at his hermitage on the Bristol Channel island of Flat Holm. It is unclear whether he is the same Cadoc as the one who settled in Brittany.

PRAYER
God of Mercy,
give us grace, as you did to Cadoc,
to turn the other cheek
and to radiate your smiling warmth
even when others misuse us.

READINGS
Psalm 131
Proverbs 15:1-18
2 Timothy 6:6-11

* transferred from 25 September

Attracta

Indomitable Irish pioneer, fifth century

A convert of Patrick's named Attracta wanted to establish a Christian community in one place, but Patrick insisted she establish it somewhere else. This proved to be a place where one disaster after another faced her. She could easily have left in a sulk, telling him, 'I told you so', but Attracta was made of sterner stuff. Everyone in the area was terrified of a wild animal which attacked people at whim; eventually Attracta killed it herself, using her metal cross to do so. Then a local bard drowned in the nearby lake; Attracta nursed and prayed over him and brought him back to life. They needed to cut and transport trees with which to build the monastery, but there were no horses to pull the timber; Attracta used deer instead. Then they realised that they had no ropes with which to tie the timber to the wagons; so she used everything that was to hand, including strands of her own hair, to create strong cords.

PRAYER

Great Overcomer,
when you give to your servants any great endeavour,
bring home to us that it is not the starting of it,
but the continuing of it until it is thoroughly finished
which brings the true glory.

Echoes a prayer of Francis Drake

READINGS
Psalm 89:19-35; 2 Kings 4:1-7; Mark 1:29-45

Wenceslas

Martyr, Prince of Bohemia, d. 929

Wenceslas was a member of Bohemia's feuding ruling family. Although Bohemia was mostly pagan, he was educated by his Christian grandmother, Ludmilla, and determined to follow Christ. At the age of 18 he became ruler, and set out Christian policies of legal justice, open government and crime clean-up. He built good relations with neighbouring Christian states, and a disciplined army. He attended worship daily. In Lent he visited barefoot the poor of struggling churches. He challenged the leader of an invading force, a feared and famed swordsman, to a duel, in order to spare the people from mass slaughter. Wenceslas won and a peace treaty was agreed. His pagan brother Boleslav assassinated him while he was in church. His last words, echoing those of his Lord, were 'May God forgive you this, my brother'. His relics were taken to Prague and became a centre for pilgrims. His statue commands Prague's Wenceslas Square.

PRAYER
All-forgiving God,
thank you for Wenceslas,
clear of purpose, full of courage and compassion.
We pray for those in leadership today
that, hostage to neither fear nor favour,
they may model forgiveness in politics,
and tread a path for the world to follow.

READINGS
Psalm 2; 2 Chronicles 31:2-3, 20-21; Matthew 25:31-46

Michael

The Angel Force leader

Michael is looked upon in Scripture as the protector of the individual against the evil forces and as the protector of the God-honouring nation against hostile forces. In the Apocrypha Michael is portrayed as 'the great captain' who also wards off the devil at people's deathbeds and escorts them to heaven. Later Christians also regarded Michael as a healer. Many Christian churches on high places are dedicated to St Michael, which means 'who is like God'; often these are associated with angelic appearances.

PRAYER
Almighty and everlasting God,
who out of your love has ordained the services of angels
and called into being Michael for our good,
through Michael and your force-field
save us and our nation
from all that would bring harm.

READINGS
Psalm 55
Daniel 12
Jude, verses 1-14

Jerome

Bible translator and scholar, d. 420

Jerome studied and was baptised in Rome, spent time in Gaul, and tried unsuccessfully to live as an ascetic monk in Aquileia. After being accused in a dream of preferring literature to Christ he became a hermit in the Syrian desert and while there learned Hebrew. Following ordination he spent time as secretary to Pope Damasus. He finally became abbot of a monastery at Bethlehem and devoted the rest of his life to study. He is best known as the translator of the Bible into Latin, known as the Vulgate, which was used in Celtic lands.

PRAYER
Word of God,
who seeks every generation,
as we recall Jerome's struggles and give thanks for his skills,
help us to use the talents you have given us
to bring your Word to others.

READINGS
Psalm 119:97-112
2 Chronicles 34:14-28
1 John 1

All angels

The Bible informs us that there are uncountable multitudes of these bodiless spirits who mediate between God and humans. The earlier biblical books describe their mission. In Isaiah and Job they are portrayed as populating the 'courts of heaven' and singing the praises of God. Angels sang at the creation of the world and at the birth of God's Son, whom they strengthened in the desert, and before his death. They model for us the worship God desires on earth.

PRAYER
Our Father in heaven,
send your angels to those
who need to be alerted to your presence;
attune us to the angelic harmonies that we cannot see,
and help us to do on earth as the angels do in heaven.

READINGS
Psalm 148
Genesis 28:10-16
Revelation 5:11-14

Guardian angels

The ancient belief that God assigns to every person an angel to guard them in body and soul is upheld in Acts 12:15 and confirmed in the case of children by Jesus. Jerome and Basil taught that sin drove these angels away. Their function is to protect the body and soul and present prayers to God on behalf of their charge (Revelation 8:3f.).

PRAYER
O Guardian angel of my right hand,
rescue me from battling floods,
guide me in the twistings and turnings of life,
and bring me to my eternal destiny.

Echoes Carmina Gadelica

READINGS
Psalm 34:1-10
Enoch 100:5

Over all the righteous and the holy, the Most High
   will appoint guardians from among the holy angels
to guard them as the apple of an eye,
until he makes an end of all wickedness and sin.
So although the righteous sleep a long sleep,
   they have nothing to fear.

Matthew 18:1-11

Seraphim

Seraphim are those angels who are like flame. In a vision the prophet Isaiah saw seraphim above the throne of Yahweh. They are sometimes identified with the fiery serpents mentioned in the Books of Moses (for example, Deuteronomy 8:15). The Hebrew word 'seraphim' is connected with the root meaning 'to burn', and because of this Christian teachers from early times identified the seraphim with the burning love of God. Thus they came to be thought of as first in the nine formations of angels.

PRAYER
Fire of God,
kindle in us a love for you so great
that we, like the seraphim,
may blaze for ever in your presence.

READINGS
Psalm 103:19-104:4
Isaiah 6:2-7
Hebrews 1:4-7

Francis of Assisi

Founder of Franciscans, d. 1226

Francis was a leading young figure in Assisi society who developed a desire to help the poor and lepers. He renounced his inheritance and even his expensive clothes, and lived in poverty. He felt God told him to rebuild his church, but came to see that this referred to the church as a community, not a building. Disciples gathered and formed a community. They went on preaching tours. Francis drew up a Rule which pledged obedience to the Church. He was horrified by the debauched ways of Christians crusading against Muslim occupation of Jerusalem's holy places, and visited the Muslim Sultan, who was deeply impressed, though not converted to Christ. Francis had a close rapport with animals. He called his preaching friars God's troubadours. He drew up a Rule for people in ordinary jobs known as the Third Order.

PRAYER
Dear God,
when the world was growing old
you moved your people, by the life of Francis,
to delight in simple things.
When the world was growing callous,
you moved your people by his bearing the marks of the cross.
Teach us to embrace your suffering love,
bear your cross, cherish the earth,
and love your children.

READINGS
Psalm 148; Proverbs 4:18-27; Luke 12:22-34

Edwin

King and martyr, d. 633

Edwin was the first pagan king of the largest English kingdom to become a Christian. He spent many years in exile because a rival prince had Northumbria's throne. In 616 he defeated his rival and sought to marry the Christian princess Ethelburga from Kent. She agreed, on condition that she brought a chaplain with her to preach and baptise, and that he, Edwin, would consider becoming a Christian. According to Bede, the counsel of Coifi, Edwin's pagan adviser, was the turning point: he said that the new religion should be adopted if it could explain the mysteries before and after human life. It built on a vision Edwin had while in exile at the East Anglian court. Edwin, along with relatives such as the girl Hilda, and thousands of subjects, was baptised at York during Easter, 627.

PRAYER

God of the indestructible kingdom,
you can rescue us from innumerable foes
and can give us more useful counsel than any human being.
Knowing this, may we put away anxieties
and let our minds and bodies rest in peace.

Echoes words spoken to Edwin

READINGS

Psalm 39:1-6; Daniel 2:1-19; Matthew 28:16-20

* transferred from 12 October

Thomas

Apostle, first century

Thomas was a twin whom Jesus called to be one of the twelve. He was zealous: when he saw what he had to do, nothing would hold him back (John 11:16). He urged the disciples to follow Christ even if it might mean death. He was inquisitive: at Jesus' last supper he acknowledged his ignorance of the place Jesus was going to and asked how he could know the way (John 14:5). He was incredulous: because of his hesitancy in accepting the disciples' story of their meeting the risen Christ, he has come down to us as a 'doubting Thomas', a sceptic. However, once Jesus allowed him to see and touch the scars on his body, Thomas' response of adoration was stirring. Tradition says that he spread the gospel in India, and its Mar Thomas Church exists to this day.

PRAYER
Mighty God, constant and true,
who in order to confirm many in the Faith
allowed your apostle Thomas
to doubt your Son's resurrection,
only to believe with all his being.
Help us, in the light of his experience and your warning,
to walk by faith, not by sight.

READINGS
Psalm 31:19-24; Habakkuk 2:1-4; John 20:24-29

* or 3 July or 21 December

Iwi

Hermit and miracle worker, seventh century

Iwi was a monk of Lindisfarne in the time of Cuthbert who asked permission to become a pilgrim for the love of God. He got in a boat and trusted that wherever it landed would be the place he should make his hermitage. The boat landed in Brittany. His healings and holiness marked that place for many years. Two hundred and fifty years after his death his relics were taken to Wilton Abbey.

PRAYER
Teach us, good Lord,
that persons from any background may launch out in faith
with you as their guide.
As once Iwi sailed to make holy an unknown place,
may we let you lead us to the place in life
to which you call us.

READINGS
Psalm 107:23-31
Isaiah 63:7-14
Acts 27:27-38

* transferred from 8 October

Enshrinement of Aidan

After Aidan died at Bamburgh on 31 August 651 his body was interred in the monks' cemetery at Lindisfarne. Under Abbot Finan (651-661) a larger wooden church was built and dedicated by Archbishop Theodore. At some point during this period Aidan's remains were placed in a shrine to the right of the altar of the new church.

PRAYER
Creator of the angels
who escorted Aidan to his glorious destiny,
Head of the Church
who raised up the Shepherd of the English
in order that his life might always be held in esteem,
may we honour Aidan by being champions of the poor
and witnesses of your love.
At our end may we enter with him into the joys of heaven.

READINGS
Psalm 103:1-18
Ecclesiasticus 44:1-15
Revelation 14:1-5

Denys

Martyr, died *c.* 250

Denys was sent from Italy with five other bishops to convert the people of Gaul. At Paris he founded a church on an island in the river Seine and was martyred there. Later an abbey was built on the site which became the burial place of French rulers. Denys is regarded as a patron saint of France.

PRAYER
Father of peoples,
as we thank you for the simple courage of Denys
in planting the Faith at the heart of a nation,
strip from us what distracts us
from going to the heart of your will.

READINGS
Psalm 27
Deuteronomy 6:4-13
2 Timothy 2:1-10

Paulinus

Bishop, d. 644

Paulinus was one of the band of missionaries sent by Pope Gregory from Rome to Canterbury to help Augustine convert the English. When Princess Ethelburga of Kent married Northumbria's King Edwin, Paulinus accompanied her and had permission to preach and baptise at the various royal centres. Edwin accepted the new religion and a church was built at York, but after Edwin was slain in battle Paulinus returned with Ethelburga to Kent and became Bishop of Rochester, leaving behind James the deacon at York.

PRAYER
God of covenant,
who sent your servant Paulinus to preach, baptise
and build up your Church,
make us ready to witness to you in strange settings,
for the greater good of your kingdom.

READINGS
Psalm 92
Isaiah 2:2-5
Matthew 28:16-20

11 OCTOBER

Kenneth

(Canice or Cainneach) died *c.* 600

Kenneth was the son of an Irish bard and a lifelong friend of Columba whom he accompanied on his missionary journey to Brude, King of the Picts, at Inverness. He became known as one of the Twelve Apostles of Ireland. After studying under Finnian of Clonard and Cadoc in Britain he established faith communities in Ireland and then in Scotland: at Inchkenneth on Mull, at Tiree, Uist and perhaps in Kintyre and Fife. His life was lived in prayer and study of the Gospels. He lived as a hermit at certain periods, enjoying close communion with nature and wild animals.

PRAYER
O God, we thank you for Kenneth,
friend of Columba, planter of churches,
holy hermit and scribe,
converser with animals.
May we learn from his strong and consistent faith
to refer all things to you,
and to love with a missionary purpose.

READINGS
Psalm 97
Isaiah 40:25-31
2 Timothy 4:1-8

Wilfred

Bishop, d. 709

Wilfred was trained at Aidan's Lindisfarne monastery but after visits to Canterbury and Rome came to disdain what he thought of as Celtic insularity, and with tireless zeal and intelligence promoted churches whose buildings, clergy and liturgy reflected Roman splendour and order. His dominance at the Synod of Whitby was largely responsible for the victory of the Roman party. Accompanied by various disputes, he became Bishop of York and then of Hexham, spending his remaining years in the monastery at Ripon. His gift to the English Church was to make it more clearly part of the Church universal, but his manner and methods did not endear him to people.

PRAYER
Sending God,
who through Wilfred
established many churches among the English,
forgive us when we seek an earthly kingdom
in which we hope to find an honoured place;
encourage us to broaden our horizons,
maintain missionary zeal
and bring grace and beauty to your Church.

READINGS
Psalm 48
2 Timothy 2:14-23
Mark 13:33-37

James the Deacon

seventh century

James probably accompanied Paulinus (10 October) on his journey from Rome to Kent, and certainly accompanied him up to Northumbria in 625 during his seven years of teaching and baptising there. When Paulinus returned to Kent on the death of King Edwin, James stayed on alone, braving the hostile regimes, and, though neither a priest nor a monk, quietly continued to preach and baptise at Catterick, near York, until his death. He pioneered in Britain the Roman method of chanting. Bede praised his constancy and nobility of soul.

PRAYER
God our Anchor,
faithful in good times and bad, in life and in death,
as we thank you for the constant service
and noble spirit of James your deacon,
we implore you to help us become
more constant and more noble
in the midst of the mishaps of life.

READINGS
Psalm 119:1-16
Proverbs 2:20-3:10
Colossians 1:1-14

* transferred from 10 October

Ethelburga

Abbess of Barking, d. 675

Ethelburga's brother, Erconwald, Bishop of London, founded a monastery for women and men at Barking and appointed her abbess. She probably ruled the whole area, and gave sound and devoted care to her sisters. While singing praises at the tombs of brothers who had died in the plague, a sudden sheet of light illumined them and moved to the south of the monastery, which they took as God guiding them to the site for a women's cemetery. Healing miracles also took place.

PRAYER
Star Kindler,
who led your people with a cloud by day and a fire by night,
and who guided Ethelburga's community
through movements in the sky,
open our eyes to your will
as revealed to us in the signs and sounds of creation.

READINGS
Psalm 78:1-16
Exodus 13:17-22
John 11:17-27

* transferred from 11 October

Teresa of Avila

Founder of Reformed Carmelites, d. 1582

Although Teresa was a sixteenth-century Roman Catholic she is included in this calendar because she reconnected people with mystical prayer and divine creativity. At the age of 20 Teresa ran away from her Spanish home to become a Carmelite nun. After many struggles with her self-will and intense mystical experiences she left to found a reformed order on the outskirts of Avila. She worked, wrote and prayed tirelessly, and travelled throughout Spain, founding with St John of the Cross new houses for men and women. Her imaginative writings on the inner life of the soul have remained classic texts.

PRAYER
Spouse of heaven,
who called Teresa to holy daring,
may we walk this royal road through joy and pain
until we know that in all things you are sufficient.

READINGS
Psalm 77:1-13
Song of Songs 2:16-3:4
1 Corinthians 13:1-11

Gall

Fisherman hermit in Switzerland, d. 630

Gall was a principal pioneer of Christianity in Switzerland. He became a monk at Bangor, in Northern Ireland, and later left for Gaul as part of Columbanus' missionary team. They founded monasteries at Annegray and Luxeuil. Exiled from that region they preached in the Lake Zurich area and were later given hermitages as bases for evangelisation at Bregenz and Arbon. The local ruler, Sigebert, offered Gall a bishopric, and the monks of Luxeuil elected him as their abbot, but he refused both offers and lived out his life as a hermit, a fisherman and an occasional itinerant preacher. There are stories of a disagreement with Columbanus, who went on alone to found a monastery at Bobbio, but after Columbanus' death his staff was sent to Gall as a sign of reconciliation. A later Benedictine monastery and the town that grew up around it in Switzerland were named after him.

PRAYER
Fisher of souls,
we thank you that Gall was true to himself
and true to you;
help us to be so too.

READINGS
Psalm 15
Proverbs 25:1-15
1 John 2:24-29

Frideswide

Abbess of Oxford, d. 727

Frideswide was the daughter of a local ruler in the west-Oxfordshire area. He endowed minster churches at Bampton and Oxford, and Frideswide became the first abbess in charge of a double monastery for both women and men at Oxford. According to a legend, she avoided seduction by the King of Mercia (her father's overlord) by escaping to a forest retreat at Binsey, and then Oxford. He became blind but regained his sight after she prayed for him. The Oxford monastery became the largest landowner and the most influential centre in the region. She was made patron of Oxford University in the early fifteenth century. Her reconstructed shrine at Christ Church, Oxford, still attracts pilgrims.

PRAYER
Gracious God,
who endowed Frideswide with good gifts,
may we who commemorate her life of charity and prayer
attain with her the rewards of the poor in spirit.

READINGS
Psalm 36
Exodus 38:9-20
Matthew 19:1-12

* transferred from 19 October

Luke

Apostle and evangelist, first century

Luke was a Greek doctor, a companion of St Paul on some of his missionary journeys, the writer of a Gospel and of the Acts of the Apostles. His Gospel uniquely includes much of the story of the birth of the Virgin Mary, and parables such as the Good Samaritan and the Lost Son. Luke's emphasis on simplicity, prayer, healing and a love that embraces women and non-Jews has won wide appeal. Tradition attributes cave paintings of the nativity to him.

PRAYER
Great Physician,
who called Luke to become a physician
and a companion of your first envoys,
and to turn into your friends
those who were strangers to you,
give your Church a compassion that embraces all,
that in her outreach, writing and art
she may transmit a universal love.

READINGS
Psalm 147
Isaiah 35:3-6
Luke 15:11-32

The Angel Michael

His appearance at Mont St Michel

According to legend, in 704 Michael appeared in a dream to Aubert, the saintly Bishop of Avranches, and asked him to build a church on Mount Tomb. He shrank from such a huge task, but the dream recurred, so he decided to 'test the spirits' by increased fasting and service to the poor. At his third appearance Michael touched his forehead with such power that a wound remained visible for all to see. Michael told Aubert he would find a stolen bull and in that place they must build. Aubert's team climbed the mount, found the bull and started to build, trusting in God to supply their needs. A later bishop saw the monastery that had been built on Mont St Michel engulfed in flames, but the monks experienced no fire, and this was taken as an angelic appearance.

PRAYER
Protector of France and of high places,
may the mountains of human pride and greed be dethroned,
and may those who, like you, reflect God's likeness
be placed in the centres of power.

READINGS
Psalm 34
Daniel 10:9-19
Revelation 11:15-19

Acca

Monk and Bishop of Hexham, d. 732

Acca was a disciple and companion of Bishop Wilfred, who on his death-bed named Acca as his successor at Hexham. He was a fine singer, adorner of church buildings and scholar; he supplied Bede and Wilfred's biographer with valuable source material.

PRAYER
For friendship and the pursuit of excellence,
we give you thanks, O God.
As we see these reflected in the life of Acca,
so may you see them reflected in us.

READINGS
Psalm 134
Ezra 7:12-23
Revelation 15

21 OCTOBER

Tuda

Abbot and Bishop of Lindisfarne, d. 664

Tuda was discipled and consecrated a bishop in southern Ireland, and came to Northumbria to help the evangelisation programme there. Following the departure of Colman and many monks from Lindisfarne after the Synod of Whitby, Tuda was made Bishop of Lindisfarne, where this good and devoted man implemented the new Roman regulations. He diligently taught the faith by word and example, and continued the simplicity, prayerfulness and freedom from avarice established by Aidan. The Irish mission continued to win the love and respect of the Northumbrian people. After a very short time as Bishop the plague took him, along with many others.

PRAYER
Overarching God,
we thank you **for** the authenticity of Tuda's faith
lived out in a changing framework.
Keep us in the beautiful attitudes:
simple, prayerful and generous.

READINGS
Psalm 119:9-20
Malachi 3:1-4
2 Timothy 1:3-14

Donatus of Ireland

Bishop of Fiesole, died *c.* 876

Donatus made a pilgrimage from Ireland to Rome, and was made Bishop of Fiesole, where he founded a hostel for Irish pilgrims which he dedicated to Brigid, whose biography he had written. His other writings include a poem in praise of Ireland and his own epitaph. There is still a convent of Irish nuns at Fiesole, near Florence, which welcomes pilgrims.

PRAYER
God of pilgrimage, our host for eternity,
as Donatus was mindful of the needs of this world's pilgrims
and of his own end,
so may we look to the needs of others
and keep on course for our eternal home.

READINGS
Psalm 132
Genesis 18:1-8
Titus 1:4-8

James

Brother of the Lord, first century

Two Gospels describe James as a brother/cousin of Jesus (Matthew 13:55, 56; John 2:12; 7:3, 10). According to varying church strands, James was a son of Mary and Joseph, or of Joseph by a former marriage, or of Mary's sister. He did not accept Jesus as Messiah until, it seems, a personal revelation of Jesus' resurrection won him to faith (1 Corinthians 15:7). After this 'the brothers of the Lord' joined with the apostles and the women in the upper room (Acts 1:14). He became a pillar of the church at Jerusalem (Acts 12, 15 and 21) and is assumed to be the writer of the Epistle of James. There are traditions that he was a Nazirite from birth and followed strict personal disciplines, that he was known as 'the man with camels' knees' because of his frequent kneeling in prayer, and that he was cruelly martyred. The tomb of St James is still to be seen in Jerusalem.

PRAYER ˷
O Christ,
who chose as a brother a man cautious of change,
faithful to tradition, yet obedient to a fresh revelation,
powerful in intercession and faithful to death,
we rejoice that you invite people
of many temperaments, races and viewpoints
to become part of your family.
Help us to treat them as our brothers and sisters too.

READINGS
Psalm 133; Genesis 33:1-11; Acts 15:12-21

Maglorius of Sark

Founder of monasteries, d. 575

Maglorius came from Ireland to train at Illtyd's great Christian community in Britain. After he became a monk and was ordained, Samson took him to Brittany where he was put in charge of the monastery at Kerfunt. He retired to a secluded spot on the coast, but crowds sought him out for counsel and healing. After healing the ruler of the nearby Channel Island of Sark of a skin disease, he was given land there where he established a monastery. He nobly served the poor through times of famine and plague, and organised their defence against raiders. He probably visited the larger neighbouring island of Jersey, tamed a feared wild creature, and was given land to establish a monastery there, too. It was said that he interpreted the words of Psalm 27:4 literally: 'One thing only do I desire, to live in the Lord's house to the end of my days', and that during the last months of his life he refused to move from his church.

PRAYER
Glorious, O God,
was the establishing of the Faith in Sark and Jersey
by the hands of your noble servant.
Establish the work of our hands
that it, too, may be glorious in your eyes.

READINGS
Psalm 27
Isaiah 58:6-12
Luke 14:15-24

Crispin and Crispinian

Shoemakers and martyrs, d. 287

Crispin and Crispinian were shoemakers who travelled to Gaul to preach the Gospel and who, like the tent-making St Paul, earned their living through their trade so as not to be a financial burden on the local Christians. Soissons, where their relics were enshrined, became a major pilgrim centre. Faversham, in Britain, also claimed that they stayed there during persecution, and Shakespeare refers to them six times. They are the patrons of shoe- and leather makers.

PRAYER
Carpenter Christ,
who learned your craft through long years of toil,
but toiled even more for the souls of humankind,
as we thank you for the resourcefulness
of these your two servants,
help us to put our best resources at your disposal,
that we, with Crispin and Crispinian,
may gain an eternal reward.

READINGS
Psalm 97
2 Chronicles 2:11-16
Acts 18:1-8

Alfred the Great

King and founder of monasteries, d. 899

Alfred was the Christian King of the West Saxons who defeated and then made peace with the invading Danes, whose king himself became a Christian, thus creating a united England. He gave half his income to founding Christian communities which, during or after his lifetime, developed education and care of the poor, the sick and travellers. He gathered around him a team of Christian scholars who made available to the clergy and others great spiritual and classical works in English. He himself translated many Christian books into English. He appointed Assur, a Celtic bishop, as his chief advisor and put Irish pilgrims to work as teachers. He evolved a legal code based on common sense and Christian mercy.

PRAYER
You are our Father and Creator,
our Highest Wisdom and Good,
our Intellectual Light and our Ruler,
our Wealth and Pride,
our Home and Country, our Life and Salvation.
Few of your servants understand you,
but at least we love you.
We ask you to command us as you will,
through Jesus Christ our Lord.

Alfred (shortened)

READINGS
Psalm 21:1-7; 2 Samuel 23:1-5; 1 Timothy 2:1-8

Eata

Abbot of Lindisfarne and Bishop of Hexham, d. 686

Eata was one of the first twelve English boys educated by Aidan at Lindisfarne. He became a monk and eventually abbot at Melrose, where he trained Cuthbert. In the 650s the king gave land at Ripon for a monastery and Eata, Cuthbert and others set it up, but returned to Melrose in 661 when Bishop Wilfred decided to impose Roman regulations there. Following the Synod of Whitby and the death of Tuda after a few months as Lindisfarne's abbot, Eata became Abbot of Lindisfarne with Cuthbert as prior. Here they worked within the new Roman framework. Eata was Bishop of Hexham from 668-671, and Bishop of Lindisfarne from 681-685 but, when Hexham again became vacant in 685, he returned to his old see so that Cuthbert could become Bishop of Lindisfarne. He was buried at Hexham and is described as a man of peace and simplicity.

PRAYER
God of Eata, Lord of the Church, help us, like Eata,
to walk in the ways of peace and simplicity,
and to serve humbly wherever you place us,
that we may be links in a divine continuity.

READINGS
Psalm 15; Joshua 22:1-5; 1 Timothy 3:1-10

* transferred from 26 October

Simon and Jude

Apostles, first century

Simon was one of the twelve apostles of Jesus who was a member of the Zealot party. He continued to be known as 'the Zealot' after he became a believer, which suggests that he was able to harness to Christ the highest ideals of that party – zeal for his nation to be free under God. Like Simon, who was overshadowed by the more famous Simon Peter, Jude was another apostle about whom little is known; he is generally thought to be the same person as Thaddeus (John 14:22) which may be his last name. Because his name was similar to that of the traitor Judas he was seldom invoked in prayer and therefore became known as the patron of lost causes!

PRAYER
Great God,
we pray for those who, like Simon and Jude,
have forgone fame or fortune to follow you
but who are overshadowed by namesakes or peers.
Assure them that you build your Church
on the foundation of the apostles,
and that each person is a living building block
for you to use.

READINGS
Psalm 118:19-29
Ezra 4:24-5:11
Luke 6:12-20

Hilarion

Monastic pioneer of Palestine, died *c.* 371

Hilarion was a pioneer of hermit life in Palestine. His parents were pagans, and he was converted to Christianity while studying at Alexandria. For a time he sought the guidance of Antony in the Egyptian desert before returning to Gaza. He gave away the wealth he inherited from his parents to live a frugal hermit life. A ministry of miracles developed and crowds engulfed him, so he went to ever more secluded places in Egypt, Libya, Sicily and Cyprus, where he died. Jerome wrote of his life.

PRAYER
Father,
as we recall the God-beckoning beauty of Hilarion's life,
who so cleanly left illusory goods
and so completely searched for deeper communion with you,
give us a greater clarity of heart we pray.

READINGS
Psalm 1
Proverbs 15:8-31
Matthew 16:21-26

* transferred from 21 October

Raphael and the seven angels

The Apocryphal Book of Tobit, chapters 5-12, tells the story of a person who accompanies a young man and whose advice results in several types of healing. The person reveals themselves as the angel Raphael who is one of seven leading angels. The pseudepigraphical Book of Enoch gives the names of six of these angels in the following prayer.

PRAYER
Holy Raphael,
bring healing to those scarred by illness.
Holy Salathiel,
bring healing to those scarred by bad memories.
Holy Jegudiel,
bring healing to those scarred by fear of spirits.
Holy Barachiel,
bring healing to those scarred by fear of people.
Holy Jeremial,
bring healing to those scarred by mistreatment.
Holy Gabriel,
bring healing to those scarred by dark deeds.

READINGS
Psalm 148; Tobit 12:6, 12-18; Luke 10:17-21

* or 24 October or 8 November

Local saints

(Halloween – Eve of All Saints)

In the Celtic, as in other traditions, it is customary to mark the lives of local people who have left a print of holiness in the area. Some churches keep their own Book of Local Saints. Since today's western world focuses at Halloween on ghouls and ghosts, it seems appropriate to provide this alternative focus on the Eve of All Saints.

PRAYER
Holy and healing God,
we thank you for your cloud of witnesses in this locality
who beckon us to live our lives in your light.
We especially remember . . .
Help us to grow strong and holy like them,
and to overcome evil with good,
that you may scatter the darkness before our path.

READINGS
Psalm 97
1 Samuel 16:14-23
Luke 10:17-23

All Saints

From the days of the New Testament the Church has recognised as its living foundation stones the apostles and other heroes of the faith whose lives have inspired many to live courageous and holy lives. Martyrs, hermits and others were added to the roll-call and by the fourth century the festival of all saints was kept. In the ninth century in the western Church it was transferred to 1 November.

PRAYER
Triune God who mothers us all,
who knits together into one fellowship
all who have embraced your love,
help us so to honour the memory
of your holy and risen ones,
and to follow their example,
that we may come with them into that glorious company
where you reign with your saints in incorruptible splendour.

READINGS
Psalm 89:1-7
Wisdom 3:1-9
Revelation 7

All souls and ancestors

In the Celtic tradition the dead are habitually remembered. First of all ancestors and, more generally, all souls are remembered, for each person who has lived is sacred, as is their memory, because, whatever the distortions, they were made to be in the likeness of God.

PRAYER
Since it was you, O Christ, who bought each soul –
at the time it gave up its life,
at the time of returning to clay,
at the time of shedding of blood,
at the time of severing of the breath,
at the time you delivered judgement –
may your peace be on your ingathering of souls.
Jesus Christ, son of gentle Mary,
your peace be upon your own ingathering.
Echoes a prayer in the Carmina Gadelica

READINGS
Psalm 23
Isaiah 29:6-9
1 Corinthians 15:42-49

Cadfan of Bardsey

fifth century

Cadfan and his wife lived in Armorica (Brittany) where he was a fine fighter for the British colonisers. Perhaps as a result of political changes he returned to Britain along with many of his clan. There he founded a major monastery on the coast at Towyn, which flourished as a place of sanctuary and healing until at least the thirteenth century. There is a tradition that Cadfan sailed across Cardigan Bay to become the first abbot of the famed Bardsey Island. The town of Llangadfan, to which he used to travel, is named after him. The Cadfan Stone in Towyn church claims that he was buried nearby.

PRAYER
Lord,
human extremity is your opportunity.
As Cadfan turned personal upheaval
into bold new church planting,
may we refuse to be cowed by disappointments,
but rather turn them into springboards
for the advance of your kingdom.

READINGS
Psalm 3; Nehemiah 2:1-8; Acts 16:1-10

* transferred from 1 November

Winefride

Healer, seventh century

The theme of the many legends of Winefride are of dying and rising, of being fatally wounded and healed. The grievous violence that was inflicted on her was transformed; her wounding became a source of healing. Her life manifests the abundantly flowing water of life that heals, transforms, and makes new and beautiful. The healing pool at her shrine at Holywell, North Wales, is well kept and frequented.

PRAYER
Healing God,
mindful of the story of Winefride,
be in our woundings and healings,
be in our dyings and risings,
to mend and restore,
to heal and make whole.
Echoes a prayer of Earle and Maddox

READINGS
Psalm 30:1-5
Jeremiah 30:12-17
Matthew 9:18-26

All saints of Ireland

Ireland is known the world over for becoming a 'land of saints and scholars' in the centuries following St Patrick's mission. Lists were drawn up of hermits, monks, nuns, clergy and others whose heroic, Christ-like lives continued to inspire the people. The Litany of Irish Saints that follows echoes that in the twelfth-century Book of Leinster.

PRAYER
We give you thanks and praise, Holy Jesus,
for the glorious procession of saints in this land
of saints and scholars.
Glory to you for the saints of Ireland.
We give you thanks for the hermits:
for three thousand anchorites who,
receiving Communion from Bishop Ibar,
experienced like Brigid the glorious feast of heaven.
We give you thanks for the monks:
for seven hundred true monks who were hidden in Rathen.
For an innumerable multitude of Fintan's monks
who lived only on herbs and water.
For the four thousand monks of Comgall.
We give you thanks for bishops:
thrice fifty bishops, Spirit filled,
whom Patrick bequeathed to Erin.
Seven holy bishops from each of our many peoples.

* transferred from 6 November

We give you thanks for heroes:
for thrice fifty royal heroes in holy orders,
true Gaels,
who went on pilgrimage together.
For eight hundred men who occupied Lemor,
the grace of God in each one of them.
We give you thanks for the youths
who gave their lives to you:
twelve youths who went with Columba to Britain;
twelve youths who went to heaven
with Molasse without sickness,
the reward of their obedience.
We give you thanks for martyrs:
thrice fifty true martyrs led by Munnu son of Tulchan.
We give you thanks for the pilgrims who crossed the seas:
thrice fifty pilgrims who crossed the sea with Buite,
twelve with Maedoc of Ferns.
Three score men who went with Brendan
to seek the land of promise.
The holy hermit whom Brendan found there,
with all the saints who fell in all the islands of the ocean.
Cormac, who sought a desert in the ocean.
We give you thanks for holy guests on Irish soil:
seven monks of Egypt in Uilaig Desert.
Romans, Saxons, foreigners,
pilgrims here for the love and learning of God.
Glory to you for the saints of Ireland.

READINGS
Psalm 107:1-9
Malachi 3:16-18
Revelation 21:22-27

Illtyd

Founder and Abbot of Llanilltyd Fawr, sixth century

Illtyd was a married soldier who, after his conversion to Christ, was trained and ordained by Bishop Germanus of Auxerre, perhaps spending time at the monastic community founded by Cassian at Marseilles. In Britain he became a hermit, but was prevailed upon by the king under whom he had served to start a monastic school. This grew into the most influential monastic community in Britain, and many of the next generation of Britain's Christian leaders were trained there. Illtyd was known as the most learned of all the Britons in the knowledge of the Old and New Testaments, philosophy, poetry, rhetoric, grammar and literature; he invented a plough which helped to make his settlement a flourishing agricultural settlement. He displayed qualities of loyalty, dedication and discipline throughout his life, and became the spiritual father of many.

PRAYER
Wise and gracious God,
who raised up Illtyd
to make many Britons wise, holy and fruitful,
prosper the work of our hands, heads and hearts
that the virtues of hard work and holy living and learning
may flourish afresh in our time.

READINGS
Psalm 119:89-104; Proverbs 1:2-8; Matthew 7:24-29

Willibrord

Apostle of Frisia, Archbishop of Utrecht, d. 739

Willibrord studied under Wilfred in Northumbria, where his father had become a hermit, and then in Ireland, before being sent as a missionary to Frankish lands. He was consecrated a bishop, and established an organised church in Frisia, building the cathedral of Utrecht and restoring an ancient church dedicated to St Martin. In 698 he founded the largest of his monasteries at Echternach (now in Luxembourg) where he died 40 years later. Alcuin said his work was based upon energetic preaching and ministry informed by prayer and sacred reading. He is known as the patron of Holland.

PRAYER
Lord,
Willibrord's life-work was a huge advance for your kingdom.
Give us, as you gave him,
the energy to accomplish your purposes,
the clarity to organise well,
and the informed faith to persevere to the end.

READINGS
Psalm 96
Isaiah 52:7-10
Romans 10:9-17

Tysilio

Abbot of Meifod, seventh century

The young Tysilio ran away from his royal family of Powys to become a monk. For seven years he took refuge in the Menai Straits, until it was safe to join the monastery at Meifod, of which he later became abbot. Following a Saxon invasion his parents' court had to relocate near to Meifod, so, in order not to be drawn into political intrigues, Tysilio moved south to Builth and then, if later accounts are correct, to Brittany. There he settled at a place named after him, Saint Sullac, where he died. He sent a Gospel Book back to his homeland as a sign of his blessing. Once, his aged former mentor was intent on making the hazardous journey to Rome. Tysilio helped to get this out of his system by trekking with him over the Snowdonia mountains, urging him to dream of the great Roman buildings as they walked.

PRAYER
Guide us, our great Mentor,
through the ups and downs of life.
Strengthen us, like Tysilio,
to leave behind what hinders our calling,
and to keep moving towards ever greater reality.

READINGS
Psalm 27:4-14
2 Samuel 22:17-34
Matthew 6:19-24

All saints of Wales

Wales is the name given by the Anglo-Saxon invaders to that part of western Britain they did not colonise. The Britons' own name for it is Cymru, meaning land of comrades. In the eighth century Mercia's King Offa built a dyke to mark the boundary. As well as its famous saints such as Illtyd, Samson, David and Asaph, the land is everywhere dotted with tokens of holy people, many of whom give their name to villages and towns, such as St Athan, St Govan or St Twynnells. There were child saints such as Tyfil, killed near Llandeilo, married couples such as Gwynllyw and Gwladys who established a hermitage near Newport, and wives such as Helen of Caernarvon. The list includes kings such as Brychan, spiritual guides such as Beuno and Brychan's soul friend Brynach, who settled with his wife on the banks of the river Nyfer. Places like Puffin Island were home to hundreds of hermits from Seriol onwards. The great pilgrimage centre, Bardsey Island, claims that over 20,000 saints are buried there.

PRAYER
O God,
when the lights went out in Europe,
your saints, the glory of Wales, shone brightly in the dark
and still light up our lives.
You who are their Crown and ours,
kindle in us the fire that blazed in them.

READINGS
Psalm 15; Ecclesiasticus 44:1-15; Revelation 19:5-10

Justus

Archbishop of Canterbury, d. 627

Justus was one of the Roman missionaries sent with Augustine by Pope Gregory to establish a uniform church in the British Isles. He was a co-signatory of a letter to Irish and British bishops urging them, it seems with little effect, to conform their customs to the Roman See. Following a resurgence of pagan forces and kings, he and other Roman bishops withdrew to France but returned upon the conversion of one of these, King Eadbald. Justus became Archbishop of Canterbury in 624. It was he who consecrated as bishop the Roman missionary Paulinus and sent him to Northumbria. It seems it was also he who by his learning and eloquence discipled King Eadbald after he had turned from the pagan to the Christian Faith. The Pope wrote that he 'guided the English Church with great love and energy'.

PRAYER
Patient Redeemer,
in the life of Justus you show us
that a person who may lack heroic virtues
or honed intuition may nevertheless,
by their faithful friendship,
lead a person from ignorance to faith.
Help us, whatever our strengths and weaknesses,
always to struggle for the Faith.

READINGS
Psalm 72:1-7; Isaiah 51:4-8; Romans 15:1-13

Martin

Monk and merciful Bishop of Tours, d. 397

Best known for giving half his cloak to a freezing beggar in whom he recognised Christ, Martin left a career as an officer in the Roman army to be 'a soldier of Christ'. After living a hermit's life in extreme conditions Martin offered himself to Hilary, the faithful Bishop of Poitiers, who asked him to establish a missionary community of hermits. Martin's brothers went to people in outlying areas who had previously been neglected by Christian missions. When, in 372, the people of Tours elected Martin to be their bishop, he used a cow stool as a sign that all his clergy should eschew status and be humble shepherds. Young people from far and wide came to experience a community of genuine, loving relationships at Tours. Among them was Ninian, who founded a similar community in north-west Britain at today's Whithorn.

PRAYER
Great God,
who called Martin from the armies of this world
to be a soldier of Christ
who established colonies of heaven,
inspire us to follow his example of humble service
and compassion for the needy,
armed with the sword of the Spirit.

READINGS
Psalm 112:1-9; Deuteronomy 15:7, 8, 10, 11;
Matthew 25:34-40

Machar

Spiritual father of Aberdeen, sixth century

In 563 Machar came with Columba from Ireland to Iona.
He traversed the larger neighbouring island of Mull telling
the people about Christ. He then travelled east to evangelise
the Picts in the region of Aberdeen. He thus came to be
regarded as the first spiritual father, or bishop, of Aberdeen.
Water from his well was at one time used for baptisms in
Aberdeen Cathedral.

PRAYER
Teach us, good Lord,
like Machar, never to take for granted
the faith community that we know and love,
but always to reach out to others
who lack the blessings we hold dear.

READINGS
Psalm 108:1-9
Jonah 3
2 Timothy 4:1-5

13 NOVEMBER

Cadwalader

King and protector of British Christians, d. 664

Although Cadwalader is regarded as a weak king, he is included in the Orthodox calendar because, as the Welsh Triads state, he was one of Britain's Three Blessed Sovereigns and he gave protection to the Christian Britons who fled from the Saxons. His father, the nominally Christian King Cadwallon, brutally treated the Anglo Saxons until the Christian Saxon King Oswald slew him at Heavenfield. Now Cadwalader headed the Britons. But he was more interested in prayer than in battles, and was nicknamed the Battle Shunner. His army was routed in 658 in Somerset. If he lacked courage, he was mild and generous. He was the last king of the (pre-Saxon) Britons, and the Book of Taliesin contains predictive poems that one day he would return to lead the Britons to victory. The red dragon was on his standard, and remains on the Welsh flag to this day.

PRAYER
King of the last judgement, immortal, holy and mighty,
you sit with the book of life and death open before you.
All mortals pass before you, one by one, like sheep.
In your Book of Life all our deeds are written.
You see our hearts, you know our every thought.
As we remember the mercy of Cadwalader,
we pray that you will have mercy on us
and make us merciful towards others.

READINGS
Psalm 103; Numbers 35:9-15; Matthew 5:1-7

361

Dyfrig

Hermit of Bardsey island, d. 560(?)

Dyfrig (Dubricius), bishop in Hereford and Gwent, was one of the earliest spiritual leaders of south-west Britain. Probably a Romano-Briton, he became the spiritual father of a family of faith communities in the Wye Valley that numbered thousands of disciples. In response to angelic visions he dedicated a church to the Holy Trinity. When Illtyd was converted he went at once to Dyfrig who spiritually directed him. Dyfrig was the bishop who discerned Samson's vocation, and ordained him a priest, as he did Deiniol. One senses in him a strong, holy and apostolic custodian of the Faith. When he aged, Dyfrig became a hermit on Bardsey Island where he lived by the work of his hands and died in good old age. Centuries later Geoffrey of Monmouth used him as a figure in his fables about King Arthur.

PRAYER
Great Shepherd of souls,
who raised Dyfrig to oversight in your Church,
may we learn from his wise counsel and holy ways
to discern your will above all and in all.

READINGS
Psalm 60:1-7
Exodus 29:27-37
1 Peter 2:1-10

Malo

Rugged apostle of Brittany, seventh century

Malo was born in Gwent. His parents had him educated at Llancarvan monastery founded by Cadoc, but when they came for him to start a career he ran to an isle and refused to leave until they agreed he could be ordained. By then he had learned the entire Psalter by heart. About 547 Malo, in common with multitudes who were fleeing the plague, emigrated to Brittany. He established an island hermitage for the the region around Aleth. He founded faith communities and built cells where converts could make retreat. Today that area is named St Malo. Malo spent time with Columbanus at Luxeuil. He was a rugged pioneer who sang psalms on horseback and loved flowers. In old age he became irritable. He could be domineering and unhappy local bishops asked him to leave and settle at Saintes.

PRAYER
Rugged and real was your servant Malo, Lord,
a man of faith, though not without faults.
You are a real God
and on earth you were tempted as we are.
Help us to be real men and real women for your sake
and for the sake of the world.

READINGS
Psalm 95; Genesis 49:22-26; Hebrews 2:10-18

* transferred from 14 November

Margaret

Queen and patron of Scotland, d. 1093

Margaret was born around 1045 in Hungary where her father 'Edward Ironside', King of Wessex, had taken refuge and married the sister of the Hungarian king. Her father was called back to England, heir apparent to the Anglo Saxon throne, but the Norman invasion changed everything. Margaret, one of the few surviving members of the Saxon royal family, sought refuge in Scotland and married the Scottish king Malcolm III. She transformed court and church life, bringing in continental culture and church practices. She established monasteries, hostels for pilgrims and revived the abbey at Iona. The queen spent most of her time in prayer, reading, needlework and providing charity to the poor. Malcolm 'saw that Christ truly dwelt in her heart so what she rejected, he rejected, what she loved, he loved.'

PRAYER
Eternal Ruler,
who gave Margaret an earthly throne
that she might advance the eternal kingdom,
and endowed her with zeal for your Church
and care for her people,
spur us, by her example, to serve you and others
with an undivided heart.

READINGS
Psalm 2
Esther 9:20-32
Philippians 4:4-9

Hilda

Abbess of Whitby, Mother of the Church, d. 680

Hilda is known as a Mother of the Church in Britain and as a Jewel in the Darkness. A niece of King Edwin, she was baptised with him and many others at York at Easter 627. Her spirituality was shaped, however, by Aidan and his Irish mission. When at the age of 36 she decided to become a nun, it was Aidan who persuaded her to pioneer in Northumbria. She became abbess of a small community by the river Wear, then of a larger one at Hartlepool, and finally of the large double monastery for men and women at Whitby. There she trained six missionary bishops and sponsored the illiterate cow herd Caedmon to become a lay monk and the first popular poet and singer in the English language. For the last six years of her life she suffered, but never ceased to give thanks publicly. She maintained her spirituality under two systems, the Roman system replacing the Irish after the synod held at her monastery in 664.

PRAYER
O God our vision,
in our mother's womb you formed us for your glory.
As your servant Hilda shone like a jewel in the Church,
so we now delight to claim her gifts of wisdom and nurture.

READINGS
Psalm 34
Isaiah 61:10-62:5
Ephesians 4:1-6

Mawes

Bishop and healer in Cornwall and Brittany, fifth century

Mawes was either a Welsh or an Irish monk who was a missionary first to Cornwall and then to Brittany. He spent much time teaching his disciples in the open air. By tradition he is the founder of the fishing village near Falmouth that bears his name. In Brittany he became the most popular saint after St Ivo. He made his settlement on the island of Modez near the coast of Leon in the Gulf of St Brieuc, which he cleared of snakes and vermin by burning the grass. Many came to him for healing; he had a particular reputation for the healing of snake bites, headaches and worms.

PRAYER
Healing God of the open spaces,
as we rejoice that Mawes,
through his naturalness, drew people to you,
help us rediscover the naturalness of faith today.

READINGS
Psalm 104:24-35
Exodus 4:1-9
Acts 7:44-50

Egbert

Archbishop of York, d. 766

Egbert, brother of Northumbria's King Eadbhert, was Bishop of York from 732-766. After three years this see became an archbishopric again for the first time since Paulinus. Bede describes him as truly faithful and imbued with divine wisdom; he wrote a long letter to him advising him on ways to root out corruption and build up the Church.

PRAYER
Lord,
you expect much from those
to whom you give great responsibility.
As we remember Egbert's long service
of the Church at York,
we pray that you will imbue us
with a proper sense of responsibility
for the work and duties we have been given.

READINGS
Psalm 7
1 Samuel 12:1-4
1 Peter 5:1-4

Edmund

King and martyr, d. 869

Edmund was nominated as King of the East Angles while still a boy. He won the hearts of his subjects by his care for the poor, wise counsel and upholding of justice. In 866 the invading Viking armies destroyed the East Anglian monasteries. Edmund refused either to recant his faith in Christ or to share rule with Ingvar, the pagan Viking ruler. He declared that his faith was more precious to him than his life, which he would never purchase by offending God, so he he was scourged, tied to a tree and killed. Some 40 years later Edmund's body was found to be incorrupt and was transferred to a shrine at Bury St Edmunds. This increased an already huge following, and his life and death have remained a rich source of inspiration.

PRAYER
God of Edmund, God of valour,
give us courage to stay true to Christ whatever the cost,
and mercy to take seriously
the needs of those less fortunate than ourselves.

READINGS
Psalm 10:10-18
Proverbs 20:28; 21:1-4, 7
Matthew 10:34-39

Eucherius

Solitary and Bishop of Lyons, d. 449

Eucherius was born into a prosperous Gallo-Roman family. He had his two sons educated at the great Lerins monastery, where Patrick of Ireland may also have trained, and later he himself became a monk there. John Cassian described him and the monastery's founder, Honoratus, as 'the two models of that house of saints'. Eucherius sought greater solitude on a neighbouring island, where he wrote a book in praise of the solitary life which he dedicated to his friend, Bishop Hilary of Poitiers. He also wrote fine letters of spiritual instruction. Such was the respect in which he was held that he was prevailed upon to become Bishop of Lyons in 435. Here he was a tireless pastor and established charitable projects and religious houses.

PRAYER
Better is one day's silent communing with you, O God,
than a thousand days ruled by money.
Yet better still, for the sake of your children,
is to obey your call to serve others.
As we thank you for Eucherius,
help us know with him the blessings of solitude and service.

READINGS
Psalm 84; Lamentations 3:22-33; 1 Timothy 6:17-21

* transferred from 16 November

Gregory

Bishop of Tours, d. 594

Gregory was the best-known early bishop of Tours after Martin. In his great work, *A History of the Franks,* Gregory reveals that he most wanted to be known for the flowering of faith and charitable works, the restoration to faith of many who had lapsed, and the rebuilding of the cathedral and other churches during his episcopate. Yet other aspects of his character were sorely tested. Tours was caught up in political feuding and Gregory was at times required to act on behalf of the king. Through it all he displayed diplomatic skills and an ability to remain true to his own convictions. He gave sanctuary, at risk to his relations with the king, to the king's grandson, who had angered his father by marrying into a hostile family. Gregory was devoted to the ways of his predecessor, Martin, and wrote a book about him, as well as books on the Desert Fathers and the saints.

PRAYER
God of turbulent cities,
as we thank you for Gregory's steady and God-guided hand
on the affairs of Tours, we pray for our cities today
and ask that incorruptible leaders
of wise counsel and spiritual energy may emerge.

READINGS
Psalm 48; Jeremiah 33:10-16; Acts 20:17-28

* transferred from 17 November

Columbanus of Ireland

Abbot of Luxeuil and Bobbio, d. 615

Columbanus is the earliest Celtic monk whose writings have come down to us. They reveal a tutored leader, with an outstanding grasp of Latin, who throughout his life forsook worldly possessions in order to be a pilgrim for the love of God. After training at the great Northern Irish monastery at Bangor he travelled the Continent, establishing several major monasteries, the last of which, Bobbio, was where he died in 615.

PRAYER
Give us, Lord, the love that does not fail;
renew in us the flame that burns for ever.
As we continually gaze on you, the Perpetual Light,
may we shine before you,
scattering this world's darkness,
giving light to others.

Echoes Columbanus

READINGS
Psalm 103:15-22
Jeremiah 2:9-13
James 1:19-24

Enfleda

Abbess of Whitby, d. 704

The daughter of Northumbria's first Christian king, Edwin, and of Princess Ethelburga of Kent, Enfleda was baptised by Paulinus at Pentecost 621. At age 7 she fled to Kent with her mother after Edwin was killed. In 642 she married Oswin, King of Northumbria, as part of a plan to re-unite the two sections of Northumbria. In 651, after her husband murdered his brother, she persuaded him to establish a monastery at Gilling as an act of reparation. She became a patron of Bishop Wilfred, and followed the Roman dates for Easter, while her husband followed the dates observed by Aidan's Irish mission. This helped to bring about the Synod of Whitby, which ruled in favour of the former. After Oswin's death in 670 Enfleda became a nun at Whitby under Hilda, and, with her daughter, succeeded her as abbess.

PRAYER
O Triune God who mothers us all,
you teach us through Enfleda
that in the emptiness of loss you can bring
to birth a new calling.
As you led Enfleda,
so lead us to move on with you after setbacks and sorrows.

READINGS
Psalm 9
Deuteronomy 6:1-13
Ephesians 2:11-22

Alnoth of Stowe

Hermit and martyr, died *c.* 700

Alnoth was a serf and cowherd attached to the monastic community of Werburga at Weedon, Northamptonshire. He became a hermit in the nearby woods of Stowe where he was murdered by thieves. His holy presence lingered long in the area.

PRAYER
In simplicity your servants live
and in simplicity they die;
vulnerable to the winds of nature and of human pride.
The landscape long retains their presence.
Teach us, like Alnoth, to live simply, die content
and enter into eternal glory.

READINGS
Psalm 11:1-5, 7
Deuteronomy 22:1-4
John 11:17-27

Aedh MacBric

Founder of monastic churches, sixth century

Aedh was disinherited when his father, a member of the Ulster royal family of Niall of the Nine Hostages, died. We may speculate that this was because his brothers regarded him as either illegitimate or too generous. Aedh sought refuge in Offaly, where he became a monk. He went on to found churches in West Meath. He became a friend of Columba, who, though far distant, was aware of his death. According to three Latin *Lives*, he performed many miracles. The ruins of a hermitage where he is believed to have meditated stand at Slieve League, which attracts an annual pilgrimage.

PRAYER
Saviour Christ,
rejected by your own, but raised up by divine power,
you ever seek us out.
When others reject us you lead us,
as you led Aedh, into your kingdom's fruitful ways.
Glory to you, our Everlasting Father.

READINGS
Psalm 27
Isaiah 41:8-20
Matthew 21:28-32

* transferred from 10 November

Leonard

Abbot and hermit, sixth century(?)

According to his *Life*, Leonard was a Frankish noble converted to Christ by Remigius, whose godfather, King Clovis, offered him a bishopric. He declined and instead became a monk at Micy and later a hermit at Noblac (now St Leonard, near Limoges). Clovis eventually rediscovered him and gave him as much land as he could ride round on a donkey in one night. Here an abbey was built, where he died and was buried. After the somewhat fanciful *Life* was written in 1025 Leonard became an icon for people across Europe. It tells of the release of a prince from prison who, in gratitude, visited Leonard and made an offering. After that, prisoners of war and even pregnant women thought of him as a patron.

PRAYER
Holy God,
through whom Abbot Leonard became a shining light,
inflame us with the same spirit of discipline
that we may ever walk with you.

READINGS
Psalm 68:1-10
Ecclesiasticus 45:1-6
Matthew 19:27-30

* transferred from 6 November

Philip the deacon

first century

Philip was chosen by the Jerusalem Christians as one of the first seven deacons in their church. They looked after the practical and pastoral needs of the church, yet Philip was not content only to serve at tables; he was a Spirit-sent evangelist. After Stephen was martyred, Philip preached in Samaria with great success. He led the high-ranking Ethiopian officer to Christ, and his four daughters all became preachers. Paul loved to stay in his home.

PRAYER
Guiding Spirit,
who led Philip to a diplomat
who was seeking enlightenment,
help us to make ready your way
by being attentive to your voice
and bold in introducing others
to your Word and Sacraments.

READINGS
Psalm 72:1-11
Isaiah 53
Acts 8:26-40

Brendan of Birr

Abbot, 'chief of the prophets of Ireland', d. 573

Brendan was known as the 'chief of the prophets of Ireland'. He founded the influential monastic community at Birr, Ireland, which was later to produce the MacRegal Gospels. He was a friend and ally of Columba. When the Synod of Meltown (Meath) decided to excommunicate Columba, who came from a hostile tribe, only Brendan stood to greet him. 'I dare not slight the man chosen by God to lead nations into life,' he explained. When Brendan died, Columba, far away on Iona, saw a vision of angels receiving his soul, and called his community to pray for Brendan.

PRAYER
Strong God, full of purpose,
Brendan reflected your character.
He knew you are always speaking
and we are slow to hear.
As we thank you for the ministry of Brendan,
like a tall, straight tree, we dedicate ourselves
to listen to you and be true to what we hear.

READINGS
Psalm 12
Proverbs 20:1-12
Matthew 3:1-14

Andrew

Apostle, martyr, patron of Scotland, first century

One of the twelve apostles, Andrew was a fisherman from Capernaum who introduced people to Jesus: his brother Simon Peter, a boy with a picnic, and some Greek seekers. Ancient legends say he preached the Gospel in other lands such as Greece. A legend preserved in a poem once attributed to Cynewulf of Lindisfarne claims he went to Ethiopia. For these reasons he is used as an icon for mission. Another legend claims that in the eighth century Regulus brought his relics from Patras to the place now called St Andrews, in Scotland, which became a major centre of evangelisation. This led to him being named patron of Scotland. The blue diagonal St Andrew Cross is part of the flag of the United Kingdom of Great Britain and Northern Island.

PRAYER
Saviour God,
whose apostle Andrew so readily responded
to your call to follow you,
inspire us by his example to follow you without delay,
to go wherever you will,
and to introduce others to you.

READINGS
Psalm 96
Isaiah 52:7-10
Matthew 4:18-22

Saints and martyrs of Scotland

Fergus the Pict, Nathanlan (who decided to show his devotion to God by spending his life cultivating the earth which fed the people in times of famine), Finan of Aberdeen, Macha, and a host of lesser-known saints join the roll-call alongside giants such as Columba, Cuthbert, Kenneth, Margaret, Mungo, Ninian and Serf.

PRAYER
In this wild and rugged land,
ennobled by wild and rugged saints,
raise up again, O God,
those who will heal the wounded heart
and untie folk who are bound.

READINGS
Psalm 117
Genesis 22:17-19
Romans 1:1-5

Tudwal

Bishop in Wales and Brittany, sixth century

Tudwal lived as a hermit in the Lleyn Peninsular (Cardigan Bay) and the remains of his first known hermitage are in St Tudwal's Island East (Ynis Tudwal). He may have emerged as spiritual father to his extended family when it emigrated *en masse* to Brittany after invasion and plague devastated Britain. He established a monastery at Lan Pabu, where a relative was the local ruler, until King Childebert I insisted he became a bishop. He gave leadership as a bishop at Treguier for the rest of his life. In art he is depicted as holding a dragon by his stole. Tréguier, Chartres, Armel and Laval all claim to house part of his remains.

PRAYER
Mighty God,
you sheltered Tudwal and his people
during their flight to Brittany
as once you sheltered the holy family
during their flight to Egypt;
shelter us in the unsettling transitions of our life.

READINGS
Psalm 91
Genesis 35:1-15
1 Peter 2:11-17

Justinian

Hermit of Ramsay, sixth century

Justinian emigrated from Brittany to Britain, where he established a hermitage on Ramsay Island off the Pembrokeshire coast, and teamed up with another hermit named Honorarius, and with David, whose base was across the water. Such trust developed between Justinian and David that David welcomed Justinian's converts into his monasteries, and Justinian went to be with David when he thought he was ill. According to legend, he once realised that his oarsmen were in fact devils; as he recited Psalm 79 they fled. He was killed by lay helpers, who, it was said, became lepers and refugees as a result.

PRAYER
O Christ,
you call us both to test the spirits and to live in unity:
learning from the life of Justinian,
may we develop relationships of trust
with our fellow believers,
and also discernment of people of ill will.

READINGS
Psalm 79
Proverbs 3:21-35
1 Peter 5:5-11

* transferred from 5 December

John of Damascus

Poet, friend of Muslims, d. 749

John was born in a Damascus that was under Muslim rule, of a father, Sergius, whom the Caliph trusted to administrate the Christian population. John learned from his father to show kindness, be generous in alms, and free Christian prisoners. He and his adopted brother were educated by Cosmos, and excelled in poetry, music and many aspects of learning. The Caliph appointed John, with his perfect Arabic, to succeed his father. When Emperor Leo III attacked the use of icons John sent a stream of letters defending their use, and was forced to leave Damascus for Jerusalem. In the desert monastery of St Sabas he was stripped of this world's trappings, learned spiritual warfare and everyday obedience. He was given the gift of writing beautiful songs, inspired by the Spirit, which expressed the deepest theology of the Church. He then wrote a great work of theology.

PRAYER
Through humility, steadfastness and ascetic labour
John gave voice to your mysteries and glories, O God,
and a world was touched.
Dear God, strip from us all that is not of you,
and let the pure gold of your gift shine out.

READINGS
Psalm 119:121-136
Daniel 10:1-11:2
1 Peter 1:1-9

Birinus

Apostle of Wessex, first Bishop of Dorchester, d. 650

Birinus was sent by the Pope to convert unevangelised English areas, but gave up the difficult task of trying to convert the pagan West Saxons. Then Oswald, the leading English king, who had embraced Christianity through the Irish way of mission, urged the West Saxons' king, Cynegils, whose daughter he was to marry, to receive instruction from Birinus. From that time doors opened and his mission work bore fruit. He baptised Cynegils and his daughter, was made the first Bishop of Dorchester, and baptised many others over the next 15 years.

PRAYER
Baptising God,
who impelled Birinus across the sea
to bring your Word to a pagan people,
immerse us in your love,
and bring many into the company of those who believe.

READINGS
Psalm 117
Deuteronomy 24:17-22
Romans 10:12-13

Nicholas

Bishop of Myra, d. 343

Nicholas, the original Santa Claus, was born in Lycia in 280 of wealthy parents who gave much of their wealth to the poor. He used his fortune to help people in need. In order not to embarrass a formerly wealthy man who intended to raise income by selling his daughters into prostitution, Nicholas went secretly at night and placed sufficient money for a dowry for the first daughter through a chimney; the money landed in a sock which had been left out to dry. This was repeated with the second daughter. Thus children were saved from abuse. This is the origin of the Christmas stocking. Later he embraced a life of solitude and prayer but the church called him to become chief pastor. Then he went to Myra where the church asked him to become bishop. Here he opened his home in hospitality and was a father to orphans. He was imprisoned for his faith by Diocletian, the Emperor who persecuted Christians from 301 until 313. He died on 6 December 343. People considered him a saint even during his lifetime.

PRAYER
Father of orphans, Guardian of the young,
who through Nicholas rescued girls in danger,
make us aware of children's hidden cries for help,
inspire us to give our young people a good start in life,
and revive in us the true spirit of Santa Claus.

READINGS
Psalm 82; Deuteronomy 10:14-19; James 1:22-27

Ambrose

Bishop of Milan, d. 397

Ambrose was respected as the governor of Northern Italy by both sides in the Church dispute about Arius' teaching, so they asked him, though he was not yet baptised, to become Bishop of Milan. Eventually he agreed and was baptised and consecrated. He became a great teacher and hymn writer, and stood against political interference in Church affairs.

PRAYER
God of fair play,
who called Ambrose from a governor's throne
to be a shepherd and champion of the people,
replenish the Church with the spirit of sound learning
and the beauty of holiness,
that she may appoint teachers like Ambrose
to guide Christian people into the fullness of the Faith.

READINGS
Psalm 96
Micah 6:6-8
2 Corinthians 5:15-21

Conception of the Virgin Mary

first century

This celebration of the conception of Mary, which dates from the seventh century, is held on this day in both the eastern and western Church. It makes us aware of the divine preparation of people to receive their Saviour, showing that 'heaven can come in the ordinary', and that mortal flesh can indeed bring Christ to the world.

PRAYER
All-merciful God,
who stooped to raise our fallen human race
by bringing Mary into the world to bear a unique child,
may we who have seen your glory reflected in manhood,
and your love made complete in weakness,
daily be renewed in your image and become like your Son.

READINGS
Psalm 97
Ecclesiasticus 24:17-22
Luke 1:26-38

Lydia

Paul's first European convert, first century

Lydia was a trader in dyed cloth. She came from Thyatira in Lydia, but worked and lived in Philippi. She was the head, presumably widowed, of a substantial household. Though a non-Jew by race, she had adopted the Jewish faith, and engaged in prayers and ritual washing by the river on the Sabbath. It seems she met Paul, Silas and Luke there, and she and her entire household were baptised. She then offered them hospitality. She was the first of their converts in Europe and it is assumed she became a valued member of the Thyatira church. She has inspired women's movements, including the contemporary Lydia Fellowship for Prayer.

PRAYER
Seeking God,
as you opened the mind of Lydia
to the message of your Son,
open the minds of people today
and bring to them messengers of your Word.

READINGS
Psalm 127
Genesis 18:1-8
Acts 16:11-15

Saints and martyrs of Asia

Many of the Jews converted to Christ on the Day of Pentecost (Acts 2:7-11) came from provinces of Asia, and some of the earliest Christian churches were in Asia. Christianity among Celts began in Asia, with St Paul's visit and letter to the Galatians. Celtic Christians felt a special affinity with the apostle John, who planted seven churches in Asia (Revelation 1:1-11). Tychicus and Trophimus (Acts 20:4) are among the earliest Asian saints mentioned by name in the Bible. According to tradition, Thomas took the Gospel to India and the Mar Thomas Church has continued to this day. Through the followers of Nestorius a monastic form of the Christian Church spread like wildfire through China at the same time as it spread through Celtic lands. Saints and martyrs have abounded in Asia ever since.

PRAYER
God of the East,
we bless you for your Asian children
whose lives have been utterly authentic
because the love of Christ consumed them.
May these stars light up their continent
and draw many more to that love
which knows no distinctions.

READINGS
Psalm 113
Genesis 11:1-9
Acts 19:1-10

Edburga

Abbess of Minster, d. 751

Edburga was a princess who in 716 built a church and a monastery at Minster-in-Thurness where Mildred had established a group of nuns. After she was buried there, healing miracles took place. Boniface wrote her a letter which recorded a monk of Much Wenlock's famous vision of the Other World.

PRAYER
Our Father in heaven,
who through Edburga
extended the boundaries of your kingdom
through building, letters and prayer,
guide us in the ways you wish us to extend your kingdom.

READINGS
Psalm 128
Isaiah 54:1-6
John 15:1-8

* transferred from 12 December

Finnian

Bishop of Clonard, died *c.* 549

Finnian travelled from his native Ireland to train in a British monastery. On his return he founded two monasteries, and then his third, most famous, at Clonard. It was said this drew over 3000 monks, many of whom were sent out with Gospel Book and Psalter to establish faith communities elsewhere. Finnian offered a rigorous study of Scripture and the early Church spiritual fathers, as well as practical skills and lessons from the British and Coptic (Egyptian) monasteries. He drew up the first known penitentiary (spiritual fitness exercises), which drew insights from Cassian and Jerome. He died of the yellow fever, having in some way put himself at risk in order to save others' lives. Many future leaders trained at Clonard, and Finnian became known as the teacher of the twelve apostles of Ireland.

PRAYER
God our teacher,
as we thank you for Finnian's great gifts
in teaching many people by word and example,
restore to us that quality of teaching
that knows no divorce between theory and practice.

READINGS
Psalm 51
Proverbs 4:10-27
2 Thessalonians 2:13-3:5

Lucy

Virgin and martyr, d. 304

Lucy was put to death at Syracuse in the persecution of Christians by the Roman emperor Diocletian. Although few facts about her survive, her life and death had enormous influence for good. Churches were dedicated to her. Stories circulated, were embroidered or invented. In Sweden, her festival on the shortest day of the year has become a festival of light: the youngest daughter, dressed in white, wakes the rest of the family with refreshments and a song. A church near Venice railway station claims to have her partially incorrupt body.

PRAYER
Immortal and Holy God,
who enabled Lucy to uphold you and gladly suffer for you,
keep us steadfast, faithful and true
that we may come with her
into the glorious fellowship of your saints.

READINGS
Psalm 22:19-29
Ecclesiasticus 2:1-9
Luke 12:4-10

John of the Cross

Virtual founder of the dispersed Carmelites, d. 1591

John was educated at Avila, Spain, and after a time with the Jesuits joined the Carmelites, who espouse much silence. He was small in build, and suffered from bouts of ill health and depression, but had a profoundly spiritual and imaginative inner life. He met Teresa of Avila, who persuaded him to help her establish a reformed type of Order. For this he was persecuted, and even briefly imprisoned. Yet these experiences prompted some of his finest poetic and mystical writings, including his famous *Dark Night of the Soul.* After ten years in charge of various new religious houses he was banished to southern Spain where he died. He finds a place in this calendar because he helped to restore an element of spirituality that was neglected after the decline of the Celtic mission.

PRAYER
Lover of souls,
who always beckons us,
even through the dark night of the soul,
teach us, through the example
of your dear son John of the Cross,
that no suffering or misfortune is so great
that we cannot remain your spouse.

READINGS
Psalm 131; Song of Songs 2:8-17; John 14:18-23

Hybald

Abbot in Lincolnshire, seventh century

Hybald, or Higebald, was the spiritual father of a community in Lincolnshire, perhaps Bardney. Bede describes him as 'a very holy and abstemious man'. When on a visit to his friend Egbert in Ireland, Egbert told him how someone in Ireland had a vision of Cedd being taken to heaven at the time of his death. Hibaldstow takes its name from his grave there and four Lincolnshire churches have been dedicated to him.

PRAYER
Holy God, holy and mighty,
who graced Hybald's travels
with stories of the victories of faith,
bless his land of Lincolnshire,
and make sacred the landscapes where we live and die.

READINGS
Psalm 9:1-12
Exodus 4:27-31
Hebrews 11:1-6

* transferred from 14 December

Ruth

Ancestor of Jesus, between the
fourteenth and the twelfth century BC

Ruth, God-honouring ancestor of Jesus, was a Moabite girl who married into the family of Elimelech of Bethlehem, whose family had sought exile in Moab for the duration of a famine at home. Her husband and father-in-law both died in Moab. By the time her mother-in-law, Naomi, was able to return to Bethlehem, Ruth had formed a deep love both of Naomi and of her God. She insisted on accompanying her home. Eventually she was married again, to Boaz of Bethlehem. She was a forebear of Jesus and because of this we can say that he had mixed race ancestry.

PRAYER
God of all peoples,
in the life of Ruth you show us how through faith
people of all races and creeds
can become part of your family.
May we cherish every human life
and have faith that people of every race
can become brothers or sisters of Bethlehem's Infant King.

READINGS
Psalm 27
Ruth 1:6-19
Matthew 1:1-16

17 DECEMBER

Jesse

Father of King David, forebear of Jesus

Today marks the beginning of the week before the celebration of Christ's birth. During the second millennium, churches in the West began on this day to invite the Triune God to come, using each day one of the names given to God in the Old Testament. One of these names is 'Root of Jesse'. The prophet Samuel discerned that he should spend time with Jesse and his fine family in his search for a God-guided king. Jesse's youngest son, David, was chosen with Jesse's blessing. Jesse is an ancestor of Jesus. The Jesse Tree has become a pre-Christmas tradition. The trunk represents Jesse. Branches represent various of his descendants. The top of the tree represents Jesus.

PRAYER
God of the generations,
thank you for Jesse's big faith and solid parenting.
Help us to be rooted and grounded in Christ,
and thus to be linked with Jesse's timeless faith.

READINGS
Psalm 72:15-20
1 Samuel 16:1-11
Romans 15:7-13

Samthann

Abbess of Clonbroney, d. 739

Samthann was born in Ulster and her foster father was a king. She was married before she became a nun at Donegal, where her spiritual and financial gifts enabled her to be generous to the numerous lepers, guests and penitents who visited the community. She became abbess of the small community of Clonbroney, which had only six cows. There her deep, mystical prayer and discernment as a soul friend, transformed many lives, including that of Maelruain of Tallaght, a leader of the (Culdee) Reform movement. The influence of this woman, 'who frequently knocked at the doors of divine mercy', spread to Salzburg and other German-speaking parts through the influence of Bishop Virgil. One of her sayings is: 'The distance to heaven is the same from every part of the earth and if a person comes close to God they cannot be far from home.'

PRAYER
Holy God,
who gave visions and spiritual discernment
to your servant Samthann,
revive in us the vocation of prayer
that bears fruit in transforming friendships,
and bring us close to you and to our eternal home.

READINGS
Psalm 119:97-112
Isaiah 63:11-14
Acts 10:9-23a

Winnibald

Missionary and Abbot of Heidenham, d. 761

Winnibald became a monk among the West Saxons in Britain and travelled much. He took a team to evangelise with Boniface in Thuringia and Bavaria where he was ordained. Later he rejoined his brother, Willibald, who was bishop of Eichstatt. Together they founded the monastery of Heidenham. This was the only eighth-century Christian community in Germany which included both men and women, and it became a centre of prayer, work and outreach. Winnibald narrowly escaped assassination by pagans and suffered from ill health. After his death at Heidenham miracles were reported at his tomb.

PRAYER
All-merciful One,
we thank you for the many hearts
Winnibald opened up to you.
Help us to be broad in our thinking
and wide in the hospitality of our hearts.

READINGS
Psalm 41
Isaiah 55:1-5
Acts 13:16-26

* transferred from 18 December

Ignatius

God-bearer of Antioch, d. 107

Ignatius had known the apostles in his youth and had been discipled by John the Evangelist. He became the second bishop of Antioch and addressed the challenge of how to maintain the cohesion of the Church now the apostles had gone. He did it by fostering a oneness of love and common hope, with the bishop as the focus of that unity: 'Where the bishop is, there is the church.' He personally witnessed to the Emperor Trajan who began to persecute Christians. 'Why do you call yourself God-bearer?' asked the man who wanted to be a god. 'Because I carry the living Christ within me!' replied Ignatius. Trajan sent him to Rome to be thrown to the lions. But at each stop on their long journey to Rome the Christians flocked to meet him, and Ignatius sent moving letters to the churches to build them up and to express his joy at being a sacrifice for Christ. The lions quickly devoured him, and his remaining bones were taken back to Antioch.

PRAYER
Deathless Saviour,
grant us, after the example of Ignatius,
to be so grounded in divine love
that we may joyfully overcome all things, even death itself,
for the joy of meeting Christ face to face.

READINGS
Psalm 16; Ezekiel 1:15-28; Romans 8:31-39

Isaiah

Prophet, eighth century BC

Isaiah was a family man who lived in Jerusalem with two sons and who rose to great influence at the court of the kings of Judah. He was called to challenge the blind materialist march of his nation at the time of King Uzziah's death (Isaiah 6) by warning that if they did not go God's way they would be invaded and exiled. Looking to the farther future, he foretold of a remnant who would be the true representative of God, and then of the possibility that only one person would in the end be capable of being Israel's representative, and that person would suffer deeply. He also foretold of a young woman who would give birth to a son named Immanuel – God with us. Isaiah was also a great orator, writer, poet and theologian.

PRAYER
Holy God,
whose glory fills the earth,
and who foresees the rise and fall of peoples,
we thank you for the unique inklings you gave Isaiah
of the coming of your Son.
May it lead us to welcome him with wonder and awe.

READINGS
Psalm 45
Isaiah 7:10-17
Romans 9:25-31

Micah

Prophet, eighth century BC

Micah proclaimed that the kingdom of Judah in which he lived would face disaster unless its people turned away from injustice and followed God's ways. If, however, they heeded his message, a period of unparalleled harmony would be ushered in. His words were recorded and are part of the Old Testament. He also prophesied that when a woman gave birth to a ruler in the little known town of Bethlehem it would be a sign that God had returned to his people.

PRAYER
Teach us, good Lord,
like Micah, to be fearless for the truth,
confront evil and speak out for justice.

READINGS
Psalm 80
Micah 5:1-3
James 2:1-17

David

King, Jesus' forebear, tenth century BC

David was a shepherd, the youngest and least prominent of Jesse's eight sons. But God led the seer Samuel to identify him as the one who would replace the failing King Saul. He was described as 'a man after God's own heart', and had outstanding qualities and skills. He was a brilliant survivor in defeat, and magnanimous in victory. He lived life to the full. His greatest sin was to take another man's wife (Bathsheba) and to arrange for him to be killed in battle. His repentance (Psalm 51) was heartfelt. He transformed the worship of his people and wrote many of the Psalms. Jews taught that their Messiah would be a descendant of David. He was an ancestor of Mary and Joseph.

PRAYER
I love you, Yahweh,
my shield, my stronghold, my place of refuge.
You are faithful to those who are faithful.
You gird me with strength,
you make me as swift as a deer,
your right hand upholds me in the fight,
you give me the strides of a giant.
For this reason I will praise you among the nations
and sing to your name.

David

READINGS
Psalm 18:30-50; 2 Samuel 23:1-7; John 7:37-43

Josiah

King, Jesus' forebear, seventh century BC

Josiah, whose name is a version of the name Jesus, was a forebear of Jesus and one of the most God-honouring kings of Israel. He succeeded his evil father Amon when he was only 8 years old. His long reign was like a burst of brilliant sunset before the darkness of moral decay, invasion and exile came upon the people. Though without a father, his mother Jedidah, meaning 'God's darling', must surely have been a saint. At the age of 16 he turned from his father's evil ways and, following the steps of his forebear David, set his heart to seek God. He purged Judah of all forms of idolatry, and rebuilt the temple. He reigned for 31 years and was only 39 when he died. There was long and deep mourning by the people, who loved him.

PRAYER
Josiah wanted to please you more than all else, O Lord.
May we please you today.
Josiah restored your word and your worship
at the heart of his nation.
Restore your word and worship at the heart of our nation.
Come, live among us and be our Saviour.

READINGS
Psalm 84
2 Chronicles 34
Matthew 1:1-17

Mary, Joseph and the shepherds

Witnesses of Jesus' birth

Mary lived at Nazareth and was engaged to be married to a local carpenter named Joseph, who could trace his family tree back to the great King David. Due to a compulsory census which required residents to return to the place of their birth, they returned to Bethlehem despite the teenage Mary being pregnant, and had to make do with a stable at the back of an inn. Some distance away were sheep grazing in fields. Certain shepherds saw a brilliant light and heard what sounded like a great choir. They were convinced that some special God-event was taking place in the village, and they excitedly found their way to the place where Jesus was born. The thing that unites these disparate characters is sensitivity and obedience to God.

PRAYER
Father,
you appointed Joseph to be guardian of Jesus
and husband to Mary.
Give to fathers, guardians and mothers
grace to make holy homes.
Give to those who work in the fields
of farming and commerce
an awareness of your presence among them.

READINGS
Psalm 100
Isaiah 7:10-17
Matthew 1:18-25

Jesus

Jesus was born in a stable at Bethlehem. It is believed the Church of the Nativity now stands on that site. His mother was Mary and to outward appearances his father was Joseph, but two of the first Christian Gospel writers were led to believe that Mary remained a virgin, and that the birth of Jesus was a unique impregnation of a woman with God's Spirit. Joseph was told in a vision to name their son Jesus, which means 'the one who saves'. Muslims believe that he was a prophet born of the virgin Mary. Messianic Jews and all Christians believe that he was the Messiah, and that he was actually divine. Many names have been given to him. In the Celtic tradition he is known as 'the Root of our Joy', 'the Healing Man' and by names such as those in the prayer below.

PRAYER

Son of the dawn, Son of the clouds,
Son of the planet, Son of the stars,
Son of the flame, Son of the light,
Son of the spheres, Son of the globe,
Son of the elements, Son of the heavens,
Son of the moon, Son of the sun.
Son of Mary of the God-mind,
and the Son of God first of all news –
glory to you.

Carmina Gadelica, adapted

READINGS
Psalm 98; Ecclesiasticus 50:22-24; Luke 2:1-20

Stephen

First martyr, first century

Stephen was one of the seven deacons in the first church of Jerusalem, chosen to oversee the practical work, such as care of widows. He was given inspired speech and his address to the Jewish council who arrested him, in which he shows the great sweep of Jewish history as leading to the birth of Jesus, the long awaited Messiah, and his urging that all people might know about this, led to his martyrdom by stoning. As he died he asked forgiveness of those who killed him, and saw Jesus standing before him. Thus, the day after Christmas, we are shown a costly way of being a bearer of Christ.

PRAYER
Jesus, born of Mary,
proclaimed by apostles,
witnessed to by martyrs,
we bless you for your birth
and for your continuing presence with us.
Today we thank you for Stephen,
the first of many witnesses who gave their life for you.
May we make with them the seamless journey
from the cradle to the cross.

READINGS
Psalm 119:161-168
Jeremiah 26:12-19
Acts 6:8; 7:51-60

27 DECEMBER

John

Apostle and Gospel writer, first century

The Church honours on this day the one who in his Gospel proclaims Jesus as God's Word who became a human being (John 1), and who is 'the disciple whom Jesus loved'. John was one of the sons of Zebedee, the fisherman, who followed Jesus, and was one of his inner circle, with his brother James and Peter. John was there at Jesus' transfiguration, next to him at the last supper, with him in his agony in the garden, with Jesus' mother standing at the foot of the cross, as a witness to Jesus' resurrection when he 'saw and believed'. He took Mary as his adopted mother, at Jesus' request, and tradition identifies him with the John who fathered many churches in the area that is now Turkey, who lived in Ephesus with Mary, and who died there at a very old age. In the Celtic tradition John is regarded as the foster son of Mary, the foster brother of Christ, and as a spiritual father. His symbol is an eagle, which soars to high vision and which, it was thought, was the only bird that could contemplate the sun directly. It was John with whom churches in Celtic lands felt a special rapport.

PRAYER
Cast the bright beams of light upon your Church
from the pages of your Word,
that, illumined by the faith of your servant John,
she may always walk in the light of your truth.

READINGS
Psalm 113; Exodus 33:7-11a; John 1:1-14

Innocent infants

first century

Herod, appointed king of the Jewish province of Palestine, was a tyrant, who brooked no rivals. When he heard from distinguished visitors that they sought to honour a baby who would become a great leader, he asked them to report back to him where the child was. They were warned in a dream to slip away without giving Herod this information. He was furious; his enquiries revealed Bethlehem as the place of this birth, and he ordered that all male infants there under the age of 2 should be killed. That act is known as 'the slaughter of the innocents' and tradition names this as 'Holy Innocents' Day'. It points us to a pattern that can be discerned throughout human life: wherever great good emerges, it evokes great evil. In modern times this day is often used to celebrate the sanctity of life and to pray for vulnerable unborn and young babies. Jesus' life was saved because God guided his parents to slip away into Egypt.

PRAYER
All-knowing God, we thank you for the example of Mary who bore your Son in her womb
and suffered persecution of her new-born child.
As we mourn the loss of the innocent Bethlehem infants,
we pray for all unborn and newly born babies,
that they may be protected, cherished
and led into the way of your salvation.

READINGS
Psalm 124; Jeremiah 31:15-17; Matthew 2:13-18

29 DECEMBER

Trophimus

Bishop of Arles, died *c.* 250

Trophimus was one of seven bishops sent from Rome at the time of the persecution of the Emperor Decius (249-251) to extend the work of evangelisation in Gaul. He was allotted the church of the Gallo-Roman city of Arles which was the metropolis of the south of Gaul and had a cosmopolitan population. Trophimus built up the faith which had been proclaimed there since the days of the apostles, and encouraged believers to stand firm in the face of persecution. He himself confessed Christ at risk to his life. The cathedral of Arles is dedicated to him.

PRAYER
Son of Mary, Son of God,
you are glorified by your saints
who risk even death to witness to you.
We thank you that knowledge of you
spread through Gaul by your servant Trophimus,
and we pray that knowledge of you
will spread through our world
by us, your unworthy servants.

READINGS
Psalm 140:1-8, 12, 13
Isaiah 61:10-62:3
Luke 2:15-21

Cornelius

First non-Jewish convert, first century

Cornelius was a commander in the Italian division of the Roman army based at Caesarea. Disgusted with the immorality of his society, he and his household turned to God as far as he understood, following Jewish practices of prayer and alms-giving. He had a vision during a siesta that he should send staff to Joppa and ask a man named Peter to visit him. Peter the apostle, who was staying at Joppa, also had a vision, that from now on he must not dismiss non-Jews as disqualified to join Christ and his Church. Peter came to Cornelius' house, informed him about Jesus, and the power of the Holy Spirit and the gift of tongues came upon Cornelius and everyone present. They were baptised and became the first non-Jewish Christians.

PRAYER
God of all peoples,
you accept people everywhere
who honour you and do what is right.
You teach us that to the pure all things are pure.
Draw into the family of Christ
people from the five continents,
the different races and religions,
the rich and the poor.
May you do in them
what you did in the household of Cornelius.

READINGS
Psalm 96; Isaiah 66:17-23; Acts 10

Saints and martyrs of Australasia

The rays of light from Christ, the eternal Word of God, have been reflected in the aspirations of holy souls in every continent, before as well as after they know of the coming of Christ to earth. So we give thanks for shining souls among the aboriginal peoples of Australasia and the Pacific region. We give thanks for missionaries, martyrs, and a host of faithful Christians for whom the light of Christ shines through the journeys, the ancestors, the land, the encounters; for those who understand the meaning of the Celtic knot – the inter-relatedness of all things; for those who understand the meaning of the circle – the elements, the sun, completeness, the rising from death of Christ. We give thanks for those who find God in the great outdoors and in the telling of stories, and for those who draw from the great artesian water basins of the Spirit.

PRAYER
O God,
I see your story in flowing streams,
in people's dreams,
in sporting teams.
As the water in the stream makes its journey to the sea,
so I will flow with your Spirit and with your saints,
on to you.

Echoes Kiwi prayers

READINGS
Psalm 90; Isaiah 30:19-26; Matthew 20:1-16

Let us go forth

Let us go forth
in the goodness of our merciful Father,
in the gentleness of our brother Jesus,
in the radiance of the Holy Spirit,
in the faith of the apostles,
in the joyful praise of the angels,
in the holiness of the saints,
in the courage of the martyrs.

Let us go forth
in the wisdom of our all-seeing Father,
in the patience of our all-loving Brother,
in the truth of the all-knowing Spirit,
in the learning of the apostles,
in the gracious guidance of the angels,
in the patience of the saints,
in the self-control of the martyrs.

Such is the path of all servants of Christ.
The path from death to life eternal.

From *Celtic Fire,* Robert Van der Weyer
(Unattributed)

Index of Saints

Caedmon	11 February	David, king,	
Cainneach	11 October	Jesus' forebear	23 December
Caleb	2 April	Deborah	3 April
Canice	11 October	Declan	24 July
Carantoc	18 May	Dedication of the	
Cassian	28 February	infant Christ	2 February
Cedd of Lastingham	7 January	Deiniol	11 September
	26 October	Denys	9 October
Ceolfrith	22 September	Derfel (Cadarn)	5 April
Ceowulf	9 January	Dichu	16 March
Chad	2 March	Dogmael	14 June
Christ the		Donan	17 April
Pantokreter	22 January	Donatus	22 October
Ciaran of		Drithelm	1 September
Clonmacnoise	9 September	Dunstan	19 May
Ciaran	4 March	Dyfrig (Dubricius)	14 November
Colman,			
Bishop of Dromore	6 June	Eadbert	6 May
Colman,		Eadfrith	7 June
monk of Iona	18 February	Eanswyth	7 September
Columba (Columcille)	9 June	Earconwald	30 April
Columbanus	23 November	Eata	27 October
Comgall	10 May	Ebbe	25 August
Conan	27 January	Edburga	11 December
Constantine	11 March	Edith of Wilton	18 September
Cornelius	30 December	Edmund	20 November
Crispin	25 October	Edwin	5 October
Crispinian	25 October	Egbert	19 November
Cummian the Tall	28 May	Egyptian martyrs	16 February
Cuthbert	20 March, 5 September	Eithne	8 May
Cyprian	15 September	Elfleda	8 February
Cyril	14 February	Elidius	8 August
Cyril, Bishop of		Elijah	13 June, 6 August
Alexandria	27 June	Elisha	15 June
		Elizabeth	31 May
		Elwyn	22 February
Daniel	9 August	Enda	21 March
Daughters of the		Endellion	29 April
King of Connaught	18 March	Enfleda	24 November
David	1 March	Enoch	20 February

Mary, mother of Jesus	
25 March, 31 May, 15 August,	
8 September, 8 December,	
24 December	
Mary, sister of Martha	
and Lazarus	29 July
Matthew	21 September
Matthias	14 May
Mawes	18 November
Mel	6 February
Melangell	27 May
Melchizadek	21 February
Methodius	14 February
Methuselah	26 February
Micah	22 December
Micaiah	19 August
Michael	29 September,
	19 October
Miriam	26 March
Mishael	13 August
Modan	28 April
Molaise	18 April
Moling	18 January
Molua	5 May
Moluag	25 June
Monesan	20 April
Monica	27 August
Moninna	5 July
Morwenna	6 July
Moses (Abbot)	14 January
Moses	28 March, 6 August
Mother Julian	9 May
Mungo (Kentigern)	13 January
Muredach	12 August
Nathan the prophet	10 June
Nectan	17 June
Nehemiah	17 August
Neot	1 August
Nicholas	6 December

Ninian	26 August, 16 September
Non	3 March
Oswald	5 August
Oswin	20 August
Oswy	15 February
Pachomius	15 May
Padarn	14 April
Palladius	7 July
Patrick	17 March
Paul Aurelian	12 March
Paul of Thebes	5 January
Paul, his conversion	25 January
Paulinus	10 October
Perpetua	7 March
Peter	29 June, 6 August
Petroc	4 June
Philip	3 May
Philip the Deacon	28 November
Phoebe	4 September
Pictish martyrs	17 April
Piran	5 March
Polycarp	23 February
Priscilla	13 February
Raphael and the	
seven angels	30 October
Remigius	23 January
Ronan	2 June
Ruadhan	15 April
Ruth	16 December
Saints and martyrs –	
of Asia	10 December
of Australasia	31 December
of England	23 April
of Europe	3 February
of Scotland	1 December
of the Americas	8 April

Bibliography

Sources consulted include the following:

Anglican Altar Services 1941 (The Faith Press Ltd)

All the Men of the Bible, Herbert Lockyer (Pickering & Inglis)

Calendar and Lectionary According to the Revised (New Style) Julian Calendar (The Orthodox Fellowship of Saint John the Baptist)

Calendar for Holy Days in *Common Worship: Services and Prayers for the Church of England* (Church House Publishing, 2000)

Early Irish Saints, John J. O'Riordain (The Columba Press, 2001)

Exciting Holiness (Canterbury Press)

General Calendar and Saints of the National Calendars in *The Divine Office* © Copyright 1974, The Hierarchies of Australia, England and Wales, Ireland (Collins, 1977)

Lives of Irish Saints, two volumes, ed. Charles Plummer (OUP)

Lives of the Irish Saints, ten volumes, John O'Hanlon (Duffy, Dublin, 1875)

Lives of the British Saints, seven volumes, Baring-Gould and Fisher (Llanerch)

Lives of Saints from the Book of Lismore, trans. William Stokes (Clarendon Press, Oxford)

Lives of the Saints, twelve volumes, Alban Butler (Burns and Oates)

Saints of England's Golden Age, compiled by Vladimir Moss (Centre for Traditionalist Orthodox Studies, California, 1997)

Saint Patrick's World, Liam De Paor (Four Courts Press, 1993)

The Celtic Year, Shirley Toulson (Element)

The Ecclesiastical History of the English People, Bede (OUP)

The New Bible Dictionary (IVF, 1962)

The Oxford Dictionary of Saints (OUP)

The Oxford Dictionary of the Christian Church (OUP)

The Spirituality of the Celtic Saints, Richard J. Woods, OP (Orbis Books, New York, 2000)

The Synaxarion: The Lives of the Saints of the Orthodox Church, six volumes (Mount Athos, 2001)

The Culdees of the British Isles, William Reeves (Llanerch, reprint 1994)

Wisdom of the Celtic Saints, Edward C. Sellner (Ave Maria Press, Indiana, 1993)

Women in a Celtic Church, Christina Harrington (OUP, 2002)